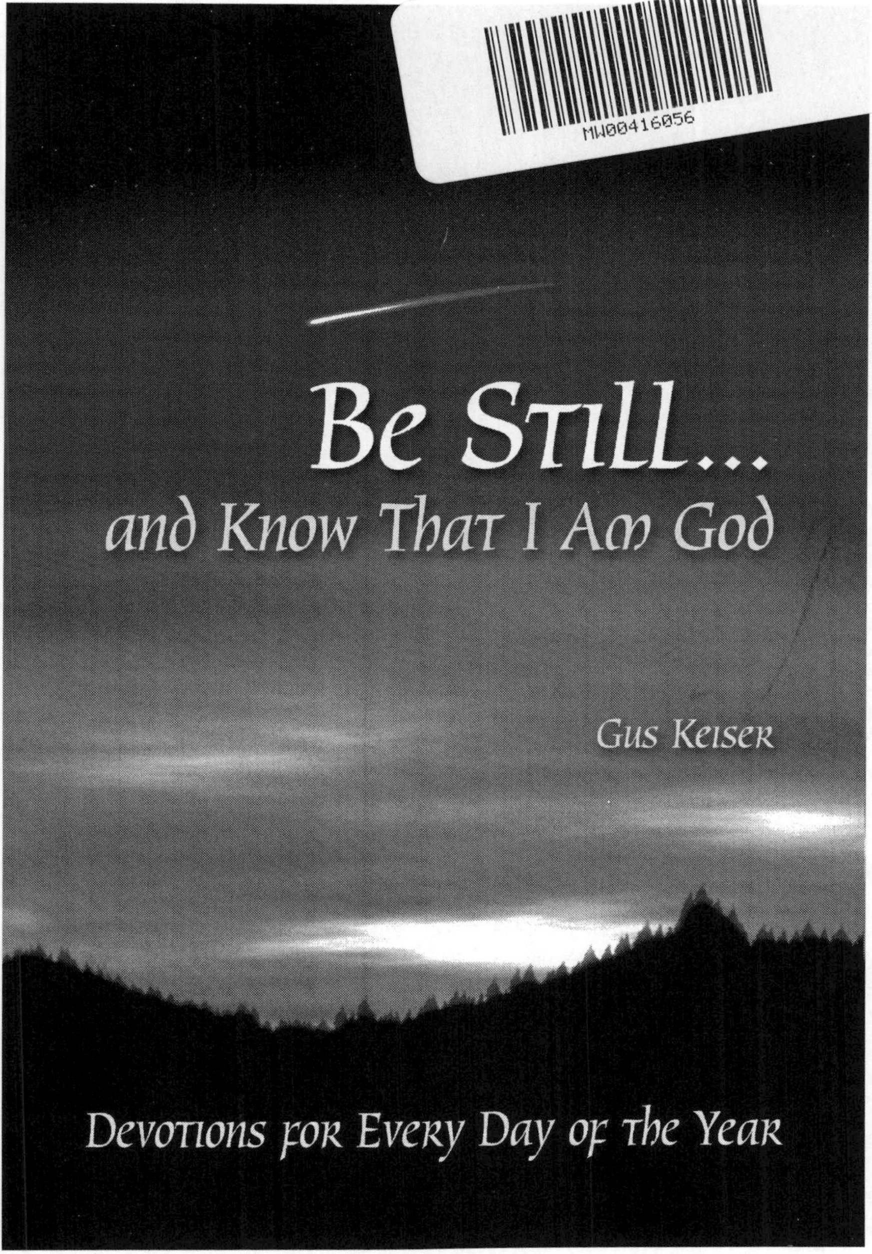
Be Still...
and Know That I Am God
Gus Keiser
Devotions for Every Day of the Year

Augsburg Books
MINNEAPOLIS

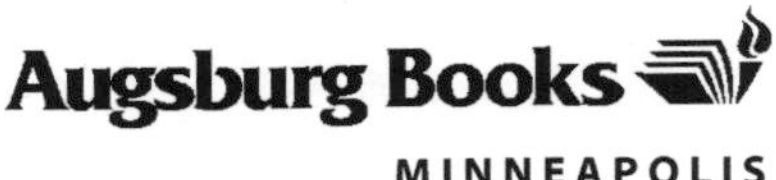

BE STILL . . . AND KNOW THAT I AM GOD
Devotions for Every Day of the Year

Large-quantity purchases or custom editions of this book are available at a discount from the publisher. For more information, contact the sales department at Augsburg Fortress, 1-800-328-4648, or write to: Sales Director, Augsburg Fortress, P. O. Box 1209, Minneapolis, MN 55440-1209.

Library of Congress Cataloging-in-Publication Data
Keiser, Gus, 1946-
Be still and know that I am God : devotions for every day of the year / Gus Keiser.
p. cm.
ISBN-13: 978-0-8066-5230-6
ISBN-10: 0-8066-5230-6 (pbk. : alk. paper)
1. Devotional calendars. I. Title.
BV4811.K37 2006
242'.2—dc22 2006006929

Editors: Mark Hinton, Susan Johnson, David Lott, Donn McClellan, Carol Throntveit, Scott Tunseth, and Alisha Seifert

Cover design by David Meyer; Cover image: meteor flying through a darkened sky. Photo © Chad Baker/Photodisc/Getty Images. Used by permission.

Book design by Michelle L. N. Cook

The paper used in this publication meets the minimum requirements of American National Standard for Information Sciences—Permanence of Paper for Printed Library Materials, ANSI Z329.48-1984.

Manufactured in the U.S.A.

With love,

To my wife, Ellie.
Your faith and your belief in me and your selfless love are what have kept me going throughout our thirty-two years together.

To two of the greatest children
a father could ever hope to have, Sunshine and Jordan.
Thank you for believing in me and for being there whenever I've needed you.

To you, God.
You have been, and continue to be,
my rock and my fortress, my refuge and my strength,
that very present help in all times.

Soli Deo Gloria! . . . to God be the glory, now and forever!

Contents

Preface

Be Still . . . And Know That I Am God began as a daily e-mail devotion that represents just one part of a personal, spiritual journey begun three years ago. I sensed God's call to begin that journey following some serious faith-based wrestling in my life that caused me to challenge my relationship with God and with the church. I am thankful that God is faithful to us, even when we struggle with the deep questions of faith and life.

With the leading of God's Spirit, I began an electronic journal of my "quiet times" that I shared online with friends and family. In my times of being still, of opening myself in prayer and reflection, God has provided me with strength and guidance, allowing me to move beyond my pain and doubt.

It is my hope and prayer that these daily "still moments" will strengthen and encourage you in your faith journey. I also hope that they will challenge you and make you ponder something new. Above all, I hope that they will help you draw closer to God, and in so doing find direction and power for living out your faith for the sake of others.

And now, I invite you to "be still" and listen for the voice of God. This time apart may just change your life. **I expect it will.**

—Gus Keiser

Day 1 / Mark 4:13-20

The Cross Won't Go In

And he said to them, "Do you not understand this parable? Then how will you understand all the parables? The sower sows the word. —Mark 4:13-14

Over the years, two of our cats have died, and we've buried them both in our backyard where we can see the small, fenced-in grave plots from our rear kitchen window. On each one we've also tapped into the ground a small wooden cross. When the cross on Buffy's grave came out one day, I went to the basement and grabbed my rubber mallet and also a bucket of water, figuring I'd have to soften up the ground since we had received very little rain that fall

When I tried to pound the cross back into the ground, it was as if I was trying to pound it into concrete. So I poured about half the contents of the bucket of water onto the spot and waited. It took several minutes before the soil became soft enough that I could pound the cross back down into the ground.

"The sower sows the word." Sometimes our lives resemble the hard ground. We resist God's life-giving word. Our hearts need softening once again to be that good soil. When I took the bucket of water out to soften Buffy's grave, I suppose I learned the method from God. It is in the waters of baptism that God's Spirit prepares our "soil" and gently but firmly places the word in our hearts and connects us to the life and death of Christ. And so, the cross *does* go in—like the seed.

Lord, let our hearts and our whole lives be the good soil for your Word. May our soil never become hardened to the point where your cross isn't able to remain in us. Amen.

Day 2 / Proverbs 14:12

My Way = Big Trouble

There is a way that seems right to a person, but its end is the way of death. —Proverbs 14:12

Hardly a day goes by that we don't wish God would give us a few "do-overs"—the chance to take back something we've said or to fulfill a promise to someone. Sometimes, the troubles we get ourselves into are just part of being human, but at other times they're directly related to the problem of sin—living one's life as if God doesn't matter.

Whenever we live life on our own terms, the momentary pleasure that gives us leaves us empty, and we cement another brick in a wall that separates us from having that intimate, vital relationship that God wants to have with us. If we really want to break down that wall and reconnect with God, we've got to face up to the fact that we need God. When we come to the point where we can truthfully admit our sin and neediness to God, only then can we start down the path to living a complete life in God's grace.

Can you identify any areas of your life where you tend to ignore God and live on your own terms? Confess those shortcomings and sins, and then commit to giving God control of all the areas of your life. What have you got to lose? Go ahead and let God be in charge of it all.

God, I know if I put my life completely in your hands, everything will be fine, but I'm not always ready to do that. I just keep trying on my own. How about a wake-up call, please, God? Amen.

Day 3 / 1 Peter 5:6-11

As I Am

And after you have suffered for a little while, the God of all grace, who has called you to his eternal glory in Christ, will himself restore, support, strengthen, and establish you.
—1 Peter 5:10

In his sermon titled "God's Omniscience," noted preacher Charles Spurgeon wrote: "God sees you as much as if there were nobody else in the world for him to look at . . . The infinite mind of God is able to grasp a million objects at once and yet to focus as much on one as if there were nothing else but that one . . . God sees you with all his eyes, with the whole of his sight . . . you . . . you . . . You . . . YOU are the particular object of his attraction at this very moment."

Some days I cling to that word of hope because everything else seems to be crashing in about me.

I know God is busy with much more important things than my minor crises, but it is comforting and encouraging to remember that God has me in his sights. When I need help to sort out everything, I can go to God in prayer and receive direction. And I am comforted in knowing that I can come just as I am. I often find myself drawn toward some words of the hymn written by Charlotte Elliot:

> "Just as I am, though tossed about
> With many a conflict, many a doubt,
> Fightings and fears within, without,
> O Lamb of God, I come, I come."

Lord of Comfort, I bring you my fears and doubts, trusting that you will help me work through them so I might, in turn, provide your comfort and assurance to others in need. Amen.

Day 4 / Matthew 25:14-30

Investing in the God Market

Well done, good and trustworthy slave . . . —Matthew 25:21

Success! It's what most of us spend our lives trying to obtain in our "success-driven" culture. Even many churches fall into the trap that puts the numbers game front and center. Success is measured by numbers alone. Just how we've come to equate numbers with "gospel success" I'm not sure. As churches, and as those involved in the work of the church, be it paid or volunteer, we need to keep one ideal firmly entrenched in our minds: God has not called his church to be successful; God has called it to be faithful.

In this difficult passage from Matthew, we tend to focus on the success of two servants and the failure of the third. Of course, the master is happy with the financial profit made by the two who are praised. But note what they are called—"trustworthy." Trust is related to faithfulness. They were faithful, and that faith emboldened them to invest God's gifts. The return on those gifts was a virtual certainty. That's the lesson. In God's kingdom, those who are faithful and trustworthy are investing in a sure thing, and God will multiply their investment.

Christ certainly calls us to strive toward excellence in all that we do for him. He calls us to invest the gifts and the talents he's given us, both as individuals and as churches, into the "God market," where our returns will be more than adequate to meet our needs and to continue to fund the work of his kingdom.

Lord, keep us faithful in all the "things" of life. Let us come to you always with complete confidence in your blessings. Let us never question or doubt that you're going to be there to provide for us. Amen.

Day 5 / John 13:12-20

Washing Dirty Feet

If I, your Lord and Teacher, have washed your feet, you also ought to wash one another's feet. —John 13:14

A thought to ponder: "You cannot wash the feet of a dirty world if you refuse to touch them." Dirty feet obviously need to be washed, but very few people want to do it. When Christ commanded the disciples to wash one another's feet, he was referring not to a literal act, but rather making a symbolic statement about the act of serving. To serve implies a type of action that will not only strengthen various muscles of our body, including the heart, but also will keep those same muscles from atrophying. When a muscle atrophies, it wastes away, decreases in size, stiffens up, and does not allow the part of the body to which it is connected to move.

At the center of the servant must lie the serving heart, which needs to do more than just beat regularly to prevent atrophy. It must be willing to love unconditionally; it must direct the body to reach out and wash even the "dirtiest and smelliest" of feet. Far too often we allow the "smell of their feet" to shape our serving of other people. You cannot wash the feet of a dirty world if you refuse to touch them. I can only hope that in our communities and in our world, towels and basins abound.

Loving God, touch the hearts of all people that they might become serving hearts. Amen.

Day 6 / Psalm 71:4-6

God, Our Hope and Trust

Rescue me, O my God, from the hand of the wicked, from the grasp of the unjust and cruel. —Psalm 71:4

One of my basic philosophies of life as I deal with people has been, "I have complete trust in you until you do something to prove to me that I can't trust you." It's a good philosophy to use in raising children, or in dealing with anyone with whom you come in contact. Beginning a relationship by showing trust in someone, even a stranger, is to live out the gospel's message.

But the minute someone violates our trust, we likely will be guarded in our future encounters with that person, even if we are willing to offer forgiveness without qualification. If we are truly to depend upon God for trust and forgiveness, we must be willing to exercise the same.

In the face of feelings of hurt and violation, we can make it through when we trust in God to be there for us and continue to fall back on these words from Psalm 55, "Cast your burden on the LORD, and he will sustain you; he will never permit the righteous to be moved." Be willing to let go and place your pain in God's hands, trusting that God's truth and judgment will prevail, both in the life of the one who hurt you, and in your own as well.

God, when I feel hurt and violated, let me rest in your arms so that my trust is renewed and I can offer the same forgiveness you have graciously given me. Amen.

Day 7 / 1 Kings 1:1-6

God's Mysterious Ways

Now Adonijah, son of Haggith exalted himself, saying, "I will be king"; he prepared for himself chariots and horsemen, and fifty men to run before him. —1 Kings 1:5

The name Adonijah probably doesn't ring a bell with most readers. He was the fourth son of David, born of David's wife Haggith. When David was near the end of his reign as king of Israel and intent on doing things God's way, he chose to name his tenth son Solomon as his successor. Solomon, you might remember, was the son that was born of Bathsheba, whom David had taken as a wife after getting rid of her husband Uriah. As the child born of this lustful affair, Solomon was not the most likely successor to David.

When Adonijah heard that Solomon was to become king at the time of his father's death, he became angry and thought he deserved to be the next king. And why not? He was the next in line. But God had other plans, and Solomon became king after David.

Sometimes God's ways are so mysterious. Just when we think we have things figured out, life in God's kingdom changes. Maybe we think we deserve a new promotion, a well-deserved bit of recognition, or a new opportunity, but it doesn't happen. At those times we can feel discouragement or even the urge to lash out. God understands our hurt, and above all we need to remember that all circumstances can work out for good for those love God. Take care not to live in the "what could have been" moments, but live in the certain knowledge that whatever happens, God is in control.

Dear God, may your will be done on earth as it is in heaven. Let it be so. Amen.

Day 8 / Philippians 2:1-4

Do You Know That You Can?

Let each of you look not to your own interests, but to the interests of others. —Philippians 2:4

One day I received an e-mail from our good friend Betty who was preparing to go to the area ravaged by hurricanes Katrina and Rita to help out with relief efforts. I could sense the apprehension in her words, but she also wrote something that reminded me again of her deep abiding faith in her Lord: "I know I can do this because I know God wants me to go."

Betty constantly exudes energy and enthusiasm, a personality with a heart filled both with love for others and with a solid love and trust in Jesus Christ. So, it didn't surprise me in the least when, in that same e-mail, she shared with us a request: "I ask for your prayers, not for me but for all the victims."

Her words brought to my mind Paul's words from today's passage: "Do nothing from selfish ambition or conceit, but in humility regard others as better than yourselves. Let each of you look not to your own interests, but to the interests of others." Especially in times of global and national disaster, we, God's church, are called to care for those in need, no matter where they are, where they are from, or what they may need. God calls people like Betty to put her normal life on hold for two weeks in order to share her life with those who, for now at least, have no life of their own.

Gracious God, let us bring calm and peace to those who are suffering the storms of life. Give us hearts that are attuned to the needs of others, and, as far as we are able, let us go and lend a hand. Amen.

Day 9 / Colossians 1:27-29

The Reflection of Christ

To them God chose to make known how great among the Gentiles are the riches of the glory of this mystery, which is Christ in you, the hope of glory. —Colossians1:27

If you are like me, looking at yourself in a mirror is tough, especially first thing in the morning. That's certainly not the face I want the world to see. I need time to clean up, wash my hair, and shave before this face is going to be seen by the eyes of anyone other than my family.

So then, once the face is all spiffed up, polished up, and ready for view, whose face do others *really* see when they look at us? Do they see the face of an unscrupulous, conniving person? Do they see the face of someone entirely too busy or too self-absorbed to give a care? Do they see the face of someone unloving or even condemning? Or do they see the face of Jesus?

As Christians, the writer to the Colossians reminds us that we have Christ within us, but we also need others to be able to "see" Christ in us. We need to proclaim him in all that we *do* so that they may experience his warmth emanating from us and receive him as we "reveal" him through our lives. Do you see Jesus Christ each time you look in your mirror? Does your life reflect Jesus to others?

I received a beautiful poem once that describes how someone observed Jesus in the loving actions of others. The poem concluded with this line:

> Though it may be a neighbor or a friend, it's always Jesus,
> I can tell by the way he serves.

Loving God, may someone see Jesus in me today. Amen.

Day 10 / Psalm 13

Anytime God, Anytime

How long, O LORD? Will you forget me forever? . . . But I trusted in your steadfast love; my heart shall rejoice in your salvation. I will sing to the LORD, because he has dealt bountifully with me. —Psalm 13:1, 5-6

We have this interminable traffic signal in town, and it has to be one that I must go through in order to get home from work each morning. This is one of those "forever lights," that makes me mutter to myself, "How long? How long?" And there are other times—as I watch the news reports of wars and tragic storms and senseless abuse that I ask the psalmist's question: "How long, O Lord? Have you forgotten about your world?"

But notice that this psalm of lament ends with the psalmist's faith shining through the pain and seemingly unanswered prayers. There is recognition that God functions at God's own pace. The God whom we serve, the One who created us and continues to sustain us, doesn't share our understanding of time. God does what God chooses to do when God chooses to do it, according to his eternal purpose.

So, if you want to complain about a "forever" light, be my guest. But when life's burdens and challenges cause you to question God's timing—and this most certainly will happen—remember that in God's good time he revealed his love for us in the death of his Son who authored our salvation. And in spite of the present pain we feel, our lives are filled with good things—bountiful blessings. The psalmist knew this. We know it.

God, help me to remember that the good that you do has nothing to do with the time in which you choose to do it, but rather it has to do with the love you show for me when you do it. Amen.

Day 11 / Corinthians 9:24-27

No Train, No Gain

Athletes exercise self-control in all things; they do it to receive a perishable garland, but we an imperishable one. —1 Corinthians 9:25

How would you react if you received a letter from the United States Olympic Committee stating they had determined that you were the most qualified person in the country to represent the United States as a marathon runner at the upcoming Olympic games? Would you view it as your big moment or as your worst nightmare?

I used to run, purely for exercise, five to seven miles a day, six days a week. But even then, I knew there was no way I was ready to run and finish a marathon. Today, that letter would be my worst nightmare. I think of the training regimen and the physical sacrifice it would take, and I cringe. I am very aware that, without major training, I could not cross the finish line in a marathon run.

When the apostle Paul compares the Christian life to an athletic contest, he is not describing an impossible physical test. But he is pointing out the fact that the Christian life is like an athletic contest, or at least like training for one. Without walking in God's word, without exercising our prayer life, without keeping fit through regular worship, and without practicing our faith through service to others, we aren't really training for the ultimate race that hands out the ultimate prize, the imperishable garland of life eternal with God.

Lord, help me to keep my eyes on your heavenly prize. Be my trainer, Lord, and lead me in your ways, strengthening me through your Word and empowering me through the gifts of your Holy Spirit, that I might run the race for you. Amen.

Day 12 / Psalm 91:9-13

Hurtling through Life

For he will command his angels concerning you to guard you in all your ways. —Psalm 91:11

In his book *Searching for God Knows What*, Don Miller says he sometimes feels like a human cannonball shot into the air to the roars of a circus crowd. Just as he reaches the apex of his flight and begins to fall back to the ring below, he says, "It occurs to me that there is no net. And I wonder: What is the use of the circus? Why should a man bother to be shot out of a cannon? Why is the crowd's applause so fleeting? And . . . Who is going to rescue me?"

Who is going to rescue me, indeed? I really like Miller's analogy because I often feel like life is a three-ring circus. There's the family ring, the work ring, and the spiritual (church) ring, and we try very hard to give our best performance in each. And at times we hurtle through life, feeling out of control and on the brink of a hard fall. Who will rescue us?

The psalmist assures us that God doesn't launch us into this world without the benefit of a safety net. God promises to lovingly protect us. Even the angels get in the act. Like great trapeze "catchers," they keep us from crashing to earth and dashing our foot—or our head or our heart—on the rocks.

So, don't worry if you sometimes feel like a human cannonball. Enjoy the ride and trust that God will break your fall. Life with God can be a blast!

God, for the assurance of your loving arms to catch me and to keep me safe, thank you. Amen.

Day 13 / Hebrews 11:1-3

Not Always What Meets the Eye

Now faith is the assurance of things hoped for, the conviction of things not seen. —Hebrews 11:1

About twenty-five years ago, our family flew to New Mexico. While there, we took a day trip to White Sands National Monument, a huge expanse of desert-like terrain, with huge sand dunes and large saguaro cactus.

Another form of plant life found at White Sands surprised me—cottonwood trees, a variety known as Rio Grande cottonwoods, that has been able to survive the extreme desert conditions. These trees grow on average to a height of about sixty to seventy feet. The interesting thing is, only about eight to ten feet of them are visible above ground. The rest of the tree and its root system is buried deep within the sand dunes. So long as a portion of its limbs and leaves can reach sunlight, the Rio Grande cottonwood will survive.

The author of the letter to the Hebrews describes faith as "the conviction of things not seen." Like that Rio Grande Cottonwood, what we can see of God's kingdom is only a fraction of the whole. Faith assures us of what is unseen. Think of this example of faith: A little girl and her mother were looking at the stars one night. The beauty of that night touched the little girl so much that she looked at her mother and asked, "If heaven is this beautiful on the wrong side, what must it be like on the other side?"

May your faith and your trust sustain you even while you wait for the whole of God's kingdom to come into view.

Lord God, keep us faithful, keep us trusting, and keep us connected to you and rooted in your word. Amen.

Day 14 / Psalm 15

We Shall Not Be Moved

Those who do these things shall never be moved. —Psalm 15:5

I searched for the origin of the song, "We Shall Not Be Moved," and found that it has been connected to the civil rights movement, the cause of labor unions, and more. The words to the chorus are:

"We shall not, we shall not be moved. We shall not, we shall not be moved. Just like a tree that's planted by the water; we shall not be moved."

Wherever it is sung, the song's message remains the same: We will stand firm in our beliefs and our principles. The psalmist lays out the principled life in Psalm 15, making it clear that those who are invited to dwell in God's tent and holy hill are expected to live by different standards than those who have little regard for their neighbors and who have no respect for God. Those who live by this higher standard will not be moved from God's favor.

But if we learn anything from the Bible, we learn that God's people—including us—often move themselves away from God and fail to live up to the standards that God's Law demands. God desires that we obey his word and his commands. On this point *God* will not be moved. The good news is that God has also planted us in sight of the water of baptism. Because God has called us by name and claimed us as his children, nothing in all creation can separate us from God. Do the demanding standards of God still apply? Of course, but all things are possible for those who are created new in Christ.

Steadfast and faithful God, thank you for calling us to be your own. Plant our feet on the rock of your word, so that even the gates of hell may not prevail against us. Amen.

Day 15 / John 10:31-32, 37-38

Do You Believe?

[Jesus said,] "If I am not doing the works of my Father, then do not believe me. But if I do them, even though you do not believe me, believe the works, so that you may know and understand that the Father is in me and I am in the Father." —John 10:37-38

Back in the winter of 1980, sports commentator Al Michaels coined a phrase that will forever live in the annals of sports history. When the U. S. Olympic hockey team was just seconds from defeating a far superior Soviet team in one of sport's most stunning upsets, Michaels shouted out that now famous question, "Do you believe in miracles?"

That "Miracle on Ice" was amazing, but it really wasn't much more than a surprise victory pulled off by an inspired team. Most of the time we reserve miracle language for those events that might be described as "an opening in the wall between this world and another." During his brief, three-year ministry, scripture records some thirty-five miracles performed by Jesus. He performed such acts as walking on water, healing the sick, casting out demons, multiplying of five loaves and two fish to feed a multitude, turning water into wine, and even raising three people from the dead. Those certainly fit the description of miracle.

While those miracles, or "works," were signs meant to point to the Father, we sometimes don't know what to do with miracles today. Do miracles still happen? Of course. I happen to think they occur all around us, all the time. They may or may not be as dramatic as the miracles attributed to Jesus. But they happen nonetheless, and they are "from God." Make it a habit to watch for them. You will be surprised at the miracles you see.

Awesome God, continue to dazzle us with your power. Keep us faithful and continue to make believers out of us, that we might rejoice over all your miraculous works, both great and small. Amen.

Day 16 / Psalm 51

Give Thanks

Create in me a clean heart, O God, and put a new and right spirit within me. —Psalm 51:10

When I reflect upon God's gifts, I am often reminded of Psalm 51, an incredible piece of writing. Why this psalm? Because it touches the very core of my faith and the reason I can rejoice. King David, to whom this psalm is attributed, was a powerful ruler and the most respected of Israel's kings. But he was also a sinner who committed adultery with Bathsheba and conspired to have her husband killed on the battlefield. In spite of his sins, he also knew that God had chosen him and continued bless him.

Some of us suffer under the mistaken impression that because we are sinners, there is no way that God can really love us. It's at those moments when we would do well to read this psalm again and again. Look at how the writer calls on and expects God to act—have mercy on me, blot out my transgressions, wash me, cleanse me, purge me, restore, sustain, deliver! The writer even asks God to "open" his lips in order to praise God.

Notice the psalm doesn't talk about how we cleanse or restore or deliver ourselves. No. Thanks be to God we don't have to do that. That's God's work, embodied now and forever in Christ Jesus. That is something to celebrate. Because of the life, death, and resurrection of Jesus Christ, you and I, along with every other person on this earth, can stand blameless before God! Isn't that amazing? Isn't that awesome? Isn't that a great reason to give thanks?

Great and awesome God, We confess that we cannot wash ourselves clean, so we call on your mercy. Deliver us from sin and help us live each day in the sure and certain knowledge that you will restore and renew us when we turn to you. Amen.

Day 17 / Psalm 138:1-3

A Holy Habit

I give you thanks, O Lord, with my whole heart. —Psalm 138:1

In his Thanksgiving Proclamation delivered in 1789, President George Washington shared the following:

> ". . . that we may unite in most humbly offering our prayers and supplications to the great Lord and Ruler of nations and beseech him to pardon our national and other transgressions . . . to render our national government a blessing to all the people by constantly being a government of wise, just, and constitutional laws, discreetly and faithfully executed and obeyed . . ."

The psalmist reminds us that we have much to be thankful for, including a country whose ideals are based on trust in God and the promise that our government will "bless" people because of its wisdom and justice. We long for that vision to be the vision that dominates our words and our actions.

I heard someone say recently that we can choose to be thankful or joyful, that it's a learned response. In spite of living in complicated and often stressful times, we would do well to choose thanksgiving as a daily practice. When we take time to say thanks, we acknowledge the Giver.

Here's an idea: write a thank you note to God for all the blessings you have received. Send it to yourself as a reminder. In fact, do this once a month, and soon the "learned response" of thanksgiving will become a holy habit.

God of abundant blessings, thank you for providing all I need, and then some! I can never thank you often enough, but help me to remember to pause often to give thanks for all, especially the gift of forgiveness and new life. Amen

Day 18 / Hebrews 12:3-11

Teach Your Children Well

God is treating you as children; for what child is there whom a parent does not discipline? Now, discipline always seems painful rather than pleasant at the time, but later it yields the peaceful fruit of righteousness to those who have been trained by it.
—Hebrews 12:7, 11

All children need discipline—discipline administered with love. Nothing bothers me more than to witness a parent disciplining a child when that parent is at the height of his or her anger. I've seen this take place in public more often than I care to think about. A child becomes obstinate in a store, and the next thing you hear is the parent screaming at the child, often belittling the child in front of others, and then, feeling they have no options left, they proceed to spank an already crying child (like that's going to cause the child to stop crying?).

How we handle the disciplining of our children is one of those seeds that we plant within them. Research studies that have been done regarding child abuse often point to the fact that those who are disciplined in an abusive way, either physically or psychologically, will often perpetuate the cycle of abusive discipline.

The idea that God disciplines us is not an easy concept for me, until I recognize that real discipline is born of love. Admittedly, we are all like rebellious children. We are often inclined to say and do things that cause pain to ourselves and to others. This is when God's Spirit gently, or not so gently, reminds us that we are not living according to our loving Parent's expectations. No one, including me, likes to be disciplined, but if the discipline is administered justly and with love, we learn and grow, and our lives will bear fruit.

Loving God, may your word be a lamp to my feet and your teaching a light to my path. Thank you for loving me enough to correct and discipline me when I need it. Amen.

Day 19 / Exodus 16:24-30

Sabbatarianism

The Lord has given you the Sabbath, therefore on the sixth day he gives you food for two days; each of you stay where you are; do not leave your place on the seventh day. So the people rested on the seventh day. —Exodus 16:30

Today's title is a made-up word that has its root in the word "Sabbath." In English, the "ism" suffix essentially transforms a simple noun into a way of life. For example, commune + ism = communism; ideal + ism = idealism; catholic + ism = Catholicism. You get the idea. The formation of the word "Sabbatarianism" is a bit more complicated, but the point is still the same. God's command to keep the Sabbath, conveyed by Moses in today's Bible reading, involves more than setting aside a specific day for rest and worship in the midst of our busy lives. Sabbatarianism is a way of life that places priority on living in communion with God. It's about trusting that God, who provided the Israelites food enough on the sixth day to last for the day of rest that followed, will also provide for our daily needs.

While I was growing up in central Pennsylvania, the observance of a Sabbath day of rest was prescribed by the state's "blue laws" that prohibited businesses from being open on Sundays. Today Sunday shopping is the norm in Pennsylvania and everywhere else. So what does that mean for Sabbatarianites like myself? Of course it means keeping our priorities straight by setting apart time in our busy lives for worship. But it also means hearing God's words to "remember the Sabbath" more as invitation than command—an invitation to live in God's presence and be sustained and renewed by God's love so that we might better thank, praise, serve and obey God every day of our lives.

Gracious Lord, help me see the Sabbath as gift, not obligation, and to eagerly keep Sabbath-time every day. Amen.

Day 20 / John 14:27

Please, Lord, a Moment's Peace?

Peace I leave with you; my peace I give to you. I do not give to you as the world gives. Do not let your hearts be troubled, and do not let them be afraid. —John 14:27

God calls us to take time out of our busy schedules to celebrate and give thanks for the gift of life . . . to take just a few peaceful minutes. For most of us, that's far easier said than done!

From the moment we awaken to the time we go to sleep, most of our lives are in constant turmoil. Each day we may face illness, fire, floods, burglary, flat tires, burned dinners, discord, insecurities, lack of money, an aching back or some other body part, the fear of terrorism—and a host of other issues.

And, for many of us, the night before offered little or no respite. It may have been a night filled with nightmares, an uncomfortable mattress, or even young children crying.

And then we awaken to yet another day, where the prospect of even a few peaceful moments is bleak at best. But if we are lucky—or if we've planned our day well—on occasion, we are able to find even a moment or two of peace: quiet time with a cup of hot chocolate or coffee, a peaceful moment in the evening to read with the phone off the hook (or our calls forwarded to another responsible person!).

Such moments are precious, and should be cultivated and protected, for our souls' sake. Christ calls to us to come to him and know his peace; part of our response is to build quiet time and space into our lives for just that encounter.

And may the peace of God, which surpasses all human understanding, keep our hearts and minds in Christ Jesus our Lord. Amen.

Day 21 / Jeremiah 20:9

God, Can You Warm These Bones, Please?

If I say, "I will not mention [the LORD], or speak any more in his name," then within me there is something like a burning fire shut up in my bones; I am weary with holding it in, and I cannot.
—Jeremiah 20:9

Jeremiah speaks of the word burning like fire in the bones. There are days of spiritual winter when we just don't feel that heat.

St. John of the Cross referred to these times as the "dark nights of the soul": such seasons are the spiritual "winter of our discontent." The sense of separation from God, of divine absence, can feel like a dismal, bone-chilling winter day. We seem so far removed from any source of spiritual warmth that we feel empty and cold, like a planet on the outer edge of the solar system.

But God reminds us—at last—that the fire doesn't go out, even if it may at times be nothing but some smoldering embers. God has placed within us the fire of the word; the breath of Holy Spirit can blow on those embers to reignite an unquenchable flame within us—a flame we can no longer hold within.

If, each day, we avail ourselves of God's word and allow that word to find a place within the deepest recesses of our being, its fire may grow to the point that it heats us, body and soul, and, in God's good time, warms the lives of others.

Start a fire within me, O God, that I might radiate the light and warmth of your word to those around me. Amen.

Day 22 / Isaiah 48:3, 6

Shouldn't You Be Talking about It?

For a long time I've let you in on the way I work: I told you what I was going to do beforehand, then I did it and it was done, and that's that . . . You have all this evidence confirmed by your own eyes and ears. Shouldn't you be talking about it? —Isaiah 48:3, 6 The Message

In ancient times, "lords" had complete and sovereign control of everything and everyone within their territory or kingdom. To acknowledge someone as "lord" meant obeying his or her ownership and authority over every aspect of your life, without question or hesitation.

There just aren't any lords like that around anymore. For most of us, the word "lord" is an antiquated word that just doesn't seem to fit into contemporary culture.

So are we being honest when we refer to Jesus as "Lord"? Perhaps there is room for us to reconsider that question's implications for our lives. Are there parts of our lives that we still regard as *ours* alone? Even when our faith in and love for Jesus Christ are very strong, do we try to reduce his presence to what is convenient and easily managed? Do we regard Jesus as someone we turn to primarily to pull us out of trouble when things get way too deep?

The message is that God is *already* way out ahead of us, working in our lives, and in our world. Perhaps the greater part of our work is not to strain toward ever greater efforts, but to simply pay attention. What is God up to? And once we discern that, how can we get involved? Shouldn't we be talking about it?

Give us grace, O Jesus, not only to call you Lord, but to give our efforts, our very lives, over to your service, obeying you with grateful hearts. Amen.

Day 23 / Romans 14:7-9

Courage

If we live, we live to the Lord, and if we die, we die to the Lord; so then, whether we live or whether we die, we are the Lord's. —Romans 14:8

The Cowardly Lion in "The Wizard of Oz" sought but one gift from the Wizard: "courage." Or, as he paraphrases his request in the film version—"the nerve."

Isn't the root of our fears and anxieties the knowledge, however we may consciously seek to suppress or evade it, that we shall die?

But what if we reoriented our thinking around a different reality? It is the same God who created all life and called it "very good" who is the Lord of the living and the dead, the God who calls upon us to give our lives over to him as our Lord. If we but reflect on that truth, so simply stated by the apostle Paul, surely we can also "trust and obey" the one who made us, whose will for us and for all creation is *shalom*, wholeness and peace.

God grant us grateful hearts—and the courage to live out our gratitude to you for the gift of life. Amen.

Day 24 / Psalm 8:1

So, What's in a Name?

O L*ORD*, *our Sovereign, how majestic is your name in all the earth! —Psalm 8:1*

If we reflect even for a moment on where we would and would not want to see our names appear, we realize the importance of a name.

God has been called by a host of names, each with its own specific meaning, yet none exhausts what scripture calls the majesty of God's identity. The book of Exodus suggests that the proper name for God in Hebrew—*Yahweh*—derives from God's solemn revelation to Moses, who had asked, "Who shall I say has sent me?" "I AM who I AM" was God's reply.

In the Hebrew Bible, *Elohim* ("God") evokes divine strength and creative power, and is often combined with other words: *Elohay Kedem*—God of the beginning; *Elohay Selichot*—God of forgiveness; *Elohay Mikarov*—God who is near. The psalms refer to God as *Elohay Yishi*—God of my salvation; and Jeremiah calls God *Elohay Chaiyam*—Living God.

Other Hebrew names of God appear in contemporary Christian music: *El Shaddai*—God the all sufficient; *El Olam*—God of eternity; *El Elyon*—the most high God; *Emmanu El*—God with us. God's proper name in the Hebrew Bible, Yahweh (YHWH), emphasizes divine care and personal concern for creation, as well as God's close and covenantal relationship with human beings.

In the New Testament, God is referred to as the Father of our Lord and Savior Jesus Christ; and Paul declares that Jesus has been given "the name that is above every name" (Phil. 2:9).

May we ever lift your name on high, great and holy God, through our praise, our worship, and our lives. Amen.

Day 25 / Lamentations 3:25-26

The Great Wait

The LORD is good to those who wait for him. . . . It is good that one should wait quietly for the salvation of the LORD. —Lamentations 3:25-26

We spend a great portion of our lives waiting: on a mundane level, for a slow computer or for a line of people waiting to be served by a clerk; at a deeper, more heartfelt level, for the arrival of loved ones traveling in bad weather or for relief for a sick child.

The Bible encourages the faithful to "wait patiently for the Lord." That's not always easy; perhaps that is not ever easy. Sometimes a holy impatience seems the better course.

But wait we must.

As Christians, we learn to wait with patience, with endurance, not only on our own behalf and that of those dearest to us, but on behalf of strangers and an anguished creation as well. We learn to wait for the "now, but not yet" of God's good time, in which God's good purposes are and will be fulfilled. We learn to wait in the calm assurance that "the Lord is good to those who wait for him."

God give us the grace to weigh our impatience against your purpose, and to give up our complacency when you would stir up in us eager anticipation to see your will done; through Christ our Lord. Amen.

Day 26 / Isaiah 9:6-7

God With Us

For a child has been born for us, a son given to us; authority rests on his shoulders; and he is named Wonderful Counselor, Mighty God, Everlasting Father, Prince of Peace. . . . The zeal of the Lord *of hosts will do this. —Isaiah 9:6-7*

Isaiah's words are often read as prophetic of the birth of Jesus as the Messiah. Whether that was what Isaiah had in mind is debated. But, the names given this marvelous child are certainly arresting, and to them we can add, from Isaiah 7, the name Immanuel, "God with us." Matthew surely regarded that as a prophecy of Jesus' birth—though he was quite aware that *Jesus*, not Immanuel, was the name Mary gave her child.

Jesus literally means "God saves." The New Testament provides many other names for this one come from God, and each gives a different glimpse into his character.

In Revelation, John first calls him the Almighty, and at the end, Alpha and Omega, beginning and end. Other New Testament writers hail him as Blessed Hope, Bridegroom, Lamb of God, Great Physician. The writer of Hebrews calls him King of Peace and of Righteousness, as well as High Priest. He is Bright Morning Star, the Stone which the builders rejected, Truth, Word of God, and of course, Savior.

More is at work here than an effort on the part of the first Christians to find adequate ways to speak about Christ. Our ancestors in faith sought names with which to speak *to* Christ, in prayer and adoration—not unlike the way we seek new endearments for those we love.

"Jesus, the name that charms our fears and bids our sorrows cease" is that "little Word" that (according to Luther's majestic hymn) shall fell the "Prince of darkness grim."

Jesus, seal your name in our minds and hearts, that we may magnify your glory by our lives. Amen.

Day 27 / Luke 2:10-11

Just the Beginning

The angel said to them, "Do not be afraid; for see—I am bringing you good news of great joy for all the people: to you is born this day in the city of David a Savior, who is the Messiah, the Lord." —Luke 2:10-11

Small town newspapers often provide a column announcing all the births at the local hospital so that everyone in town can offer the family their best wishes. There's nothing like the anticipation and joy experienced by parents of a newborn child.

It's easy for Christians to imagine that the birth of Jesus was "like that—but more." As if not only had Joseph and Mary been eagerly anticipating their child's birth, but the people of the countryside—indeed, the Jewish people as a whole—had been waiting long years, centuries, for this particular child's birth.

That's a distorted imagination, of course. What Israel had eagerly awaited is just what Mary extols in her song of praise: God's decisive action to scatter "the proud in their conceits," to bring down the powerful from their thrones, to lift up the lowly, to fill the hungry with good things—and send the rich away empty (Luke 1:51-53). As thrilling as the angel's announcement to the shepherds of Judea in Luke 2, a quick reading of the morning papers tells us we're still waiting for that announcement to see its fruition. Surely we could use a little more scattering, more bringing down, more lifting up, more filling with good things, and more sending away!

Your kingdom come, O Father, your will be done, on earth as in heaven—speedily and in our day! Amen.

Day 28 / John 1:14

Incarnation Every Day

And the Word became flesh and lived among us, and we have seen his glory, the glory as of a father's only son, full of grace and truth. —John 1:14

We often associate the theme of incarnation of the Word—along with other Scripture passages, like the angels' proclamation to the shepherds in the Gospel of Luke—with the season of Christmas. But the truth of the Word's incarnation cannot be limited to one season of the year.

That's important to bear in mind. Otherwise, we find ourselves surprised, even dismayed, by news reports of violence, injustice, and war anywhere in the world during the Christmas holidays.

God's Word is no more incarnate on Christmas Day than at any other day of the year. And we—the church—are no less Christ's body on earth today than on that first Pentecost. Why should any indignity or violence done to human beings seem a greater affront to the glory of God, in whose image we are made, on one day than on another?

The wonder of the incarnation is, we confess, an abiding reality in our anguished world: the presence, the nearness of a God who cares enough to stand with us. But God is not simply a companion in suffering. The peace Luke's angels proclaim is the hope at the heart of our faith—a radical, joyous, urgent hope for nothing less than the full and holy peace of God's reign.

Lord, make us instruments of your peace—this day and always. Amen.

Day 29 / Matthew 25:31-32

Take Your Seat, Jesus

When the Son of Man comes in his glory, and all the angels with him, then he will sit on the throne of his glory. All the nations will be gathered before him. . . . —Matthew 25:31-32

It's one thing to confess that Jesus "ascended into heaven and is seated at the right hand of God." That language is comfortably religious, abstract—*distant,* "up there" in heaven.

It's another thing to contemplate Jesus as seated to give judgment—not as a general truth, but giving judgment *of our lives.* What, something in us protests, gives *him* that right? Who is Jesus to judge: wasn't one of his own teachings "judge *not*"?

But of course we gave Jesus that authority when we accepted his invitation to belong to him. We give him that authority again, ever new, each time we call him "Lord."

We are pretty independent-thinking people. Many of us don't readily take direction from others. We consider it a mark of freedom to be able to answer to no one. But how realistic is that?

We are all responsible to different people for different aspects of our lives. Belonging to Christ is a deep responsibility of the heart, and that means making ourselves accountable to the truth of the gospel. How do we make that accountability specific and concrete in our daily lives?

Direct our eyes, our thoughts, our hearts, O God. Make us yours in truth, ready to respond to you in trust and love. Amen.

Day 30 / Romans 8:27

Self-Examination

And God, who searches the heart, knows what is the mind of the Spirit, because the Spirit intercedes for the saints according to the will of God. —Romans 8:27

There may be no more sensitive topic than that of spiritual self-examination—perhaps because we so often think of self-examination primarily as preoccupation with what we've done wrong. It's to our benefit to hear the wisdom of another Christian, Jonathan Edwards, regarding self-examination. Here are a few of the Resolutions he made for himself in 1723.

- Resolved, constantly, with the utmost niceness and diligence, and the strictest scrutiny, to be looking into the state of my soul, that I may know whether I have truly an interest in Christ or not; that when I come to die, I may not have any negligence respecting this to repent of . . .
- Resolved, to confess frankly to myself all that which I find in myself, either infirmity or sin; and, if it be what concerns religion, also to confess the whole case to God and implore needed help . . .
- Resolved, to exercise myself all my life long, with the greatest openness I am capable of, to declare my ways to God and lay open my soul to him: all my sins, temptations, difficulties . . .
- Resolved, to endeavor to my utmost to deny whatever is not most agreeable to a good, and universally sweet and benevolent, quiet, peaceable, contented, easy, compassionate, generous, humble, meek, modest, submissive, obliging, diligent, and industrious, charitable, even, patient, moderate, forgiving, sincere temper; and to do at all times what such a temper would lead me to; and to examine strictly every week whether I have done so.

Search me and know me, after thy will; while I am waiting, yielded and still. Amen.

Day 31 / Romans 12:10-11

Ambition

Outdo one another in showing honor. Do not lag in zeal, be ardent in spirit, serve the Lord. —Romans 12:10-11

We may be tempted to imagine that ambition, competitiveness, and striving to excel are somehow unworthy motives for a Christian. Yet Paul seeks to stir up just these motives among the Christians in Rome.

Consider as well the tone of some of the resolutions Jonathan Edwards framed for his own spiritual edification (in 1722–23):

- Resolved, to strive to my utmost every week to be brought higher in religion, and to a higher exercise of grace, than I was the week before . . .
- Resolved, never to say anything at all against anybody, but when it is perfectly agreeable to the highest degree of Christian honor, and of love to mankind, agreeable to the lowest humility, and sense of my own faults and failings, and agreeable to the golden rule . . .
- Resolved, to be strictly and firmly faithful to my trust, that in Proverbs 20:6, "A faithful man who can find?" may not be partly fulfilled in me . . .
- Resolved, always to do what I can toward making, maintaining, establishing, and preserving peace.

Cause me so to walk in your Spirit, O God, that I may fulfill your just requirement; through Christ. Amen.

Day 32 / *John* 1:14

Pitching the Tent

And the Word became flesh and lived among us, and we have seen his glory, the glory as of a father's only son, full of grace and truth. —John 1:14

A tent is a valuable shelter: it protects us, keeps us warm, dry, safe from the elements. A tent is also portable; we can pull up stakes and be on the move quickly. It's not an accident that when God chose to dwell among a people on the move—Israel on their march from bondage to the promised land—the structure of choice was the "tent of meeting" of Exodus 25.

The language used in the Fourth Gospel for the incarnation evokes Israel's campsites on their journey through the wilderness: literally, "the Word became flesh and pitched a tent among us." God promises to "make camp" with us, to shelter us.

One of the most popular songs during the American Civil War was written by a concert singer on the eve of his induction into military service. Walter Kittredge put to music his apprehension and the hope—so widely shared—that a horrible war would soon have an end.

> We're tenting tonight on the old campground; give us a song to cheer.
> Our weary hearts, a song of home, and friends we love so dear.
> Many are the hearts that are weary tonight, wishing for the war to cease;
> Many are the hearts that are looking for the right, to see the dawn of peace.
> Tenting tonight, tenting tonight, tenting on the old camp ground.

Lord, pitch your tent and dwell among us; and keep us always on the move toward the attainment of your promises. Amen.

Day 33 / Matthew 4:1-4

From the Mouth of God

Then Jesus was led up by Spirit into the wilderness to be tempted by the devil. He fasted forty days and forty nights, and afterwards he was famished. The tempter came and said to him, "If you are the Son of God, command these stones to become loaves of bread."
—Matthew 4:1-4

Even a glancing familiarity with the current political scene shows just how powerful words are. People on different sides of a controversial issue will work very hard to reframe and rename, and to shape our perceptions of reality.

There is plenty of reframing and renaming in the temptation scene in Matthew's Gospel. The temptation to make bread is more than a taunt regarding Jesus' self-imposed hunger; it's a challenge to prove himself as Son of God—able, by implication, to feed all the hungry of Judea with his miraculous powers!

Jesus parries the temptation with a word of Scripture: "One does not live by bread alone, but by every word that comes from the mouth of God" (Matt. 4:4). Yes, he has the power to provide bread miraculously, and he will do so—but on God's terms, not Satan's.

How do we find our way through the myriad claims and counterclaims in modern media? Our touchstone may be in Jesus' responses to the second and third of Satan's temptations. As the Message translation puts it, "Don't you dare test the Lord your God . . . 'Worship the Lord your God, and serve him only.'"

God, give us the grace of discerning minds—and hearts to do your will! Amen.

Day 34 / Mark 8:29

The Real Jesus

[Jesus] asked [his disciples], "But who do you say that I am?" Peter answered him, "You are the Messiah." —Mark 8:29

In churches, classrooms, news magazines, and, yes, on prime-time TV, Jesus remains a controversial figure. Starting in the early eighteenth century, many scholars have interpreted the Bible as a collection of historical documents. From this perspective, the Gospels can be seen as theological writings composed to promote the emergent Christian faith. The search for the historical Jesus—the "real" Jesus—thus involves getting behind or beneath the surface of the Gospels.

Those of us who want to relate personally to the figure of Jesus ask a somewhat different set of questions: What was the historical Jesus like? Was he the solemn, ever-serious Savior of church art? Or did he also know laughter, frustration, wonder, and perplexity, as we all do? The Christian affirmation that he was fully human suggests a positive answer to that last question, but that's not the way Jesus is usually portrayed.

It is the humanity of Jesus that makes him accessible, approachable. Is the apprehensiveness we sometimes feel about a too-relevant Jesus an indication that we don't want Jesus to get too close? Do efforts to enforce a single authoritative vision of Jesus have the effect of keeping Jesus at a distance?

What do we make of Jesus? It's an important question. But it's just as important to ask: What will we let Jesus make of us?

Can we, at last, join in the intimate prayer of Charles Wesley:

Jesus, lover of my soul, let me to thy bosom fly! Amen.

Day 35 / Jeremiah 30:18-20

Things Will Get Better

I'll turn things around for Jacob. I'll compassionately come in and rebuild homes. The town will be rebuilt on its old foundation; the mansions will be splendid again. Thanksgivings will pour out of the windows; laughter will spill through the doors. Things will get better and better. —Jeremiah 30:18-20 (The Message translation)

After twenty-nine chapters of solemn warnings, at long last, in Jeremiah 30, God speaks a message of hope. The prophet had tried everything possible to get the people to listen to God's message, only to anger the people enough to threaten his life. God has threatened the destruction of Jerusalem and exile in Babylon. But God loves his people, and in chapter 30 we read God's promise that things will get better.

The daily news gives the impression of a world of doom and gloom worthy of a Jeremiah. These are indeed serious times, calling for our serious efforts to respond to God with all our hearts. But these are not hopeless times—not so long as the God who spoke through Jeremiah speaks in our own day as well, and we have the courage to listen.

Oh, that we would be willing to put our trust in the same promise of deliverance today!

Living God, our times are in your hands. Give us courage to live in these difficult days with genuine hope for your future. Amen.

Day 36 / Isaiah 53:4

The Ragman

Surely he has borne our infirmities and carried our diseases;
yet we accounted him stricken, struck down by God, and afflicted.
—Isaiah 53:4

The Book of Jesus is a collection of short writings, impressions, and characterizations about the person of Jesus by a variety of authors, ancient and contemporary. It includes an excerpt from Walter Wangerin's wonderful story, "The Ragman" (from *Ragman: And Other Cries of Faith,* first published in 1984).

The ragman pushed his cart through the streets of his community, collecting rags and other throw-away objects, then selling them to obtain the meager amount of money on which he lived. But the ragman not only exchanges new rags for old; in collecting discarded rags from people, he also takes on their pains and sufferings. The story is narrated by an observer who follows the ragman through the streets of the city, at last watching as the ragman ends his journey on the city dump, dying there in near obscurity. The observer falls asleep in the dump, only to awaken on a Sunday morning to find the ragman transformed into the living Christ.

The observer's words conclude the story:

> "Well, then I lowered my head and, trembling for all that I had seen, I myself walked up to the Ragman. I told him my name with shame, for I was a sorry figure next to him. Then I took off all my clothes in that place, and I said to him with dear yearning in my voice: 'Dress me.' He dressed me. My Lord, he put new rags on me, and I am a wonder beside him. The Ragman, the Ragman, the Christ!"

Clothe us, O Christ, with your glory, even as we go through the humble routines of our day. Amen.

Day 37 / Luke 13:6-7

Better Check the Fruit

A man had a fig tree planted in his vineyard; and he came looking for fruit on it and found none. So he said to the gardener, ". . . Cut it down! Why should it be wasting the soil?" —Luke 13:6-7

Some people are natural gardeners, born with a green thumb. Everything they plant grows and flourishes—not just flowers, but food: fresh tomatoes, radishes, onions, strawberries, watermelon, any number of herbs. They naturally expect the sweat they put into the soil to be rewarded.

The point of Jesus' parable is that the principle carries over to our relationship with God, as well. God wants more than simply to shower down blessings on us. We may think of God's work in our lives as the careful cultivation of a garden, and blessings as our spiritual manure. God expects us, naturally enough, to yield fruit.

When we plant corn, we expect to get corn; when we plant tomatoes, we expect to get tomatoes. When God plants the Spirit in our lives, we're expected to produce the "fruit of the Spirit"—"love, joy, peace, patience, kindness, generosity, faithfulness, gentleness, and self-control" (Galatians 5:22-23). Only the quality of the fruit we bear gives evidence of our aliveness in the Spirit.

Lord God, let my life be good soil, that I might produce in abundance the fruit of your love in this hungry world. Amen.

Day 38 / Hebrews 12:1-4

Who Indeed?

Therefore, since we are surrounded by such a great cloud of witnesses, let us throw off everything that hinders and the sin that so easily entangles, and let us run with perseverance the race marked out for us. —Hebrews 12:1 (NIV)

If asked to name great role models of serving Christ in daily life, many of us might first name high profile individuals like Albert Schweitzer and Mother Theresa. Then there are parents, grandparents, Sunday school teachers, youth leaders, and others who each in his or her own way have shown us by example what it means to live and share God's love and grace. All are among the "great cloud of witnesses" mentioned in today's passage.

But if asked to name the greatest role model, there is only one answer: Jesus Christ, the most significant and influential role model of all time. It is Christ indeed who best guides and leads us as we grow in faith and service and strive to be role models to others. Like most role models, our human weaknesses will trip us up from time to time, and we will stumble in the "race marked out for us." At those times, the cloud of witnesses here on earth and Christ in heaven above will be there to provide what we need to persevere.

God, thank you for the cloud of witnesses who have modeled a life of faith for me. Thank you most of all for Christ, the Word and the Way that I want to follow all the days of my life. Amen.

Day 39 / Deuteronomy 29:16-20

The God of the Roundabout Way

You know how we lived in the land of Egypt, and how we came through the midst of the nations through which you passed. —Deuteronomy 29:16

Our passage today speaks to only one of many, many times that the actions of the people must have tried God's patience. And perhaps, God tried the patience of some of the people as well. "What is with this forty-year roundabout journey in the wilderness? Isn't enough, enough, God?" many must have complained. But ours is often the *God of the Roundabout Way,* and God functions that way I think so that we can learn and understand patience—the very patience God has with us. Patience helps us to slow down and examine what is really happening around us. What dangers are lurking that could interrupt our journey? Are we even on the right route?

We need to be a more patient people—to trust in God's promises, to be satisfied with the manna in the wilderness and the water from the rock. We need to place our trust and our lives in God's hands, letting God direct our paths. No matter how roundabout the way, there is much to learn in the route God takes us on. Just follow. God will lead you out of the desert and into the promised land.

God, you are patient with us and our mistakes; help us to exercise that same patience and understanding with everyone else. In the name of your Son, Jesus Christ, we pray. Amen.

Day 40 / Psalm 91:14-16

Website Responding

When they call to me, I will answer them; I will be with them in trouble, I will rescue them and honor them. —Psalm 91:15

We live in a society that expects almost instantaneous communication and information access. Cell phones, the Internet, on-the-spot television reporting, satellite communications, and so forth have made our access to virtually any type of information almost guaranteed. And when that access is denied for any reason, we become frustrated.

Fortunately, denied access to God is never a problem. In the psalm for today, God's accessibility is firmly guaranteed: "When they call to me, I will answer them." When we need God's input and attention, when we seek God out, the response will never be, "I'm away from my desk. Please leave a message and I'll get back to you as soon as possible," or "Website not responding." God will always be "in" and accessible. When God calls on us, will we be able to say the same?

Gracious and ever-present God, thank you for your steadfast faithfulness. Help me to be as open to you as you are to me. Amen.

Day 41 / Corinthians 12:20-22

Who Packs Your Parachute?

On the contrary, the members of the body that seem to be weaker are indispensable. —1 Corinthians 12:22

Jet fighter pilot Charles Plum had flown seventy-five combat missions during the Vietnam War when his plane was destroyed by a surface-to-air missile. Plum ejected safely, but was captured by the North Vietnamese and endured six years in a Communist prison camp. In his lectures about that experience, Plum often shares an incident in which a man approached him and his wife in a restaurant. "You're Plum!" the man exclaimed. "You flew jet fighters in Vietnam off the aircraft carrier, Kitty Hawk. You were shot down!"

"How in the world did you know that?" asked Plum.

"I packed your parachute," the man replied. "I guess it worked!"

"It sure did," Plum said. "If your chute hadn't worked, I wouldn't be here today."

That night, Plum couldn't sleep. How many times, he wondered, had he passed that man on the ship and not even said good morning, ignoring him because he was "just a sailor," not a fellow pilot. And yet, with each parachute he packed, that man held in his hands the fate of the person who would wear it.

Who aren't you noticing? Whose importance are you failing to acknowledge? Or, as Plum asks those to whom he speaks, "Who's packing your parachute?"

God, you place in our hands the lives of others. Teach us to pack with care the "parachute" of your love that it may someday save a life. Amen.

Day 42 / Mark 4:35-41

Please Still the Storm, Jesus

They woke him up and said to him, "Teacher, do you not care that we are perishing?" —Mark 4:38

Having been in storms where I was very afraid, I have some sense of the fear and panic that the disciples must have been feeling in today's passage. What I wouldn't have given in any of those situations to hear Jesus speak those words, "Peace, be still." But I wonder how I would have reacted to his words and to the ceasing of the storm? Mark tells us that the only reactions of the disciples were that they were awestruck and uncertain.

I've spent the better part of my life trusting and serving God. So, why is it that when the storms of life strike, a first reaction is to pull a "disciple," to begin to panic? Like the disciples, I feel tossed and blown about, so caught up in uncertainty and fear that I forget that I am not alone, that Jesus stands beside me. My own humanity diverts me from the divine. Part of Jesus' love, however, is to break through our humanity, to stretch out his hand in the midst of our fear and say, "Peace, be still." My panic grows out of my need to be in control; my peace lies in turning that control over to God.

Give me your peace, Christ, and help me to be still so that I can hear your voice and be comforted by your word. Loving Christ, into your hands I commend my spirit and my life. Amen.

Day 43 / Colossians 4:2-4

Not the Prose, but the Purpose

Devote yourselves to prayer, keeping alert in it with thanksgiving.
—Colossians 4:2

Some time ago, I received the following Short Message Service (SMS) text in an e-mail:

> dad@heaven, urspshl, we want wot u want &urth2b like hvn. Giv us food, &4giv r sins lyk we 4giv uvaz. Don't test us! Save us! Bcos we kno ur boss, ur tuf, &ur cool 4 eva! Ok? (*) Or, for those not literate in SMS text: Dad at heaven, you're special. We want what you want and earth to be like heaven. Give us food and forgive our sins like we forgive others. Don't test us! Save us! Because we know you're boss, you're tough, and you're cool forever. Okay?

Considering it is still difficult for some to accept changing "thy kingdom come" to "your kingdom come" in the Lord's Prayer, there's no real likelihood of the SMS version taking hold. Language is important. For Paul, however, the greater importance was the purpose of prayer in the lives of the people, not language. Prayer is our way of communicating with God. It's far less about language and far more about coming to God in open, honest words. And it's there, in that quiet time alone with God, that God hears us and we hear God.

God, let us think less about pretty words and more about honest talk when we pray, knowing it is our open hearts you desire more than anything. Amen.

Day 44 / 2 Corinthians 11:3

Wholehearted Commitment

But I am afraid that as the serpent deceived Eve by its cunning, your thoughts will be led astray from a sincere and pure devotion to Christ. —2 Corinthians 11:3

A few years ago in the United Kingdom, track defects caused a train traveling 117 miles per hour to derail. Four people died and more than 30 were injured. An investigation revealed that the company responsible for maintaining the tracks had failed to meet its commitments on track repairs.

Most of us have been or know someone who has been hurt because of a half-hearted commitment, perhaps in sports, friendship, marriage, or business. Half-hearted commitment to Christ is nothing new, either. Often, half-hearted Christians are more committed to a program, congregation, or their idea of the "rules" of Christian living than they are to letting Christ lead their lives. But programs and churches can let people down. And following "rules" can become sterile, confining, and routine. Jesus never lets us down. A commitment to Jesus is about relationship, not rules. Whole-hearted commitment to Jesus is a daily revelation and adventure that brings freedom and life. The good news is that, even when we may slip into half-hearted commitment to Jesus, and no matter how derailed our lives may become, Jesus is always fully committed to us.

Understanding God, I know that I get my priorities confused sometimes. Help me remember that you and you only are my Lord and my God. Amen.

Day 45 / Isaiah 43

A Personal Message

I have summoned you by name; you are mine. —*Isaiah 43:1* (NIV)

The forty-third chapter of Isaiah is one of the most beautiful passages in the Bible. In this chapter, God is speaking directly to his people, and although God's words are addressed to Israel, they are yours and mine also. Take time to read again the first four verses of this chapter, and allow them to be God's very personal word to you. God has summoned you by name; you *are* God's. You are precious and honored in God's sight because God loves you.

What if you decided to make your life an experiment of living in the love of God? Every morning, let your first words be, "I am the one that God loves!" And every night, just as your head hits the pillow and you're about to doze off to sleep, let your last words be, "God loves me!" Whenever you're tempted to despair because you've blown it big time, remind yourself of God's never-failing love by saying, "I am precious in God's sight." When you are tempted to sin, to dishonor God, to lash out in anger and hurt someone; when you're afraid, anxious, or lonely; at all times remember that God knows you by name. You are God's beloved.

God, thank you for being there for me and loving me! Amen.

Day 46 / Mark 15:21-24

Make a Difference

They compelled a passer-by . . . to carry his cross; it was Simon of Cyrene, the father of Alexander and Rufus. —Mark 15:21

On that horrible day of Jesus' death, as he was being forced to carry the heavy weight of the cross, struggling through the streets of Jerusalem, bloody and weak from the beatings he had received, one person cared. There is question as to why Simon of Cyrene did what he did. Both Matthew and Mark indicate Simon was compelled to do so out of compassion, while Luke suggests that Simon was seized and forced to carry the cross. I like Mark's account, because Mark is the only gospel writer to mention Simon's sons, Alexander and Rufus. Even if Simon's service was a forced act, I think the fact that he did what was needed, that he helped a suffering person, was an incredible witness to those two young boys.

Christ calls each of us to look after our neighbor, no matter how insignificant or trivial the act may seem. You may never know or understand how meaningful your acts of kindness may be, or the impact it may have on the life of the one you serve or another who notices. Your words and actions are a witness to Christ's love. Make a difference.

God, open my heart, ears, and eyes to the needs of others; then guide and direct me so that others will see and come to know your love. Amen.

Day 47 / Nehemiah 2:4-5, 6:15

Don't Just Dream It, Do It!

Then the king said to me, "What do you request?" So I prayed to the God of heaven. . . . The wall was finished . . . in fifty-two days.
—Nehemiah 2:4; 6:15

It's truly is amazing what one person can do when he or she not only dreams, but acts. Nehemiah displayed courage and put himself in harm's way in order to see God's work accomplished. Perhaps, in order to make a difference in our world, what we need in the church today is for God's people to have a little more courage!

The challenge, I think, is threefold. First, let's ask ourselves the question: "What would we attempt to do for God if we knew that we could not fail?" Secondly, let's pray, asking God to give us wisdom in those dreams and to provide us with courage to move from dreams to action. Third, let's act! Imagine how the world might change if each one of us pursued our dreams for making a difference until those dreams become reality.

Lord God, make us not only dreamers of the word, but doers. Amen.

Day 48 / Matthew 12:46-50

We're Family

For whoever does the will of my Father in heaven is my brother and sister and mother. —Matthew 12:50

For many, family includes not only those to whom we are related genetically or through marriage or adoption, but also those with whom we have a special or committed relationship, those people who chose to be in relationship with us and are the ones we most trust and turn to for love and support. That last part is perhaps what truly defines family for many of us: those whom we most trust and turn to for love and support. Legal family is one thing; emotional family is another.

The Christian family is bound together by the blood of Christ: rich and poor, old and young, Protestant and Catholic, from the other side of town and from the other side of the world, we stand together as God's children, God's family. We may not always get along, and we may not always like each other, but we share a desire to do God's will and spread the gospel. Let's remember that. Let's act as family in the best sense of that word. Let's not just call ourselves the family of God, let's act in a way that lets the world know we *are* the family of God.

Lord God, thank you. When we forget, remind us that we are family, and that how we act toward and support each other is a witness to the world. Let that witness be only to your glory. Amen.

Day 49 / 1 Peter 1:22-25

Good News or Best News?

The grass withers, and the flower falls, but the word of the Lord endures forever. —1 Peter 1:24-25

Not so long ago, I had one of those days that seem to be nothing more than one piece of bad news after the other. When I finally had the chance to find a quiet corner of respite, Peter's words came to mind: "The grass withers, and the flower falls, but the word of the Lord endures forever." With each negative word I had received, my hope and good mood withered, and my flower of optimism faded and fell. But Peter's words reminded me that all the bad news I had had that day was related to material things, none of which can last forever. God's word, however, does endure forever. That word, Peter says in verse 25 is "the good news that was announced to you"—the good news that in love, Christ, God's Word, has given his life for us. Even during those times of our deepest despair and hopelessness, that Word lives among us. The good news is not only good news, it is the best news of all.

What a great comfort it is to know, God, that, even on our worst days, we can always count on your Son, the good news of the gospel, to raise us up and give us hope for not only that day, but all the days of our lives. Amen.

Day 50 / Matthew 7:1-5

Seeing Clearly

You hypocrite, first take the log out of your own eye. —Matthew 7:5

Dave Burchett begins his book, *When Bad Christians Happen to Good People*, with this self-realization:

> I am a hypocrite. I can be arrogant and selfish. I have been known to stretch, conceal, or slightly massage the truth. I am sometimes inconsiderate and insecure. I struggle with lust and impure thoughts. My ego often rages out of control, and I battle foolish pride. I can be lazy and foolhardy with my time. I get angry, petty, and ill-tempered. I am sarcastic and cynical. I am a Christian.

Suffice it to say, I have my own list of shortcomings. We all do. Romans 3:23 puts it up front and center: "All have sinned and fall short of the glory of God." We are all sinners. We are all hypocrites, prone to seeing faults in others more easily and quickly than in ourselves. And yet, God loves and forgives us in spite of it. Perhaps if we stop to think of that more often, we will be less judgmental toward others and more apt to model God's love and forgiveness. Perhaps then we can at least be *better* Christians to *all* people.

God, I'm trying, and you know that. And you know I can't do it alone. Help me to be more giving and less judgmental, and to honor the name of Christ that I carry. Amen.

Day 51 / Philippians 3:12-14

Your Personal Best

I press on toward the goal for the prize of the heavenly call of God in Christ Jesus. —Philippians 3:14

The prize Paul speaks of in his letter to the Philippians is not a prize to be earned, but a gift to be cherished and used. To be called to do the work of God's kingdom is to be singled out, set apart, and placed on holy ground. Our goal as Christians should be to answer that call, to use the gifts with which God has blessed us to serve him and others to the best of our abilities.

What is it that you can do for others on behalf of God today? What can you do or say to further the kingdom of God in our world? How greatly are you willing to challenge yourself as God's servant? Think big. Set your goals high—as high as the heavens, for, with God as your personal trainer, your "personal best" is bound to surprise you.

God, without your strength and without your support, we can do nothing. Continue to challenge us in our service to you; not with the goal of receiving more and more of your blessings, but rather to give more and more of your love to others. Amen.

Day 52 / Psalm 105:1-6

I Love to Tell It

O give thanks to the Lord, call on his name, make known his deeds among the peoples. —Psalm 105:1

It was an autumn morning in 1966, and I was nine years old. My parents never attended church, and neither did I, but my friend Bob had invited me to go to Sunday school. The person leading the opening asked everyone to turn to a particular page in the Sunday school hymnal, and we stood and sang "I Love to Tell the Story."

I know I didn't pay close attention to the words that day—I guess because I had no idea about what it was they were singing. But as the years went on and I became more involved in the church, those words began to make more and more sense to me. They became part of my reason for working and teaching in the church because they describe who I am to this day—one who really loves to tell the story of Jesus and his love. What a fantastic and powerful story it is. It the story of God, who loved us so much that he sent his Son to live and teach among us, the Son, Jesus, who died a horrible death on the cross and rose again for our salvation.

God, help me to tell the story of how, out of your great love for us, you gave your son's life so that we might know life eternal with you in heaven. Amen.

Day 53 / Luke 19:1-10

Grumpy No More

For the Son of Man came to seek out and to save the lost. —Luke 19:10

In one of the most poignant and powerful scenes in the film *Snow White,* the dwarfs attempt to "wash up" Grumpy, who stubbornly tries to resist their efforts. He kicks and screams, but to no avail. In the end, their cleansing act is not what changes Grumpy. No amount of soap and water alone is able to do it. It took Snow White's sweet kiss to truly change Grumpy, just as we cannot change without the "kiss" of Christ.

Zacchaeus realized this, which is why he readily welcomed Jesus into his home to share a meal. Zaccheaus could have easily dined alone and, through his own soul-searching, realized the errors of his ways and come to the decision to give back the money he had stolen. But it was only through that direct contact (the "kiss") with Christ that true change came about—a change so dramatic, powerful, and lasting, that it caused Jesus to exclaim, "Today salvation has come to this house, because he too is a son of Abraham" (Luke 19:9).

Dear God, through your touch, change us. Take away our doubts, tear down our walls, and fill us with your love. Cleanse us with your blood that we may be as "white as snow." Amen.

Day 54 / John 15:13

God's Lifesavers

Greater love has no one than this, that he lay down his life for his friends. —John 15:13 (NIV)

When our son, Jordan, was five, he swallowed a piece of hot-dog that became lodged in his windpipe. Using every first-aid method I knew, I was unable to clear his throat and he collapsed in my arms. Instinctively, I began mouth-to-mouth resuscitation, making sure the first breath I blew into him was the strongest one I could provide. Within seconds, he began to regain consciousness. The paramedics, who arrived shortly after he came around, said that apparently that breath was forceful enough to have blown free whatever was obstructing his airway, and that he would be fine. I had saved my son's life.

Our lifesaver is Jesus Christ. As much as I love my son, I know there is no love as great as Christ's love for me, or for my son, or for you—for all of us. Parents often say they would give their own lives to save their children, but would we give our children's lives to save others? God did. God gave Jesus to die and rise again so that we would know salvation and life eternal. There isn't more to give than that.

Dear God, nothing we can give or do compares to your gift of Christ for us. It is a gift too great to keep to ourselves. Guide us to be a small part of your life-saving team by sharing the story with others. Amen.

Day 55 / Matthew 18:18-20

There Beside Us

For where two or three are gathered in my name, I am there among them. —Matthew 18:20

Why is it that Jesus gets so much more of our attention when life is difficult? Christ wants to be a part of our lives; he wants to be with us in good times and bad. And, invisible as he may be to the human eye, Christ is with us. Perhaps if we took time to remember that, we would do many things differently. I suspect we at least would attempt to live more positively, to treat each other better, and to go that "extra mile" for those around us. If Jesus truly walked beside us—if we could see and touch him—only the rudest among us would fail to introduce him to those we meet. We might even help them get to know each other better. We probably also would be more likely to include him in our decisions and ask his opinion. When there was work to be done, we would invite him to be part of that, as well. And we would want him to join in our celebrations, not just in our sorrows. It's something to think about, isn't it? Maybe it is time to make our "invisible friend" much more visible to the world.

Jesus, you are with us at all times. Keep that knowledge in our minds and hearts. Amen.

Day 56 / Jeremiah 31:31-34

Heart Surgery

I will put my law within them, and I will write it on their hearts; and I will be their God, and they shall be my people. —Jeremiah 31:33

In the center of Martin Luther's seal, the Luther Rose, is a heart. On that heart is a rose, and on that rose is a cross. There in visual form are God's law and God's love right where God told Jeremiah they would be put—the cross of Jesus Christ depicted on a blood-red rose on the human heart.

God told Jeremiah that the law would be written upon the hearts of the people so that they might internalize it and make it a part of their being. We often think of the heart as the center of love. And that is what the cross on the heart of Luther's Rose is about—the phenomenal gift we have been given through the death and resurrection of God's Son Jesus Christ—a "heart surgery" that places God at the very center of our hearts.

Create in us clean hearts, O God. Repair our hearts, broken by sin, and give us new life in you. Give us hearts that beat strong and supply strength to our bodies and minds that we might serve you with renewed power. Amen.

Day 57 / John 1:4-5, 8

Never Eclipsed

The light shines in the darkness, and the darkness did not overcome it. —John 1:5

Tonight was the last total lunar eclipse for awhile. I just looked outside, and even though the moon now rests completely in the shadow of the earth, you can still see a faint glow from the moon—a faint light, a sense of hope, an awareness that we are not totally cut off from the sun's light.

God's Son is the source of light for our way and warmth for our souls. And even while the sin of this world may, at times, overshadow us, we are never totally separated from the Christ, the Light of the world.

Shortly, the moon will begin to emerge from out of the earth's shadow, and the light of the sun will again reflect the presence of it. Christ's resurrection represents our emergence from the shadow of sin and death, emergence into that glorious light that needs to reflect from us—the glorious light of the Son.

God, let your light so shine within and from me that others may know the love and the power of your living Word. Amen.

Day 58/ Job 11:13-19

God, I Can't See You

And your life will be brighter than the noonday; its darkness will be like the morning. —Job 11:17

In one of his essays, the great Spanish mystic St. John of the Cross uses the phrase, "the dark night of the soul." He describes this dark night as the lowest point in the spiritual journey, that point where all seems hopeless and lost, the point where one begins to cry out in desperation, "God, I can't see you!"

Many of the great people in the scriptures experienced this dark night; Job was certainly one. Even Jesus, as he hung there on the cross, screamed out to God, "My God, my God, why have you forsaken me" (Matt. 27:46)? Remember, however, that Christ's dark night was followed by the glorious light of resurrection. And so, in your dark nights, when the world attacks and attempts to destroy your body and soul, when the future looks its darkest, when you haven't the strength to go on, remember also Jesus' other words, the words of promise he left to the disciples and to us: "And remember, I am with you always, to the end of the age" (Matt. 28:20).

God, I need your help at all times and in all things. But only by your grace am I able to entrust my life to you without hesitation and without reservation. Grant me such grace. Amen.

Day 59 / Matthew 3:13-17

Milestones

And a voice from heaven said, "This is my Son, the Beloved, with whom I am well pleased." —Matthew 3:17

Along the edge of the road, on the westbound side of the old Lincoln Highway (much of route 30 in Pennsylvania), is a small, stone obelisk. It is a milestone. As defined by Webster's Dictionary, a milestone is a stone used to show the distance in miles from someplace. If you look closely at the weathered and faded engravings on the stone, you can see initials and numbers that were carved into this stone to show the distance from the stone to points east and west of its location. For travelers during the time it was being used, it represented for them the accomplishment of a distance traveled from the last marker. It was for them a sign that they had made it to the next post, thus the other meaning for the word "milestone," a significant event.

Jesus' baptism was a milestone in his life, as our baptisms are in ours. In baptism, we are named and claimed by God. In baptism, God says, "This is my child, in whom I am well pleased."

God, thank you for the gift of baptism, the gift of life in your love and protection. You have claimed me, and I am gladly yours. Amen.

Day 60 / Psalm 34:1-10

God Speaks Peace

I sought the Lord, and he answered me, and delivered me from all my fears. —Psalm 34:4

Someone once told me that, in order wait on the Lord, we must be willing to "come apart." We must be willing to give up control and let God lead. The circumstances confronting us may not seem to change, but God's word of peace will calm our terrified hearts. And the noise and the fury of that storm that surrounds us can be shut out by God's presence, and we will find, if only for a little while, that peace of Christ which certainly surpasses all our human understanding.

The struggles of life are always going to be there. I'm always going to be wrestling with one problem or another. But it's precisely at those times that I need to wait for God and God's word. You see, God has never failed me. God's never failed to meet me wherever I am in my life. God comes to me with grace and with a promise: "All is well. Go ahead, step out in faith, and see."

God, too often my fears tempt me to try to solve it all on my own, even when I know I can't. Remind me in those times that with you and in you I will find my direction and my peace. Amen.

Day 61 / Psalm 37:7-9

I Don't Wait Well

Be still before the LORD, and wait patiently for him. —Psalm 37:7

I don't wait well, and so when what I had hoped would happen during a lunchtime meeting today didn't, more than a little frustration set in. The decision I had hoped to revel in with my family today has been put on hold for several more days. To make matters worse, the discussion at the meeting brought back very angry, very bitter, and repressed feelings that I thought I had long since buried.

At some point this afternoon, I dozed off in my den chair, only to wake up later with these words ringing in my mind: "Be still before the Lord and wait patiently for him." My need-to-know button having been pushed, I pulled out a Bible concordance and went looking for the source of these words. I found them, buried in the thirty-seventh psalm. In the midst of my frustration, God led me back to the stillness of his presence, the stillness I needed to begin to quiet my soul, reorder my mind, and gain a sense of perspective on this day and the days to come.

Lord, you are our refuge in the time of trouble. When trouble and frustration arise, lead us to your peace and strength and wisdom. Help us to "wait well." In Christ's name. Amen.

Day 62 / 1 Corinthians 15:51-58

A Rebel with a Cause

Therefore, my beloved, be steadfast, immovable, always excelling in the work of the Lord, because you know that in the Lord your labor is not in vain. —1 Corinthians 15:58

Mike Yaconelli was killed in a one-car accident late one night. With his death, Christianity has lost a powerful, challenging voice—and I have lost a good and respected friend. Mike will be missed by those of us who appreciated his bluntness and his candor. He truly was a rebel with a cause, and that cause was to help us each realize what Christ's real message was: to love God with all our heart and with all our soul and with all our mind, and to love our neighbor—regardless of his or her color, lifestyle, or standing—as ourselves. Mike—"steadfast, immovable, and always excelling in the work of the Lord,"—understood Christ's message and lived to share it. His labor was not in vain.

I will miss Mike, and my prayers go out to Karla and their children. Go in peace, Mike, for you have served your Lord. Amen.

Lord, grant peace to all those who are dealing with loss. Fill their emptiness with your love and their days with your grace. Amen.

Day 63 / Matthew 15:32-37

The Church Bakery

All of them ate and were filled. —Matthew 15:37

Over the door of a small general store in a village close to where I lived thirty years ago hung a sign that read, "Bake Shop." Inside the store you could find candy, canned foods, magazines, comic books, a pinball machine, and you could even buy a cup of coffee or a soda (pop), but *no bread!*

Some churches are a lot like that little general store. Hanging outside are signs like, "The First Church of Christ," "Christ Lutheran Church," or some other name referring to Christ. Some may even promise nourishment for the soul. Inside, however, one may discover diversion, entertainment, social activities, or social action (including food!), but there's nary a loaf of bread for the starving soul. In wanting to draw people in, the good news gets left out. Souls hungry for God's grace and forgiveness leave still wanting.

We are called by Christ to answer both the spiritual and physical needs of those around us. Like Christ in our passage today, let us first offer the Bread of Life and then the bread.

Feed us, Bread of Life, that we may share your bread with the hungry souls that surround us each day. Amen.

Day 64 / 1 Chronicles 16:23-27

The Boss

Declare his glory among the nations, his marvelous works among all the peoples. —1 Chronicles 16:24

From time to time I've run across cars with a bumper sticker that reads, "My Boss is a Jewish Carpenter." In the work world, the right boss can make all the difference. A true sense of "we're in this together" can make even the worst of situations bearable. Most people who have worked in both situations discover they are far happier working for less money in a place where they feel known and valued than if they are earning much more in a place in which they are merely invisible, dispensable cogs in a machine designed only to get the job done. No matter how large or small the company, it is the person at the top who sets the standard for how everyone else will be treated.

Most of us are "the boss" of someone else, even if it is only on those occasions when we hire work to be done in our home or yard. Whose standards do we live by in those situations? What message do we send about who is the boss in our lives? Do they know you work for a Jewish carpenter—for Christ?

Dear Lord, I count it a great privilege to be able to serve you in all that I say and do. Guide me to treat others in ways that declare your glory! Amen.

Day 65 / Revelation 7:13-17

God's Laundromat

These are they who have come out of the great ordeal; they have washed their robes and made them white in the blood of the Lamb. —Revelation 7:14

Clean clothing makes us feel good about ourselves and ready to face the world. The people in today's passage wear robes laundered to a gleaming white, a white that no detergent on the market could ever produce. The writer of Revelation tells us that these robes were made white "in the blood of the lamb." They were made white by the greatest cleansing power of all times, the blood that was shed by Christ. And it is that blood that not only cleanses garments, but also cleanses us of our sins. Think of it as "God's Laundromat": open twenty-four hours a day, no load too big, no stain irremovable, and results guaranteed. When we bring God the dirty laundry that is our life, God's cleaning is quick, thorough, and complete.

God, let Christ's blood flow over us, so that our lives may be cleansed for your service. Amen.

Day 66 / Revelation 21:5-8

Read the Whole Word

I am the Alpha and the Omega, the beginning and the end. —Revelation 21:6

Aoccdrnig to a rseearch stduy at Cmabrgde Uinervtisy, it deosn't mttaer in waht oredr the lteters in a wrod are; the olny iprmotnat tihng is taht the frist and lsat lteter be at the rghit pclae. The rset can be a toatl mses and you can sitll raed it wouthit a porbelm. Tihs is bcuseae the huamn mnid deos not raed ervey lteter by istlef, but the wrod as a wlohe.

The above paragraph exemplifies the findings of a Cambridge University study that showed that as long as the first and last letters of any word are in their correct positions, then regardless of how the other letters are arranged in the word, we are still able to decode, or read, the word.

Reading God's word is similar, but different. God stands firmly at the beginning and end (Genesis 1:1, Revelation 22:20-21), but we each decode or read a bit differently what comes in between. This is not because the truth of the gospel changes, it is because we change. It happens in part through maturity and life experiences. It happens also because the more we read and study God's word—the whole word—the more God's truth is revealed to us.

Loving God, fill us with your message of love and freedom, that it might bring sight to the blind and set all humanity free. Amen.

Day 67 / Matthew 7:7-11

Jehovah Jireh

Ask, and it will be given to you; search, and you will find; knock, and the door will be opened for you. —Matthew 7:7

One of the most powerful stories of trust can be found in Genesis 22. There, God calls upon Abraham to sacrifice his son Isaac, the son he and Sarah thought they would never have, but who in their old age was born in fulfillment of God's promise. At the last moment, God's angel directs Abraham to a thicket where he finds a ram, which he uses as a substitute for Isaac on the altar of sacrifice. In rejoicing, Abraham gives that place a name: *Jehovah Jireh,* which literally translated means, "The Lord will provide."

Abraham understood the true meaning of the name he chose. He understood that the Lord will provide those things that we really need. On that mountain, Abraham was ready to give to God in response to what he discerned to be God's need, a display of faithfulness and trust. But from this situation, Abraham came to understand that it is God who will provide, that God knows our needs, and that when we ask, God will provide.

God, let us always come to you with a discerning heart, so that our requests are for what we need, not just what we want. For your love, your patience, and your provisions, we offer our thanks. Amen.

Day 68 / Hebrews 2:1-4

I Didn't See That Sign Before

Therefore we must pay greater attention to what we have heard, so that we do not drift away from it. —Hebrews 2:1

The sign said, "Do Not Pass." For fifteen years, Mike had driven that stretch of road, but he couldn't recall having ever noticed it before. Yet, its weather-beaten appearance indicated that it must have been there for some time. The sign was there for a very good reason: to warn drivers that on this particular slow curve to the left, passing another car would be extremely dangerous. Suddenly, it occurred to Mike that his familiarity had turned into a dangerous complacency.

God's word provides many "road signs" to direct how we live or "drive" our lives. And we, too, can let our familiarity breed a complacency in which we fail to see or hear the laws and teachings by which God—out of love and concern for us—wants us to regulate our lives. Perhaps it's time to slow down, pay attention to the road, and be sure the route we're on is where God wants us.

God, as we travel this road of life, guide us to do so with eyes and hearts wide open, so that we never miss the "signs of your gracious love" that you place along our way. In the name of your precious Son, Jesus Christ, we pray. Amen.

Day 69 / Isaiah 25:1-4

Shelter

For you have been a refuge to the poor, a refuge to the needy in their distress, a shelter from the rainstorm and a shade from the heat. —Isaiah 25:4

For a number of months, I worked in a program that provides housing, meals, and support to adolescents who, for a variety of reasons, have been court-remanded to the program. Later I became director of a shelter for homeless men. While the first shelter is a locked facility and the second is not, both are places that provide protection and care.

Much like the Hebrew people, these adolescents and homeless men need shelter from their "enemies." These enemies may be abusive parents, drug and/or alcohol use, prior criminal behavior, joblessness, or inability to cope with the demands of society. And so, along with the necessities of food, clothing, and lodging, these folks need education in career, life, and coping skills; treatment for addictions; and help to find permanent jobs and housing. They need, too, the shelter of the loving hand of God. God calls us to be that loving hand, that extension of his love to the hurting of this world. God calls us to be a refuge to the poor and needy in the midst of their despair; God calls us to be his shelter for others.

God, build us up through your grace, that we may be that shelter for all who seek the safety and security that is found only in your presence. Amen.

Day 70 / Ephesians 4:25-26

Anger Management

Be angry but do not sin; do not let the sun go down on your anger.
—Ephesians 4:26

For Christians, there is a righteous, Godly anger that energizes us to action, to right the wrong, to defend the innocent. However, anger can easily become sin when it turns to hate and retribution. It is at those times that we're all prone to fly off the handle and act in ways that are as inappropriate and hurtful, if not more, as what caused us to become angry in the first place. Or, we might find ourselves storing up our anger and then becoming bitter and resentful.

As Christians, there are several things that we can do to take some measure of control over our anger before it takes control of us:

- Yell at God first! God already knows you are upset.
- Ask God for understanding about the situation and to reveal to you the root of your anger.
- Turn the whole situation over to God. Forgive those who have hurt you, and let God deal with them.
- Pray for the Holy Spirit to be at work in you, to know inner peace.

Lord, let the peace of God that passes all human understanding keep my heart and mind in Christ Jesus. Amen.

Day 71 / Exodus 15:26

Rapha

I am the Lord who heals you. —Exodus 15:26

One of the many names used to describe God is the "Great Physician." That title comes from the Old Testament word *Rapha,* which means "the Lord who heals." In many ways, God, the great healer, acts like our modern day doctors:

- God examines us. God watches over us and knows our every need.
- God consults with us. God interacts with us through prayer, listens to our needs, and offers guidance and direction.
- God works on us. Sometimes we need surgery to clean and treat the wounds of life that afflict us.
- God oversees our rehabilitation. Once God brings about healing, God follows our "case," providing the healing medicine of God's word and love and giving protective care as we heal.

What a joy it is to be the child of Rapha, . . . the Great Healer!

In our times of trouble and wounding, we call out to you , O Lord, and you save us from our distress. You heal us with your command and save us from the sting of death. We thank you, Lord, for you constant love for us, and for the wonderful things you continue to do for us. With songs of praise and hands of a servant, we rejoice in telling others of you, O Great Physician! Amen.

Day 72 / Psalm 37:3-6

One Step at a Time

Commit your way to the Lord; trust in him, and he will act. —Psalm 37: 5

During the course of our lifetimes, we are required to make millions of decisions. Some are small and seemingly insignificant. Others are major, life-altering decisions involving issues such as marriage, jobs, and education. For the most part, we make these decisions based on the best information we have available to us at the time.

But with any of these decisions, great or small, if we're willing to take our choices to God and lay them before him, God will help us to know what's in our heart and what we need to consider before we make any decision. Unfortunately, far too many people are fearful of making decisions. Afraid it may be the wrong decision, they end up making no decision at all.

However, if we're willing to live our lives to the fullest, and we're willing to keep an open line of communication with God through daily prayer, we can be assured that God will be there to lead us through the good times as well as the difficult times of our lives, one prayer and one step at a time.

God, through the power and the presence of your Holy Spirit, continue to lead me along the path of life. And when the going becomes difficult and the way uncertain, take me by the hand and walk with me, one step at a time. Amen.

Day 73 / Ephesians 2:10

The Power of One

For we are what he has made us, created in Christ Jesus for good works, which God prepared beforehand to be our way of life. —Ephesians 2:10

English author and priest Cannon William F. Farrar wrote:

> I am only one, but I am one;
> I cannot do everything
> But I can do something.
> What I can do, I ought to do
> And what I ought to do
> By the grace of God, I will do.

A common affliction in our society is the belief that a person has to have power, money, and giftedness to make a difference. And yet, while the "movers and shakers" among us might focus attention on the needs of the world and get things rolling, not even the most powerful, wealthy, or gifted among us can do everything. Few grand gestures get far or create lasting change without the buy-in of the "common people." It the sum total of individual smaller responses that create real change. God has purposely designed you for accomplishing lasting good works in Christ's name, be it through "grand gestures" or one small, but significant, deed at a time.

Lord, I can do something. Grant me the insight, desire, and grace to do it—in your name and to your glory. Amen.

Day 74 / Jeremiah 31:1-3

A Love Everlasting

I have loved you with an everlasting love; therefore I have continued my faithfulness to you. —Jeremiah 31:3

It is the rare person who goes through life without deep disappointment. For some, efforts to do everything right seem to crumble into one hurt or "failure" after another. At those times, knowing there is someone who loves you, will stand by you, and believes in you is vital. In that knowledge, it is possible to look forward rather than becoming lost in the past. In that knowledge is hope.

Sadly, there are many in our world who have no family or loved ones who are there for them in times of distress. They are alone. That is, unless someone notices and lets them know that someone does care. As the community of Christ, we are called to be that "someone." For someone who feels completely alone in the midst of deepest disappointment, our loving voices, presence, and support are more than a reminder that God's love and faithfulness never fail—they are part of that love and faithfulness given through us.

Loving God, enfold us in your loving arms and never let us go. Amen.

Day 75 / 1 Corinthians 10:1-4

Make Mine a Rock

For they drank from the spiritual rock that followed them, and the rock was Christ. —1 Corinthians 10:4

In 1975, in a conversation with friends, Gary Dahl, a California salesman, who complained about virtually every pet under the sun, and then proceeded to tell them that he, however, had found the perfect pet. No problems, no maintenance. The pet? A rock. Out of that conversation emerged the pet rock craze that eventually earned Dahl well over a million dollars during the one-year history of the fad.

Jesus is our rock. He's our fortress. He's our deliverer. He's the one in whom we are able to take refuge. He is the force that brings us strength, the one to whom we turn to brighten even the dreariest of days, and the one who will take away our stress and flood us with his peace. Perhaps having a rock around isn't such a bad idea—not a pet rock, but a prayer rock, a rock to remind us of the never-failing presence and love of our Lord Jesus Christ.

Be my rock and my redeemer, Lord. Stay close to me always; be the rock upon which I can stand to withstand even the fiercest of life's storms. Amen.

Day 76 / Ephesians 5:14-20

Perfect Picture . . . Print It!

Be careful then how you live, not as unwise people but as wise. —Ephesians 5:15

Dewitt Jones, the award winning video and still photographer, was a regular contributor for almost twenty years to both *National Geographic* and *National Geographic Traveler.* He offers the following as keys to his success:

- **A good camera with the right lenses.** Different lenses give different perspectives. Experiment to find the right lens for the shot.
- **Attention to focus.** For some shots you want the whole picture to be razor sharp; in others the viewer may actually see more if only the subject in the foreground is clearly in focus.
- **Creative instincts and lots of shots.** There is more than one "right way" to shoot a particular shot, and an important shoot might need hundreds of rolls of film out of which only fifty or so will be used.

When Dewitt Jones empties his camera, he knows he has given the shoot his best. Can you say the same of how you live your life? Do you see life through the lens of faith? Are you focused on God's will, rather than your own will for your life? Is your heart and spirit listening for new direction? If so, you are shooting the "picture of a lifetime?"

Let us see life through the lens of your love, God. Give us perspective, bring your will into focus, and provide us with creative spirits to live that will in our lives. Amen.

Day 77 / Joshua 24:14-15

Sweet Words

As for me and my household, we will serve the LORD. —Joshua 24:15

Jenny Lind, the "Swedish Nightingale," was already famous throughout Europe when P. T. Barnum brought her to the United States for a multi-city tour. A smashing success, Lind's fame grew, as well as her fortunes. Yet at the height of her career, the "sweetest voice in the world" unexpectedly left it all behind and never returned.

When a friend went to visit her in her retirement, he found Lind sitting alone on a beach with a Bible resting on her knees and gazing at a magnificent sunset. After catching up on each other's lives, the friend asked Lind, "How is it you came to abandon the stage at the peak of your career?"

For a minute or so, Lind didn't answer. But then she turned to her friend, and said, "When everyday made me think less of this (laying a finger on her Bible), and nothing at all of that (pointing to the sunset), what else could I do?"

Has the busyness of life robbed you of some of God's most precious gifts? There is nothing as precious as your relationship with God, family, and friends. And there is no career that can bring fulfillment if it keeps you from serving the Lord.

God, let the first song I sing today be sung to you, and let me include you in all that I do and say this day. Amen.

Day 78 / Numbers 11:1-9

McManna

When the dew fell on the camp in the night, the manna would fall with it. —Numbers 11:9

The people of Judah were becoming complacent and distant from God. They were so busy taking God and God's care of them for granted that they never noticed the decay that was taking place from within and the enemies that were gathering around them. They were rapidly becoming their own "McMe, McNow" society. They were more concerned with their physical hunger than with their relationship with God. God answers their desire for food, but does it in a way that illustrates the need for more than physical sustenance.

Like the Israelites, we, too, need to be glad for the manna that rains into our lives. We need to eat of it slowly, and to savor the goodness and the nourishment it provides. And from its goodness we will receive the strength to run and not be weary ,and to walk with him and not faint.

God, we come to you with a hunger for your word. Set before us that heavenly feast, that we might be filled with the manna of your love, your mercy, and your power. Amen.

Day 79 / 2 Samuel 5:17-25

Ask Early and Often

David did just as the LORD had commanded him. —2 Samuel 5:25

The late author and theologian A.W. Tozer wrote, "It is not what a man does that determines whether his work is sacred or secular, but why he does it."

In today's text, we get a glimpse into the life of Israel's greatest king, and we discover that King David sought God's guidance in all things, great and small alike.

We would be wise to follow David's example, but unfortunately we aren't inclined to do so. Too often we act first and ask for God's blessing afterwards. Or, if things go badly, we turn to God for help getting out of the mess we've created.

Is there anything too small to need God's guidance? Although there's much to be said for keeping the lines of communication open, I don't think we need to have God weigh in on many of the mundane decisions we make each day. On the other hand, it is good to seek God's help in making decisions about major issues or those involving the needs and concerns of others.

The Bible tells us that David "inquired of the Lord." We can do the same by bringing our questions to God in prayer and seeking God's wisdom in scripture. Then we must listen carefully for God's response. And, finally, we must follow God's lead, trusting all the while that God's plan is best.

Loving God, bless us, lead us, and continue to turn our hearts and minds toward you. Amen.

Day 80 / Luke 11:1-4

Dinner with Dad

Jesus said to them, "When you pray, say: 'Father.'" —Luke 11:2

A fitful night in the midst of a hectic week had left me almost too weary to function. I settled into the chair in my den and dozed off immediately. Barely five minutes later, I was awakened by a phone call from my son asking me to dinner that evening. I was a little surprised by the invitation since this wasn't a special occasion, but I was pleased he had called and eagerly agreed to meet him.

I really enjoy these one-on-one times with my son, especially since his work schedule and mine don't often allow us much time together. I appreciate that he took it upon himself that day to initiate dinner with dad.

The same is true of our relationship with our heavenly Father. God rejoices when we call and waits with open and loving arms to share our joys and comfort us in our sorrows. God looks forward to time together with us in prayer, in worship, and in communion around the Lord's table where God, our Father, pours out grace upon us and feeds us with the word. Imagine God's delight when we call and say, "Hi Dad, would you like to get together for dinner?"

Father God, thank you for loving me and hearing me when I call to share my joys and sorrows, dreams and fears, successes and failures. Your presence in my life provides me with all that I need. Thanks, Dad. Amen.

Day 81 / Acts 1:6-8

God's Message Board

But you will receive power when the Holy Spirit has come upon you; and you will be my witnesses in Jerusalem, in all Judea and Samaria, and to the ends of the earth. —Acts 1:8

Many churches use message boards to hint at the focus for Sunday services, or to share pithy messages about faith. I recently saw one that proclaimed, "Sign Broken . . . Message Inside." It stuck with me, and it wasn't long before today's passage from the first chapter of Acts came to mind: "and you will be my witnesses in Jerusalem, in all Judea and Samaria, and to the ends of the earth."

Jesus directed his disciples to proclaim the gospel to the world, and he calls us to do the same. We proclaim God's message of love and forgiveness by living lives of faith. But, too often, our "sign" is broken. Our lives offer no outward expression of the message that has been placed within us. There is little indication in our words or actions that we are followers of Jesus.

We are God's message board. But we are signs broken by sin. God's forgiveness repairs us and enables us to proclaim God's message to the world. Be God's message board. Be God's witness where you live, work, and play, and to the ends of the earth.

Lord, may the message of your love and forgiveness be proclaimed through all we say and do. Amen.

Day 82 / Psalm 88:1-7, 13-14

Hear Me!

O Lord, *God of my salvation, when, at night, I cry out in your presence, let my prayer come before you; incline your ear to my cry.* —Psalm 88:1-2

Have you heard the story about the passenger who tried to get the cab driver's attention by leaning over the seat and tapping him on the shoulder? The startled driver lost control of the cab, drove over the curb, and stopped just inches from a plate-glass window. When the shock wore off, he apologized saying, "I'm sorry I overreacted, but today is my first day as a cab driver. I've been driving a hearse for the last twenty-five years."

Fear can cause us to overreact, or it can paralyze us. But, as the psalmist understood, fear looms larger when we are left to face it alone. Then, like a young child afraid of the dark, we cast aside our bravado and scream at the top of our lungs for the comfort of God's presence

Why is it that we turn to God only as a matter of last resort? We wait until our backs are against the wall before we swallow our foolish pride and ask for help. And even then we hold onto the mistaken illusion that we have something to offer God in exchange for God's willingness to come to our aid.

There will be plenty of dark times when we will cry desperately for God's help. But why wait? God hears just as well in the light.

Holy Comforter, receive me into your arms, with all my fears, all my doubts, and all my sins. Hear my cries and then dry my tears with the comfort of your presence and assurance of your love. Amen.

Day 83 / James 1:22-27

It's Not Either/Or

But be doers of the word, and not merely hearers who deceive themselves. —James 1:22

Have you seen the advertisement where a man holding a cell phone asks, "Can you hear me now?" A moment later he moves to a new spot and asks the same question. We never see or hear the person on the other phone, but it's apparent that he heard the question and responded affirmatively.

Today's Bible text tells us that we must be doers of God's word. In order for that to happen, we must first hear what God is doing and what God calls us to do. That's not as easy as it seems. It's difficult to discern God's voice amidst the cacophony of sounds in our busy lives. Our hearing improves when we gather with other believers for worship and study. We become better attuned to God's voice through frequent reflection and prayer.

How do we move from hearing to doing? An elderly pastor suggested to me that when I finish hearing or reading the word of God, I should immediately ask myself two questions: "What must I do now?" and "How must I change?" God's word is a living word that demands a response from us. This living word has power to effect change in us and through us. We "do" God's word when we proclaim through our words and our deeds that Jesus is Lord of our lives.

Lord, improve our hearing and grant us courage to act upon what we hear so that we might bring your word of love and life to the world. Amen.

Day 84 / Mark 9:14-24

Saying Is Not Believing

I believe, help my unbelief! —Mark 9:24

The very angry driver handed over his driver's license and car registration to the police officer with the challenge, "I can't imagine what possible reason you would have for stopping me."

After studying the cards, the officer returned them saying, "I'm sorry about this mistake. You see, I pulled up behind your car while you were leaning on the horn, giving that woman in front of you some significant finger gestures, and cussing a blue streak at her. When I saw the 'What Would Jesus Do?' decal in your rear window, the 'Follow Me to Sunday School' bumper sticker, and the chrome-plated Christian fish emblem on your car trunk, I just assumed that you must have stolen the car."

Sadly there are times when my behavior makes a mockery of what I claim to believe. Does this mean that I'm a phony Christian? I don't think so. I think it points to the fact that following Jesus isn't easy and that doubt goes hand-in-hand with faith.

The father in today's text knew this. But rather than allow doubt to triumph over his fledgling faith, the man called upon Jesus to grant him the ability to love God for what he could see and to trust God for what he couldn't. We learn from the rest of the story that Jesus did just that.

God, don't let our doubts hinder our relationship with you. Lead us to greater faith through them. Amen.

Day 85 / Joshua 24:14-15

What Were You Thinking?

Choose this day whom you will serve . . . —Joshua 24:15

In light of the number of near accidents that I've witnessed lately, I'm beginning to wonder about the abilities of many drivers to exercise good judgment on our streets and highways.

Today's text asks us to show good judgment when choosing whom we will serve. If I believe "it's all about me," then I'm likely to choose a god who promises instant gratification of all my selfish desires. If I follow Joshua's lead, I will choose the God who has already chosen me and forgives my poor judgment time and time again. I will choose the God who offers eternal life over "the good life."

The choice isn't easy, and it's a choice we need to make each and every day.

Yesterday an impatient driver chose to make a left-hand turn directly in front of me as I was entering the intersection. I screeched to a stop just in time. As I sat in my car, furious about what had happened, the driver pulled up beside me and rolled down his window. "Oh great," I thought, "now I'm going to get chewed out by this guy for his mistake." I rolled down my window and scowled at him.

"I want to apologize for what I just did," he said. "It showed very poor judgment on my part. I usually am a pretty good driver." With that he drove away.

Ouch!

Lord, I choose to serve you. Help me exercise good judgment in how I live my life so others may come to know you through me. Amen.

Day 86 / *Joshua 18:1*

Still the Center

Then the whole congregation of the Israelites assembled at Shiloh, and set up the tent of meeting there. —Joshua 18:1

The Empire State Building, Sears Tower, and Space Needle are prominent buildings that contribute to the identity of the cities in which they are located. In the community in which I live, the courthouse with its gold dome bears that distinction.

There was a time when the church was the most prominent building in town. Its towering steeple was clearly visible to all who lived and labored below. The church also served as the center for the religious and social life of the community.

By contrast, the most prominent structure for the Israelites wasn't a building at all, but a tent. The Tent of Meeting was the community center for a nomadic people constantly seeking greener pastures for their herds. Prescribed by God down to the finest details of its design, the Tabernacle was erected in the center of the camp and provided a visible reminder of God's presence and God's steadfast love for them.

The church no longer figures so prominently in community life, but for all who follow Christ it continues to play the central role in our spiritual growth and development. Here we offer praise and worship to God who gathers us around the Lord's table to be fed with the body and blood of Jesus and then sends us forth to bear the good news of God's saving love to a world in need of God's grace.

Dear God, call us away from the busyness of our lives to join with your church to sing praises to you and to offer ourselves for service in your holy name. Amen.

Day 87 / Matthew 11:28-30

The Resting Place

Come to me, all you that are weary and are carrying heavy burdens, and I will give you rest. —Matthew 11:28

I slept well last night and awoke feeling rested for the first time in several days. I guess it's tough to admit that, even though I can still function sleep-deprived for a couple of days, my aging body doesn't recover as quickly as it did when I was young. I must heed my body's warning signals and get the rest I need.

In the same way, Jesus' words of invitation in today's text are offered for our well-being. We live very demanding lives. Our days are filled to overflowing with commitments, appointments, social engagements, and family activities. We've convinced ourselves that we need to be everywhere and we need do everything. In an effort to live up to these expectations, we choose not to hear the cries of body and soul for much needed rest.

Jesus' invitation to seek our rest in him is a wake-up call to weary followers. He isn't asking us to ignore our responsibilities. Rather, Jesus is reminding us that one thing is needed. In each and every day, we need time alone with our Savior. Jesus' presence will provide the strength we need to meet the demands of each day. Jesus' arms will provide the rest we need to live our busy lives faithfully.

Lord Jesus, draw me into your presence. Refresh my body, renew my spirit, and send me out once again to bear your name and do your will. Amen.

Day 88 / Luke 10:1-12

The Second String

After this the Lord appointed seventy others and sent them on ahead of him in pairs to every town and place where he himself intended to go. —Luke 10:1

Were you a "second-stringer?" Were you good enough to make the team and contribute to the cause but not make the starting line-up? Today's text is for second-stringers.

The ninth chapter of Luke's gospel tells us that the starting line-up—Jesus' twelve disciples—had already been sent out with authority to proclaim the kingdom of God, to heal, and to cast out demons. Now it was time for the "second-string" to go and bring in the harvest from the seeds previously sown.

Who were the seventy? I believe they were your basic, run-of-the-mill, garden-variety followers. They had families, jobs, and daily responsibilities just like you and me. What they lacked in background and expertise was more than made up for by the fact that Jesus called them just as he had called the twelve.

Jesus prepared his "starters" and his "second-stringers" in much the same way, providing basic instructions about how to pack for the journey and how to handle those who would reject them, their message, or both. Then he sent out these ordinary people to do extraordinary things by the power of his name.

That same commission is given to us today. Jesus chooses us for his team who will bring hope to the hopeless and healing to the hurting. With the Holy Spirit's power we have what it takes to serve God right where we are . . . limitations and all.

Put me in, God. I'm ready to serve! Amen.

Day 89 / Philippians 4:4-7

The Source of All Joy

Rejoice in the Lord always; again I will say, Rejoice. —Philippians 4:4

For the most part, I am a joyful person. I've always been an optimist about my life and the lives of others. Even in the face of world calamities, including natural disasters, civil unrest, war, and scandal, I continue to have hope for the future and to possess a genuine sense of joy.

To what do I attribute this gift? As with all good gifts, I know that my ability to rejoice even in adversity comes from God. St. Augustine explained it this way in his *Confessions:*

> There is joy which is not given to the ungodly, but to those who love Thee for Thine own sake, whose joy Thou Thyself art. And this is the happy life, to rejoice to Thee, of Thee, for Thee; this is it, and there is no other.

The joy that God provides is deeper and richer than mere happiness. God's joy is imbued with a sense of peace and is founded in trust that God's purpose can and will be accomplished. In his letter to the Philippians, St. Paul reminds us to rejoice, not in our circumstances or even in the blessings we have, but rather to rejoice in our God from whom all blessings flow. "*Rejoice in the Lord,*" Paul reminds us. It's good advice for this day and everyday.

Help us find our joy in you, Lord, knowing that all good gifts come from your hand. Amen.

Day 90 / Psalm 27

To See God's Face

Your face, Lord, do I seek. Do not hide your face from me. —Psalm 27:8-9

If God offered you the opportunity to experience God's blessings in particular ways, what would you include on your wish list? I would probably begin by asking for good health, satisfaction in my work, opportunities to explore my interests and use my abilities, a great family, and a good night's sleep.

Suppose that God approved your list and encouraged you to add to it with the promise that you would be given everything on it. There was, however, one condition. If you accepted God's offer, you would never again see God's face.

The thought of being bereft of God's countenance, even in exchange for everything I have ever wanted, is more than I can bear. I need assurance that, no matter how often I sin, God's face will never be hidden from me because I know that I have no life apart from God's forgiveness.

The truth is that we need face-time with God more than anything else, for to see the face of God is to know God's presence and to experience God's peace.

Lord, bless us and keep us. Make your face to shine upon us and be gracious to us. Lift up your countenance upon us this day, and give us peace. Amen.

Day 91 / Micah 6:6-8

What Does God Require?

What does the Lord require of you but to do justice, and to love kindness, and to walk humbly with your God? —Micah 6:8

I was saddened to learn of the death of Rosa Parks, the courageous black woman known as the mother of America's civil rights movement. If I could have preached for her funeral, I would have used today's Bible passage for my text because Rosa Parks was all about doing justice.

When confronted with the demand to give up her bus seat to a white man, Rosa Parks refused, choosing instead to grab onto God's hand, to find courage in God's strength, and to walk humbly into a jail cell and onto the pages of history. She spent the rest of her life seeking justice for all who suffered persecution and discrimination because of the color of their skin.

In a speech she gave in 1988, Mrs. Parks remarked, "I am leaving this legacy to all of you . . . to bring peace, justice, equality, love and a fulfillment of what our lives should be."

Whether delivered through the voice of an Old Testament prophet or of a twentieth-century black woman, the message is the same. As children of God and followers of Jesus, we must faithfully pursue justice for all God's children. We can begin by treating our coworkers and all whom we meet this day with kindness and compassion according to our Lord's example.

Lord, help us see where justice is needed and then pursue it with courage and tenacity. Amen.

Day 92 / Mark 1:1-45

What's the Rush?

And the Spirit immediately drove him out into the wilderness. —Mark 1:12

The word "immediately" or "at once" occurs over and over in the Gospel of Mark. From this we might conclude that Jesus spent the three years of his ministry dashing madly about the countryside healing, teaching, and performing miracles. (Maybe that's why Mark's gospel is the shortest of the four!) I think a better explanation is that this is Mark's way of pointing to important moments in Jesus' ministry that convey a sense of urgency to act or respond.

When we spend our days rushing from one commitment to the next, we risk losing the ability to discern between what is important and what is truly urgent. I know that when my priorities get confused, I may continue to check items off my "to do" list, but the people I love don't get the attention they need and deserve.

The Gospel of Mark assures us that Jesus kept his priorities straight. Jesus understood that the life-changing and life-giving ministry with which God had entrusted him was carried out in intimate moments with people who came to him for a host of reasons. Jesus offered to all the assurance of God's love for them. In the same way, God calls us to a sense of urgency, not hurry, to carry out the work we have been given using the talents, gifts, and abilities that God provides.

God, grant us the ability to discern the urgent moments of our lives so that your love might flow through us to others. Amen.

Day 93 / Romans 8:18-25

Worth It All in the End

I consider that the sufferings of this present time are not worth comparing with the glory about to be revealed to us. —Romans 8:18

I've heard that, in an attempt to stem the decline in Australia's birthrate, the Australian government offered financial compensation to new mothers. I'm curious if the promise of a "baby bonus" helped ease the discomforts of pregnancy and the ordeal of labor.

In today's text, the apostle Paul acknowledges that following Jesus does not insure that our lives will be without pain and struggle. As Paul well knew, the very opposite is more likely the case. Chances are good that we will encounter resistance, ridicule, and even rejection in our attempts to faithfully proclaim God's message of forgiveness and salvation to a sinful world. So that makes me wonder, does God offer a bonus to help ease the difficulties of our lives today?

Paul says that our hope for a future with God beyond our lives here on earth helps us bear present trials. This hope is founded on Jesus' death and resurrection and poured out upon us in the waters of baptism. Just as pregnancy gives way to the birth of new life, Jesus promises that life here on earth will give way to life eternal in God's presence with believers of every age who endured suffering while waiting with patience for God's promises to come true.

That's a pretty remarkable bonus, don't you think?

Loving God, grant us courage to live faithfully as we wait patiently for the glory that is to come. Amen.

Day 94 / Romans 1:1-6

Whose Am I?

Paul, a servant of Jesus Christ, called to be an apostle, set apart for the gospel of God . . . —Romans 1:1

Who am I? I remember asking my mother that question one day while sitting in the kitchen of our house, in tears over I don't remember what. Sadly, I don't recall much about the rest of our conversation, but I figure either she did provide some helpful advice, or God has seen to it that I've managed to gain at least some sense of who I am.

Of course, the answer to who we are is something that constantly changes and evolves. Our identity can be affected by our age, our life circumstances, our job title, and more.

The answer to the question, "Who am I," is often up for grabs. But, as Christians, we should never have any doubt as to *whose* we are. The Apostle Paul in today's passage leaves no doubt, either in the minds of those to whom his letter has been sent, or in his own mind. *"Paul, a servant of Jesus Christ, called to be an apostle, set apart for the gospel of God . . ."* This one-time tent maker (his vocation, not his identity) is now a worker with Jesus in God's kingdom.

A little later in his letter to the Romans, Paul reminds them that "all have sinned and fall short of the glory of God" (3:23). So, yes, we are sinners. But sin shouldn't be the thing that defines us. We are more. We are *redeemed* sinners, beloved children of God, set apart and called to be servants of Jesus. That is our holy identity.

Loving God, what a joy it is to know that, in the midst of this confused world, there will always be one certainty: that I am and always will be yours. Amen.

Day 95 / Psalm 105:1-2

Tell of His Wonderful Works

O give thanks to the Lord, call on his name, make known his deeds among the peoples. —Psalm 105:1

Remember that duck in the TV commercials for an insurance company whose acronym-name sounds like "quack"? I especially recall the one in which a man brings the duck to a pet store, saying he's returning it because it says only one word. I found the ad clever and funny—until it soon became so irritating that I told myself I'd never buy that insurance.

Advertisers want their commercials, irritating or not, to *sell.* A commercial for a national chain of pizza shops did that for me. It showed a slice of pizza, then the face of a woman whose mouth alternately formed "o-o-o" or "ah-h-h." I was ready to order every time I saw the ad.

Is it possible for God's word to affect us—positively or negatively—in these same ways? "In the beginning was the Word . . ." (John 1:1). We've heard those and other words so often that we can repeat them from memory. But is that fact any guarantee that they still hold *meaning* for us?

Could even the most devout Christian become *desensitized* to the Word? I hope not! As Christ-followers, it's up to us to carry out the Great Commission. Christ has placed his message in our hearts and on our lips—and it's time for us to tell it on the mountains, in our work places, and everywhere.

God, empower me through your Spirit, so that everyday I want to "love to tell the story," your story, to those who will listen and to those who won't. Amen.

Day 96 / Hebrews 3:12-14

Support One Another

But exhort one another every day, as long as it is called 'today,' so that none of you may be hardened by the deceitfulness of sin. —Hebrews 3:13

"CU Barrel Man" may be the most loyal fan of the University of Colorado's Buffaloes football team. Win or lose, rain, snow, or shine, he's at every home game, wearing a barrel held by suspenders and a fake buffalo skin. He walks among the seats, ringing a cow bell. Fans and players love him.

I recall a professor at a church college saying, "People rise to the standard expected of them." I've played football before home crowds and can attest to the fact that it really makes a difference when you know they believe in you. That applies in the Christian life, too. We *need* other Christians around us to offer encouragement and support. I've known many people who insisted that they didn't want anything to do with a church and were content to worship in their own way. But the adage that "it takes a congregation to raise a Christian" has it exactly right.

We need to offer our fellow Christians our own versions of the support offered by Barrel Man. Above all, we need to keep in continual contact with them and not be afraid to ask, "So, how's your walk with the Lord going?" We need to be their partners in Christ so that, like the Christians Paul addresses in Hebrews, they will hold on to their confidence in Jesus Christ and be firm to the end.

Lord, we can't be Christian on our own. We need you and we need one another. Feed us, fill us, and send us forth in your name. Amen.

Day 97 / Matthew 4:21-22

Do Something Different

Immediately they left the boat and their father, and followed him.
—Matthew 4:22

It's late evening. I'm writing and eating—an apple Danish that should have been part of my breakfast today. Heavy rains required several nocturnal trips to the basement to vacuum up water, so I woke up groggy, ate my oatmeal, and forgot the Danish.

Sometimes doing something different can be at least as enjoyable as my Danish is now. Sometimes it's good to get out of our ruts and routines. Consider James and John. Scripture doesn't tell us how old the brothers were or give us any clue how long they had been in the fishing business with their father. We can only speculate that they had been fishing most days for some time.

Along comes this itinerant rabbi and, apparently without hesitating, they break from their routine and lives until now and follow him. Soon they're joined by ten others who also have responded to Jesus' call. Other rabbis in Jesus' time were followed by their own disciples, but no other group went where this one did.

When was the last time you took a truly bold step along your *spiritual* journey? Allow God to lead you, with no reservations. Touch the life of someone else with the gift of God's word—or deeds—and make a difference. Change your prayer method, perhaps by asking less and thanking more. You'll be glad you did. God will, too.

God, help me to be bold in following you, as were James and John. Help me to leap in faith knowing that, with you, life is always a great adventure! Amen

Day 98 / Psalm 139:7-12

Omnipresence

Where can I go from your spirit? Or where can I flee from your presence? —Psalm 139:7

If you're not familiar with the TV show *Joan of Arcadia*, Joan is a high-school junior who, although not really into God, is visited by and has conversations with God as he shows himself in a variety of guises. In one episode, Joan is at her computer and online when God, now a woman, appears on a pop-up and speaks to her. Remarks Joan: "Now God's like a pop-up. You never know when she's going to show up, and you can't get rid of her."

The psalmist—Psalm 139 is ascribed to David—almost certainly never imagined those annoying computer pop-ups. But as he makes clear in today's text, God is *everywhere*. Even if we flee or try to hide, God will be there. Whether I am in heaven or Sheol, says the psalmist, "You are there." Even if I fly to "the farthest limits of the sea," the psalmist says, "your hand shall lead me, and your right hand shall hold me fast."

We're left with three important attributes of God: You never know when he's going to show up in your life; when he does, you couldn't get rid of him if you tried; and he's everywhere—among earthquake victims, political prisoners, starving families around the world, at the far reaches of the seas, and in you and me. We can run but we can't hide!

God, I rejoice and offer thanks for your eternal presence. Amen.

Day 99 / Matthew 16:13-16

He Is the Christ

[Jesus] said to them, "But who do you say that I am?"
—Matthew 16:15

In his book, *Speaking My Mind,* Tony Campolo quotes this description of Jesus: "He is the living being, without beginning, without end. He is the Word, discriminating and integrating. He is to the world the ringstone of the ring. The plane of inscription, the sign by which the king deals his coffer. . ."

"Ringstone" and "plane" may not be to us be familiar names or adjectives for Jesus, but it's a pretty accurate description of the Jesus we know. The author, says Campolo, was the Muslim mystic Ibn al-Arabi (1164–1240), who put great emphasis on Christ and spoke of Jesus as the Word, the Spirit, and "God's tongue."

Especially since September 11, 2001, Americans and others have used too broad a brush to paint all Muslims as terrorists or Christ-haters. Muslims aren't Christian. But they *do* believe, as the Koran says, that Jesus is the author of creation, lived a sinless life, performed many miracles, ascended into heaven, and will come again.

"Who do you say that I am?" With Peter, we answer, "The Messiah." But that profession is no warrant for us to judge or condemn the beliefs or nonbeliefs of others. We are to preach the gospel wherever we go and to whomever we meet—and leave the judgment of their salvation in the hands of God.

God, help us to be slow to anger and condemnation, and even slower to judgment. Amen.

Day 100 / Psalm 34:8

Take Your Medicine

O taste and see that the Lord is good; happy are those who take refuge in him. —Psalm 34:8

A man who hadn't been feeling well went to see his doctor, who gave him an examination, diagnosed a problem, and wrote out a prescription that he said would likely make the patient feel better within a few days. But instead of getting the prescription filled, the man tacked it to his bulletin board. He never filled the prescription, and the illness never went away.

Would you think of doing what that sick man did?

The same scenario applies to how we handle our lives as followers of Jesus Christ. God's holy word is "medicine" we need to live spiritually healthy lives. God's words show us how to live in harmony with him.

Sometimes we Christians are like that patient, resisting and evading what's good for us. But if we want to live more spiritually fulfilling lives, we've got to take our medicine. And after we've done it, we will find that we're able to live a more confident existence, with a better understanding of God's will for our lives.

Lord, give us that "spoonful of sugar" that is the goodness of your word, whose very sweetness brings nourishment, healing, and wholeness to our lives. Amen.

Day 101 / John 8:12

The Laws of the Lighthouse

Again Jesus spoke to them, saying, "I am the light of the world." —John 8:12

It was a stormy night on an angry sea. In the distance, the captain spotted a light that appeared to be another ship, heading straight toward his ship. He had his signalman flash a message: "Change your course 10 degrees to port." The response: "Please alter your course 30 degrees to starboard." After another exchange of messages, the captain, now angry, signaled "I am the captain and this is a battleship!" The response: "I am a lighthouse, and you are heading for the rocks!"

Here are some lights I look for: When no one is watching, live as if someone is . . . Pray twice as much as you fret . . . Listen twice as much as you speak . . . Treat people like angels; you will meet some and help make some . . . Don't feel guilty for God's goodness . . . Live your liturgy.

Come on, be that lighthouse, sharing the light of Christ with all the world, so that they won't crash upon the rocks.

This little light of mine, I'm gonna let it shine! I'm gonna let it shine, Lord, because it is the light of your countenance and your promise for this suffering world! Amen.

Day 102 / 1 Chronicles 29:10-19

Bless You, God

Then David blessed the LORD in the presence of all the assembly; David said: "Blessed are you, O LORD, the God of our ancestor Israel, for ever and ever." —1 Chronicles 29:10

It was the end of the glorious reign of David, a forty-year time of prosperity and proximity to the God of the Israelites. God's people flourished under David's kingship; now was the time for transition. The mantle of responsibility would be passed on to David's son, Solomon.

God had prepared Solomon and had given him an awesome responsibility with which to start his reign: building the temple. God had had David draw plans and gather the gold, silver, wood, and other materials needed. But God told David he would not be the builder because he had done too much fighting. So David relinquished the task to his son. Solomon's coronation became a time of celebration. And in the midst of their joy, the people remembered who had brought them to this point, and with David they blessed God and raised their voices in praise and thanksgiving.

David's prayer, which continues through verse 19, is an inspiring example of how we should daily offer blessings to God. "Who am I, and what is my people," David asks, "that we should be able to make this freewill-offering? For all things come from you, and of your own have we given you" (1 Chron. 29:14). Notice how David's words humble himself and lift up God, thanking and blessing God for all that he had done for his people.

God, we offer our blessings to you for all that we have and all that you have led us to become. Remind us anew each day that all we have, all we are, and all you call us to be is your gift. Let us always be thankful to you. Amen.

Day 103 / John 9:1-12

A Tough Choice

Jesus answered, "Neither this man nor his parents sinned; he was born blind so that God's works might be revealed in him." —John 9:3

While I was growing up, my mother regularly reminded me about the "starving kids in India" who would love to have what I refused to eat. That would often lead to her tales of growing up in the Great Depression, when "times were really tough." Looking back, I realize that what she was trying to get across was not that my eating that food was going to feed children in India, but rather that I needed to be more thankful for how good I had it. I think my mother was also trying to help me understand that there were a good number of people in my own little world who could have benefited from the scraps I left on my plate.

Taken alone, today's text of Jesus' healing of the blind man is a miracle story. Jesus is asked, "Who sinned?" Neither the man nor his parents, Jesus answers. He was born blind so that "God's works might be revealed in him." Did God *create* blindness, cancer, and other human woes just to impress us now and then by healing them? But that misses the main point: It's that Jesus, in his ministry, reached out to virtually every important human need he encountered—and that as his disciples we're charged with doing the same.

God, those who are poor are indeed always with us, especially those who are poor in your Spirit. Enrich us, Lord, by your word, through your Son's example, and in our serving in your name. Amen.

Day 104 / John 21:4-6

Do You Have Enough Bait?

[Jesus] said to them, "Cast the net to the right side of the boat, and you will find some." So they cast it, and now they were not able to haul it in because there were so many fish. —John 21:6

When I was a young boy, my dad took me along when he went fishing. I think he hoped that I'd find it fun, and we could spend time doing it together. I never learned to like fishing. I did, however, learn some fishing basics—like knowing when and where to fish, using the right bait, and that even the best fishermen (and women) have those days when the fish just aren't biting.

Jesus said to Simon and Andrew, "Follow me and I will make you fish for people" (Mark 1:17). I love that analogy (except when I think too much about fish flopping unhappily on a stringer). We're called by Christ to be fishers for people. And the waters around us are teeming with fish of every size, shape, and description.

According to the Barna Research Group, about one-third of Americans are unchurched, and one-third of them already profess a personal relationship with Christ. Clearly, the seas around us are ripe for fishing for disciples. What's holding us back? The wrong bait? Throwing our nets over the wrong side of the boat? Just as it's the rare fish that jumps into the boat, few of the "fish" Jesus calls us to catch will come into the church on their own. We need to bait our hooks with the good food of the gospel!

I'd like to think I'm older and wiser now, God. How about if you teach me so we can be fishin' buddies? Amen.

Day 105 / Isaiah 38:4-6, 14

Everlasting Arms

Go and say to Hezekiah, "Thus says the LORD, the God of your ancestor David: I have heard your prayer, I have seen your tears." —Isaiah 38:5

I volunteered in ministry with a Church of God youth group. The meetings started with singing, including old gospel and campfire songs. Most of the songs were new to this Lutheran, but I liked singing them and many are lodged in my memory, including "Jesus saves and keeps me; and he's the one I'm waiting for; every day with Jesus is sweeter than the day before."

Is that a great song of faith, sentimental schmaltz—or both? My back hurts. The basement leaks. Friends are agonizing over job changes. Every day is sweeter than the day before? Not in my journey of faith.

Even as Christians, we face obstacles and setbacks. It's what I do with those bad days that helps or hinders my faith. All Jesus asks is that we hang in there with him.

In today's text, Isaiah and King Hezekiah are going through crises of faith. It's not one of those "sweet times" with God for either. But God offers hope and promise as he speaks to Isaiah, telling him to trust in his promise of deliverance and security.

In that youth group, I learned another song that promises our security in Christ. In its refrain we sing: "Leaning, leaning; safe and secure from all alarms; leaning, leaning; leaning on the everlasting arms" (WOV 780).

So, hang in there and don't lose hope, my fellow Christ-walkers. On those not-so-sweet days, just lean yourself on the everlasting arms of Christ your Savior. Amen.

Day 106 / John 6:35

Going Home

Jesus said to them, "I am the bread of life. Whoever comes to me will never be hungry, and whoever believes in me will never be thirsty." —John 6:35

I was sitting in church waiting to take my place at the communion table. I was half listening to the music the organist was playing when I realized I was hearing something both very familiar and out of place. It was the Largo or "Going Home" movement of the Czech composer Antonin Dvorak's symphony *From the New World*. It never fails to stir me.

In the late 1800s, the wife of a wealthy New York merchant founded the National Conservatory of Music for promising African American musicians. She enticed Dvorak to come to America to teach and inspire the students. He embraced African American music and used its melodies in *From the New World,* which captures the struggles and triumphs of all who had come to the new world.

America represented promise and hope for millions of people—although it was long delayed for African Americans. Hope and promise also are a central theme in today's text, in which Jesus, the bread of life, assures us that if we follow him we will never be truly thirsty or hungry.

Later at that service, our organist played "Let Us Break Bread Together." Just as Jesus called us to his table to "break bread together on our knees," so he promises that he will come again so that we can go home to share the great heavenly banquet together with him in his Father's kingdom.

Lord, you speak to us in many ways, reminding us that through your sacrifice we have been freed from sin and death, and that we can look forward with joy to a time when we will make our home with you. Amen.

Day 107 / Matthew 27:15-23

The Mind of Barabbas

Pilate said to them, "Then what should I do with Jesus who is called the Messiah?" All of them said, "Let him be crucified!" —Matthew 27:22

Meet Barabbas—although it's not certain that was his actual name. He was a notorious criminal and had been sentenced to die by crucifixion. Suddenly, his fate changed. It was a custom at the Passover feast to release a prisoner of the people's choice, and they—influenced by the religious leaders—chose Barabbas over Jesus. Jesus—kind, miracle worker, lover of those who are poor and children, humble, forgiving—had hurt no one. But the crowd chose Barabbas, and Jesus was handed over to be crucified.

What do you suppose was going on in the mind of Barabbas, now a free man, while the innocent Jesus hung in his place on the cross? Did Pilate's words—"What should I do with Jesus?"—keep ringing in his ears? What did he do with his life from that point? After all, his destiny, both earthly and eternal, depended on his response to those six words of a Roman leader who, in the midst of confusion and anger, asked: "What should I do with Jesus?"

What's your answer to that question?

In at least one way, Lord, I'm very much like Barabbas. I've been given freedom from my sins because Jesus went to the cross in my place. And all I can say is thank you, Lord. Amen.

Day 108 / Romans 3:21-26

Good for Goodness' Sake?

They are now justified by his grace as a gift, through the redemption that is in Christ Jesus. —Romans 3:24

Have you heard that old song "Last Kiss," in which two teens are thrown from their vehicle in a crash? Just before she dies, he gives her one last kiss. In the song, he says, "The Lord took her away from me. She's gone to heaven. So I've got to be good so I can see my baby when I leave this ol' world."

Those phrases "the Lord took her" and "I've got to be good" are totally out of sync with Christ's teachings, and especially with Paul's words in today's text. I should have a perforated tongue for all the times I've bitten it when someone says, following a death, "God needed another angel" or "How could a God of love let so-and-so die?" Ours is not a God who would, for his own purposes, take anyone's life.

And *being good* is neither a guarantee that heaven's door will open for us when we die nor a way we can gain God's favor now. In Mark's gospel, a man asks Jesus, "Good Teacher, what must I do to inherit eternal life?" Jesus responds, "Why do you call me good? No one is good but God alone" (Mark 10:17-18). Mark and Paul make it clear: No amount of good works will secure for us the goodness of God. Grace is God's free gift!

God, send me a shovel so I can bury my pride, my self-reliance, and my arrogance. Help me to remember your Son's words, "No one is good but God alone." It is your goodness that loves and keeps me. Amen.

Day 109 / Mark 1:2-3

As Simple as 1-2-3

As it is written in the prophet Isaiah, "See, I am sending my messenger ahead of you, who will prepare your way . . . " —Mark 1:2

As I'm writing, two related stories dominate the news here in Boston: an approaching snowstorm and Sunday's football playoff game. My wife and I just returned from the supermarket, where they're running low on the big-three storm supplies: bread, milk, and toilet paper. We bought a Boston crème pie! If the storm comes, we'll be advised to (1) limit shoveling to thirty minutes, (2) avoid unnecessary travel, and (3) stay tuned for more information.

All we need to do to prepare for almost *anything*, it seems, is follow steps 1, 2, and 3. By coincidence, today's text is Mark 1:2-3. Mark opens his gospel with the words of the prophet Isaiah, who alerts the people to a coming messenger, John the Baptist, who will tell the people to prepare the way of the Lord.

And what are we as Christians today to *do* for Christ? (1) Avail ourselves of his word each day; (2) call upon him in prayer; and (3) trust, by faith, in his promise of forgiveness and eternal life.

See, life in Christ really *is* as simple as 1-2-3—if we prepare ourselves to (1) enter his kingdom through baptism by water and the Holy Spirit; (2) take up our cross and follow him; and (3) in the words of Paul and Silas, "Believe on the Lord Jesus, and you will be saved, you and your household."

Gracious God, prepare our hearts, minds, and bodies anew each day so that we might offer ourselves in service to you through the work of your kingdom here on earth. Amen.

Day 110 / Matthew 13:24-30

Weeding

Let both of them grow together until the harvest; and at harvest time I will tell the reapers, "Collect the weeds first and bind them in bundles to be burned, but gather the wheat into my barn."
—Matthew 13:30

The husband went to another state to start a new job. The wife stayed behind to sell the house and arrange the move, then joined her spouse. But a series of crises left her exhausted and depressed. Finally settled in their new house, the couple went to look at a boat an elderly man was selling. They didn't buy it, but the woman told the seller she admired his rose garden—which had one tall weed. It was his wife's garden, the seller said. With his permission, the woman pulled the weed.

The woman tried to fit into her new community. She joined a garden club. But her loneliness and depression only deepened. Then one day the phone rang. Elaine, the caller, was a garden club member offering some plants. The new resident, sensing she'd found a friend, began describing her miserable experience. Elaine offered to phone every morning to help the woman get her life back on track. Helped by Elaine's calls, the woman made steady progress. Elaine invited the couple to visit, and when they did they immediately spotted—that rose garden. Elaine, it turned out, was ill and bed-ridden. The woman continued to pull weeds from Elaine's garden, and Elaine continued to help the woman pull weeds from her soul.

The enemy sows weeds of doubt, greed, and pain, but with his hands to guide ours, Jesus will help us beautify the "gardens" of those around us while he pulls "weeds" to strengthen and beautify our souls.

Lord, help us tend to the needs of our "garden" and to the gardens of those around us. Take our hands, Lord, as we pull those ugly weeds of hate, pain, and uncertainty so that the beauty of Jesus may be seen in us. Amen.

Day 111 / Ephesians 3:14-19

Walk a Little Closer, God

I pray that, according to the riches of his glory, he may grant that you may be strengthened in your inner being with power through his Spirit. —Ephesians 3:16

In an old gospel hymn, we sing:

> I am weak, but thou art strong. Jesus keep me from all wrong.
> I'll be satisfied as long as I walk, let me walk close to thee.

I *do* feel weak—after five hours in the cold clearing the parking lot and walkways after a snowstorm. Most of us recover quickly from sore muscles, but what about those times when we're worn out mentally, emotionally, and spiritually?

Jesus spoke to those times of weakness when he shared the beatitudes with the crowd on that hillside. He spoke of the poor in spirit, the meek, those hungering and thirsting for righteousness, those persecuted for the sake of righteousness, and those who are reviled against or spoken of falsely.

I love those words of promise in today's text. Often it's when we are at our weakest that God helps us find the strength of the Spirit that he has placed within us. And when we do, we grasp the hand that God extends and walk closer to him.

Join me as I end *my* long and tiring day with these words of Martin Luther:

I thank you, my heavenly Father, through Jesus Christ, your dear Son, that you have graciously kept me this day. And I pray that you would forgive me all my sins where I have done wrong, and graciously keep me this night. For into your hands I commend myself, my (tired) body and soul and all things. Let your holy angel be with me, that the evil foe may have no power over me. Amen.

Day 112 / Matthew 4:18-19

So, Why Not?

"Follow me, and I will make you fish for people." —Matthew 4:19

Today I passed a sign outside the downtown Methodist church that said: "I Don't Feel Like It." Was it a reference to folks who just don't feel like attending church this particular Sunday? The title of the Sunday sermon? Whatever the background, it was an intriguing location for the sign. What if many of us Christians just didn't feel like doing worship or ministry?

Today's text, the calling of Peter and Andrew, is familiar. We know what happens next. But what if Andrew and Peter had responded, "We don't feel like it?" There might have been two fewer places around the table at the Last Supper, and Jesus wouldn't have had *that* rock on which to build his church—all because someone "didn't feel like it."

We all face times and situations when we don't feel like it. The problem gets serious when that attitude becomes our prevalent thought or behavior and a lame excuse for reducing our response to God's call or dropping out altogether.

As followers of the risen Christ, we can rejoice in the fact that Jesus didn't use those words when it came to suffering and dying on the cross for us. They are words we will never hear when we come to him in prayer

So, sing his praises, rejoice in worship, and at least feel like shouting at the top of your lungs.

I believe with all my being in the God who is my strength and my salvation! Amen.

Day 113 / John 3:25-30

God, You Shrunk Your Kids

He must increase, but I must decrease. —John 3:30

I work with a woman who's under five feet tall. Once I kidded her about her size. She said she has a condition that has left her about two inches shorter than she was. This is *not* what John the Baptist is referring to when he tells his disciples, "He must increase, but I must decrease." The point, for Christians, is that we should feel *relatively* smaller as Christ becomes ever larger in our lives.

Jesus is important in my life, but on too many days I don't feel Jesus present, and I struggle to live out his words. Several years ago, I began to read some of the ancient and contemporary works on Christian spirituality. They helped me examine my relationship with God—and I wasn't totally pleased with what I discovered. Too often, I was content to allow God to play second fiddle in my life, and despite some gains, that remains true.

Jesus made it clear what he expects of us when he said that anyone who does not take up his cross and follow him cannot be his disciple. We need to pray daily for God to give us the strength to each day deny ourselves—and be ready to do what he wants done.

Apart from you, Lord, our lives account for nothing. Increase your power and presence in our lives, even if it costs us in terms of earthly wealth, position, and aspirations. Amen.

Day 114 / Ephesians 4:11-13

Minister to Whom?

The gifts he gave were that some would be apostles, some prophets, some evangelists, some pastors and teachers. —Ephesians 4:11

Chip Brogden's "The Songbird and the Flower" (*www.watchman.net/articles/songbird.html*) is the story of an ordinary-appearing songbird that each morning sings to the Lord. A squirrel, a deer, and other animals discover her talent, and soon she's busy leading music in their congregation. With the encouragement of a fox and some eagles, the bird launches an international ministry and sells her CDs to support it. She's also exhausted. In a canyon she happens on a beautiful flower whose only calling is to minister to the Lord. The flower helps the bird see that she's become so busy that, "I went into the ministry, but I missed my calling." The bird returns to its nest, and the Lord gives her new songs to sing.

Some may find that story too cute, but it makes its point. God has given each of us a special bundle of gifts, and we're to use them in ministry "for building up the body of Christ." Some of us need help in identifying our gifts. Most of us, even if our gifts were developed and used, have—at least by middle age—had our own versions of the songbird's experience. The pressures and expectations of jobs, families, and congregations leave us frustrated and exhausted, and we're not effectively using our best gifts. We, like that bird, need to return to our special gifts for ministry and service.

God, grant us the wisdom to discern your true calling as we minister in your name. Amen.

Day 115 / Psalm 40:1-5

Nothing Left but Trust

Happy are those who make the LORD *their trust, who do not turn to the proud, to those who go astray after false gods.* —*Psalm 40:4*

The last week or two have for me been one of those "almost Job" periods. I want to take charge of things so that I can have some control over their outcome. But then I get the sense that God is using different ways and people to remind me to wait patiently and that he is "inclining his ear to me and hearing my cries of anguish and uncertainty." It seems as if each time I begin to doubt or to question God's presence and plan, something or someone provides something to redirect my focus.

That happened yesterday when a friend sent me a piece by an unknown author that reminded me how we lose sight of just where God is in our lives. It also resurrected memories of my work with persons with intellectual disabilities and the profound thoughts and truths that emerged from minds thought to be simple or childlike.

Kevin, that author's intellectually disabled brother, believes God lives under his bed, that Santa Claus puts the packages under the tree, and that angels keep airplanes aloft. He never shrinks from a job. He believes everyone tells the truth. He trusts God, his closest companion. The writer suspects that Kevin "comprehends things I can never learn."

We as God's children need more of that trust, and we need to figure out where God is in our lives.

Thanks Lord, for the power of your word when I need it most. Keep me grounded in your love. When I'm inclined to go off on those "I can solve it myself" moments, snatch me back into your kingdom and still me with your peace. Amen.

Day 116 / Psalm 91:14-16

Love-Affair with God

Those who love me, I will deliver; I will protect those who know my name. —Psalm 91:14

One Sunday our pastor preached about "a love-affair with God." Look more closely at today's text—and all of Psalm 91. God says, "I will deliver . . . protect . . . answer . . . be with them in trouble . . . rescue and honor them." It's no coincidence that those words bear a striking resemblance to the vows in the traditional marriage ceremony.

In *Finding God in the Questions*, Timothy Johnson writes that moral conscience and the *drive toward relationship* are basic characteristics "that seem to be the most primal level of human thought and behavior" and least likely to result from "accidental biology and evolution alone." *Hardwired to Connect*, a study by the YMCA and Dartmouth Medical School published by the Institute for American Values, argues that our brains are "hard-wired" for relationships and that adolescents must to develop meaningful relationships if their moral and religious needs are to be met as adults. Simply put: If we are to have any chance of successfully connecting with our fellow human beings, we need to be connected to God.

I like the idea of using the image of the cross to represent those connections. On the cross, arms outstretched, Jesus reached out to embrace the world, while the vertical part of the cross represents the connection—the "love-affair"—between us and our Creator.

God, you hang on to us with a never-ending ferociousness. Don't ever let go of us. Keep us connected to you through the gift of your saving grace. Amen.

Day 117 / Psalm 119:129-136

S.A.C.K. Somebody Today

The unfolding of your words gives light; it imparts understanding to the simple. —Psalm 119:130

Joseph Brackett Jr., a Shaker elder, wrote the hymn "The Gift to be Simple" in 1848. The Shakers began in England in the middle of the eighteenth century and relocated to America, where their numbers peaked about a century later. They lived a simple lifestyle and had a variety of cottage industries, most famously their furniture. They often sang as they worked, including these lines:

When true simplicity is gained,
To bow and to bend we shan't be ashamed.
To turn, turn will be our delight,
'Til by turning, turning we come round right.

'Tis the gift to have friends and a true friend to be,
'Tis the gift to think of others not to only think of me,
And when we hear what others really think and really feel,
Then we'll all live together with a love that is real.

Today only a few Shakers remain in a couple of places in the United States—in part because the sect practiced celibacy. By orthodox Christian standards, they were radical, if not heretical. Still, their concepts of simplicity and their willingness to "think of others and not only of me" and to listen to what others think and feel are ideals we as Christians should espouse.

Here's your challenge for today and every day: Without fanfare, S.A.C.K. someone! That's **S**imple **A**ct of **C**hristian **K**indness. Do it because it's what Christ has called you to do.

God, help us to receive your love and, in turn, to extend your love to others through simple acts of Christian kindness. Amen.

Day 118 / Ecclesiastes 5:1-2

Focus, Christian-son

Guard your steps when you go to the house of God; to draw near to listen is better than the sacrifice offered by fools; for they do not know how to keep from doing evil. —Ecclesiastes 5:1

He was a first-time visitor to the suburban church. The pastor began the sermon. The visitor liked the pastor's style of delivery and the biblical substance of the message. Soon, however, he was distracted. A boy crumpled his bulletin while repeatedly kicking the hymnal rack. Members of one family were deep in a conversation. An elderly man snored.

Martin Luther, the visitor recalled, had reminded *his* congregation that the preaching of the gospel is the very word of God and that behavior that causes someone to neglect or ignore the sermon—which *then* often ran more than an hour—is a sin. I've switched from pulpit to pew, but I've watched that behavior from the pulpit—as well as those sometimes few trying their best to give ear to God's word.

At basketball games, you'll often see people trying to disrupt the shooter's concentration during foul shots. But a good shooter maintains focus and won't let that happen. In the second *Karate Kid* movie, Daniel-son, as Mr. Miyagi refers to him, is challenged to break several slabs of ice with his hand. When he has second thoughts as more slabs are added, Miyagi's counsel is: "Focus, Daniel-son!"

Maybe congregations can communicate Luther's message to folks whose manners could use some work. Meanwhile, for that visitor and others who want to listen, our best advice is, "Focus, Christian-son! (and –daughter!).

God, we live in an age where distractions are so plentiful and engaging. Let your Holy Spirit guide and direct us so that we are always true to your word, both in our attention to it and in living it out each day. Amen.

Day 119 / Matthew 6:19-21

Forget the U-Haul

For where your treasure is, there your heart will be also.
—Matthew 6:21

I stopped as we allowed a funeral procession to pass. When I was a pastor, I found myself in many of those. Once again I noticed that no U-Haul trailer was attached to the hearse. This person was going to his or her earthly rest without money, house, or other possessions. Whoever first said, "You can't take it with you" got it right.

I love the parable of the Rich Fool in Luke 12. It's one of few that Jesus *prefaces* with the basic point: "Take care! Be on your guard against all kinds of greed; for one's life does not consist in the abundance of possessions." Then he tells the story of the man so rich he needs bigger barns for his grain and goods—and smugly tells himself, "Soul, you have ample goods laid up for many years; relax, eat, drink, be merry." To which God replies: "You fool! This very night your life is being demanded of you. And the things you have prepared, whose will they be?" (Luke 12:15-20).

There's nothing wrong with enjoying life and God's other gifts. But if we live with the mistaken assumption that the more we have the more we can celebrate, we've lost sight of God's intent. Remember, God assures us that he will supply us with the things we *need*, not all that we might want.

So Lord, give us this day our daily bread, because we certainly don't need the entire supermarket! Because on the day of our death you will supply for us the greatest banquet ever prepared. And what an incredible feast it's going to be! Amen.

Day 120 / Matthew 6:1-6

Clean Hands and Pure Heart

Beware of practicing your piety before others in order to be seen by them; for then you have no reward from your Father in heaven. —Matthew 6:1

Shel Silverstein wrote a delightful tale called, *The Giving Tree*, in which a boy has a friendship with a *tree*. When he's young, he swings in the tree's branches, picks apples, and plays King of the Forest. He asks for favors each time he visits, and the tree gives without questioning or asking for anything in return. The tree never brags about all she has done for him. She loves the boy and does her good deeds with a pure heart.

Too often our actions are good, but our motives hollow or selfish. God knows sincere faith and loves a pure heart. We must be willing to give and serve in response to God's love, not for personal gain, others' approval or recognition, or self-gratification. We should serve and give even if no one notices because there is one who always sees. That's the message in today's text from Matthew.

During my pastorate at one church, the mother of a generous family would each year ask for the name of a less-fortunate family in the church. Her son would leave food and gifts on the family's porch with a note that said, "In the name of Jesus Christ, have a Merry Christmas." It was signed "His joyous servants."

With a pure heart and without recognition, we can do that kind of sharing in Jesus' name any time of the year.

God, may our gifts always be from our heart and in loving response to your sustaining grace. Amen.

Day 121 / Mark 9:7-8

In a Fog

Then a cloud overshadowed them, and from the cloud there came a voice, "This is my Son, the Beloved; listen to him!" —Mark 9:7

We have thick fog here sometimes, making driving scary and dangerous. We all feel more comfortable when we can see where we're headed.

There are many days when I find myself in another kind of fog. I can't see what lies ahead—and that bothers me. The demands of work, family, and even church cloud my ability to see God's way clearly. My fog is also partly the result of my unwillingness to deal with the challenges to faith that life presents. I don't want to think about the fact that Jesus had to suffer and die in order to experience the resurrection. I want to see God's glory now!

In my current state of "fogginess," I find comfort in the words of a hymn (*With One Voice*, 733):

> Our Father, we have wandered and hidden from your face;
> In foolishness have squandered your legacy of grace.
> But now, in exile dwelling, we rise with fear and shame,
> As, distant and compelling, we hear you call our name.

Today's text tells us that God called to Peter, James, and John from within a cloud, "This is my Son, the Beloved; listen to him!" That same God calls to us. If we move toward that voice, we'll feel a hand grasping ours and leading us out of the fog and into the glory of the Lord.

Faithful and loving God, you call to us through the fog. Help us hear your voice. Lead us where you would have us go and to those whom you would have us serve along the way. Amen.

Day 122 / Romans 4:13-16, 20-21

Promises, Promises

For the promise that he would inherit the world did not come to Abraham or to his descendants through the law but through the righteousness of faith. —Romans 4:13

In Romans, Paul explains to the people that their righteousness with God can come only through faith. Abraham, he reminds them, grew strong in faith because he trusted God's promise that he would become the father of many nations.

So it must be with the promises *we* make. Whether to God or another person, we have promises to keep and perhaps many miles to go before our final sleep. Our parents or sponsors made promises and accepted obligations at our baptisms, and we did the same when we were confirmed.

In one chapter of his 1609 *Introduction to the Devout Life*, the mystic St. Francis De Sales renews the promises made at his baptism, "conscious" that he has often betrayed them. Should he "transgress" these renewed promises, he vows that "with the grace of the Holy Spirit" he will "lift myself up immediately and return to God's mercy, with no delay or sloth whatsoever."

God challenges us to look inward, to examine our relationship with him, and to remember our promise to serve him in word and deed. Will we go the miles to keep those promises?

In that same chapter, St. Francis de Sales prayed:

May it please thee, O God, to confirm and accept this sacrifice of my heart, and to grant me the grace to carry it out. O God, the God of my heart, I adore thee now and forever. Amen.

Day 123 / Isaiah 45: 9-12

Cracked Pots

Woe to you who strive with your Maker, earthen vessels with the potter! —Isaiah 45:9

We're thrown into this world just as a potter throws the clay on his wheel. The Master Potter wraps his creative hands around us and pounds, molds, and works us. He's molding a son or daughter of the kingdom—you!

During trying or painful times in our lives, we wonder, "What's happening to me?" Maybe it's the Potter shaping or reshaping you in ways you don't at the moment understand or appreciate.

In order for a piece of pottery to be created, the clay that is being molded in the hands of the craftsman has to be moldable so that he is able to shape it from worthless earth to a thing of beauty. The beauty of the final creation is what the Potter has in mind as he shapes and molds us.

Before worrying about what kind of person we're becoming, we should first celebrate the kind of man or woman God has given us the *potential* to be. We need to remember that God's molding and shaping isn't a one-time thing, but an ongoing process. What God has in store for our lives will be beautiful—if we are willing to remain pliable in his loving hands. May your heart stay soft and open to the Potter's work!

God, what a joy it is to know that you place the highest value on us, even in our damaged condition. What a joy it is to know that, as your created vessels, you use us to pour out your love to others. Amen.

Day 124 / Matthew 15:1-9

Not Just Your Personal Jesus

[Jesus] answered them, "And why do you break the commandment of God for the sake of your tradition?" —Matthew 15:3

After worship, we got into a discussion about the sermon preached by our intern. Overall, it was solid and well delivered. He talked about the reflective nature of Lent. Then, however, he suggested that we can gain a better understanding of ourselves by looking—figuratively—in a mirror. When we do that, however, do we see ourselves as we are or as we *think* we are?

The New Testament scholar N.T. Wright wrote, "The longer you look at Jesus, the more you will want to serve him in his world." Yes, but too often our Jesus isn't the one of the Scriptures but one we've invented to suit our needs. If that's our Jesus, we're due for a serious reality check, because that's not the Jesus of the Gospels. It's great to develop a personal relationship with Jesus—and dangerous to *customize* him for our own purposes.

In today's text, the Pharisees and scribes charge that Jesus' disciples are breaking some traditional religious rules. Jesus replies that it's *they* who are breaking one of God's commandments, allowing a tradition to trump God's word.

Take a close look at yourself and your relation to the Christ of the cross. But look deeper than the surface of your skin. Search your heart and follow Jesus—the real Jesus of the Gospels.

God of truth, help us to be truthful in our worship and our service to you. Help us to love you for who you are and not who we want you to be. Amen.

Day 125 / Proverbs 3:5-7

Follow the Leader

In all your ways acknowledge him, and he will make straight your paths. —Proverbs 3:6

Someone once asked the noted African American botanist George Washington Carver the secret of his success. He responded, "It's simple. It's found in the Bible: 'In all your ways acknowledge him, and he will make straight your paths.'"

Sound advice, don't you think, especially as we make our way along the Lenten path to the cross of Jesus? At the end of each piece of music that Johann Sebastian Bach wrote, he penned *Soli Deo Gloria*—to God the glory. Whenever Bach penned those words, he meant what he said. He had a deep, abiding faith and never questioned that his musical gifts came from God.

Think about the gifts that God has given you—whether it's music, teaching, computers, athletics, being a good listener, or whatever. When was the last time you used them to the glory of God—or acknowledged them in thankful prayer?

The paths of our lives are smooth, difficult, crooked, and sometimes seemingly impossible. The writer of Proverbs tells us that if we are willing to acknowledge God in all we say and do, then even the most crooked of life's paths will be made straight. Even the path to Christ's cross.

God, guide our feet as you lead us along the paths of life. And help us to always be thankful to you for who we are and for what you have called us to do for those around us. Soli Deo Gloria! Amen.

Day 126 / 1 Corinthians 3:16-17

Really See

Do you not know that you are God's temple and that God's Spirit dwells in you? —1 Corinthians 3:16

I remember reading Thornton Wilder's play *Our Town* when I was in high school. Emily Webb, the protagonist, dies during the birth of her second child. Buried in the local cemetery, she's allowed to return for one day of her life. She chooses what she remembers as one of her happiest days, her twelfth birthday. Once there, however, she discovers that people are "living in the dark" and uninterested in *really* seeing one another. Forgetting that nobody can see her, she pleads for her mother to just once look at her, to look at her and really see her. How many other Emilys exist all around us, making similar silent pleas? And it's not just people. All God' creation is screaming out those words. But we're too busy to hear their cries.

To take the time to see God in our world, in ourselves, and in others is to live fully in God's loving embrace. It is to hold firmly and tenderly the integrity of all creation. To see and be seen with eyes of love—God's love—is to understand and cherish the Creator and his creation.

Take all of me, Lord, for I am yours alone. Surround me with your love and grace, and bless me with your vision to see all of your creation and to be the caring steward you have called me to be. In the name of your Son, Jesus Christ. Amen.

Day 127 / Matthew 6:1 and 12:34-37

Are We Trying (Very)?

You brood of vipers! How can you speak good things, when you are evil? For out of the abundance of the heart the mouth speaks. —Matthew 12:34

The pastor, using the story of Nicodemus and Jesus, commented that when many of us are asked if we are Christians, we respond, "I'm trying to be." But, he said, "We are either Christians or we're not—there's no 'trying' about it." He argued that too many Christ followers haven't fully accepted their baptism.

Good point, but it got me thinking about that *other* meaning of "trying Christians." Most of us have encountered (and, if we're honest, probably been) those folks who exhaust all patience and understanding.

In today's text, Jesus finds the Pharisees and other religious leaders so trying that he shouts, "You brood of vipers!" These guardians of the law were daily hammering away at Jesus' character, his message, and his association with the "wrong" kind of people.

Jesus' ministry and ultimate sacrifice demonstrated God's love in words and action. Says the writer of 1 John: "Beloved, since God loved us so much, we also ought to love one another. No one has ever seen God; if we love one another, God lives in us, and his love is perfected in us" (1 John 4:11-12).

That love has no room for Pharisaic words or behaviors. Through that love we have been received into God's kingdom and don't have keep "trying" to be Christians. Christianity isn't primarily something we *do*. It's first about who and whose we are.

God, remind us daily that we are yours through our baptism into your kingdom. Be patient with us, God, as we keep trying to understand both the scope and the joy of that gift. Amen.

Day 128 / *John* 21:1-12

Dawn of a New Day

[Jesus] said to them, "Cast the net to the right side of the boat, and you will find some." So they cast it, and now they were not able to haul it in because there were so many fish. —John 21:6

There's an old Pueblo Indian belief that the sun would not rise if they were not there to welcome it. Does it perhaps reflect a universal longing, when we're asleep, to greet the new dawn?

It was after Easter and after the risen Christ had been with Thomas and the other disciples. Peter decided to go fishing, and the other disciples joined him. They spent all night out on the water, but time and again their nets came up empty. Frustrated with their luck and probably cold and still distraught over the loss of their earthly leader, they must have been eager for the morning.

Shortly after dawn, a voice on shore—it was Jesus, but the disciples didn't know it—tells them to cast their nets on the right side of the boat. They follow instructions, and soon they're hauling ashore a net with 153 large fish. The risen Christ invites them to a breakfast of bread and fish. It was, John says, "the third time that Jesus appeared to the disciples after he was raised from the dead" (John 21:14).

So, how do we greet the dawn of our days? Is morning just the start of another routine day—or do we greet it as another opportunity to hear the voice of Christ calling out to us with words of promise and assurance?

Loving God, call us into your presence at the dawning of each new day so that we might bask in the glow of your radiance. Illumine our paths, warm our hearts, and feed us to fullness with the bread of your word. Amen.

Day 129 / Ephesians 4: 1-3, 17-19

You Can Do It!

I therefore, the prisoner in the Lord, beg you to lead a life worthy of the calling to which you have been called. —Ephesians 4:1

Watchman Nee was a leader in the underground church movement in communist China and was in prison most of the last twenty years of his life. His book *Sit, Walk, Stand*, organized around three verses in Ephesians, reminds us that we're seated with Christ in heaven; instructs us how to walk in ways that honor Christ; and encourages us to stand firm in times of spiritual struggle (Ephesians 2:6, 4:1, and 6:11).

Walking, for most of us, is something we take for granted and is barely a conscious effort. But it wasn't always that easy. I remember when our daughter Sunshine learned to walk. She raised herself up in her crib at some three months, and took her first steps, some *backwards*, at eight months. We'd offer helping hands and say, "C'mon, you can do it!" Soon she could.

The gentle encouragement and modest instruction that most parents offer their would-be toddlers is a good model for how we Christians should treat one another as we walk together in faith. Especially for infants in the faith, of whatever age, taking those first steps can be scary.

Too often we offer criticism, ridicule, or silence instead of encouragement and wise counsel—to new and longtime Christians alike. Instead, we need to heed Paul's advice that we're to bear "with one another in love," demonstrating patience, humility, and gentleness.

Together we stand. Guide our feet, hold our hands. Precious Lord, take our hands and lead us home. Amen.

Day 130 / Hebrews 12:1-2

Godly Discipline

Therefore, since we are surrounded by so great a cloud of witnesses, let us also lay aside every weight and the sin that clings so closely, and let us run with perseverance the race that is set before us. —Hebrews 12:1

The anonymous writer of the letter to the Hebrews says we're to run the race with "perseverance." After surgery a decade ago, my doctor advised me to walk to strengthen muscles that had been cut. One step led to another, and I became a serious runner for a few years, at my peak doing five to seven miles three days a week. I became able to block out everything and everybody around me, concentrating on the run and my goal of completing it. I was a disciplined runner.

Discipline has several meanings, including punishment, training, and self-control. *Christian discipline* isn't about the first of those, but it is about the other two. It often involves avoiding or postponing more immediate pleasures or temptations in order to reach an important, long-range goal in this "race" that here means the Christian life.

The writer of Hebrews reminds us to focus our lives on Jesus always. Christ is not only our *goal* in this race but the very *source* of our life and faith. He's the perfecter of our faith, living in us and providing the power and direction for our lives.

Lord God, set our eyes on the prize: eternity with your Son Jesus Christ. Guide our feet and strengthen our bodies so that we might run without ceasing, into the loving arms of Christ. Amen.

Day 131 / Daniel 9:14-15

Righteous-mess?

So the Lord kept watch over this calamity until he brought it upon us. Indeed, the Lord our God is right in all that he has done; for we have disobeyed his voice. —Daniel 9:14

Pastors and theologians often use the words *righteous* and *righteousness*, but they're not ones most of the rest of use in everyday conversations. Here's a useful if oversimplified definition: *righteous* means it's in God's character to always do the right thing—and that God defines what's right.

Still, when we hear about hundreds or thousands of people killed in tsunamis, earthquakes, or hurricanes, or of one innocent teen killed in a drug-related drive-by shooting, we ask: "Where is God when these things happen?" Theologians explain that we live in a "between time" and that we are, as Luther said, at once saints and sinners. Part of us accepts that, but the tragedies still don't compute.

A life of faith in God includes learning to live with things we don't understand. Why does a righteous God harden Pharaoh's heart, then punish him and all Egypt? From a human perspective, something's wrong with that picture. But from a perspective of faith, I still believe God is righteous. God sees the big picture, we can't. God is, we're not.

Do you, like me, have a list of things you don't understand and hope to one day ask God? Don't wait. Ask them now or anytime in your prayers. But keep knowing and believing that God is righteous and will always do the right thing. Live by faith, not by sight.

God, there are a lot of things that happen in life that, for us Christians, don't seem to make sense. But we just have to trust in you and in your mercy. Keep us faithful because, other than you, we have nothing. Amen.

Day 132 / Psalm 32:1-5

Silly Rabbit!

Happy are those whose transgression is forgiven, whose sin is covered. —Psalm 32:1

Remember the children's song about Little Rabbit Fufu, a naughty rabbit who goes through the forest picking up the field mice and bopping them on the head? Each time he does it, the Good Fairy warns him to stop or she'll turn him into a goon—and after her third warning, she does.

The Good Fairy had a limit to her forgiveness; God doesn't. In today's Psalm text, David expresses joy for God's forgiveness. It's a joy not common in the Books of the Law (Genesis–Deuteronomy) in the Old Testament. Those books are filled with accounts of the unfaithfulness of God's people, his repeated warnings through the prophets, their temporary punishment, and—here the Fufu story and the Bible part company—God's willingness to forgive.

There's a bit of Little Rabbit Fufu in all of us. We're slow to heed God's warnings. I figure Fufu just didn't care for field mice or had self-esteem issues. What are our excuses—a need to feel superior to others and to God or the influence of evil in our world? Whatever our excuses have been, God is willing to forgive us if we come to him with an open and confessing heart.

We pray, "Forgive us our sins as we forgive those who sin against us." Thank goodness God's forgiveness isn't conditioned on our compliance with the second part of that petition!

God, thanks for understanding and caring for us. Teach us to value all lives, including our own. Help us to stop bopping others and to instead give them the kind of love and care you show us. Amen.

Day 133 / John 4:1-9

Don't Go There!

The Samaritan woman said to him, "How is it that you, a Jew, ask a drink of me, a woman of Samaria?" (Jews do not share things in common with Samaritans.) —John 4:9

What is it with Jesus? He's always going places he shouldn't, hanging out with the wrong kind of people, and he often ends up ticking off the Pharisees. In today's text (the story continues through verse 26), he stops to rest at Jacob's well in Samaria, an alien place for Jews. "Give me a drink," he says to a woman who has come for water. She's a Samaritan woman of low reputation—she's had five husbands and now is living with another man. Jesus tells her of a new kind of water that will bring eternal life. When she tells Jesus, "I know that Messiah is coming," he replies, "I am he" (John 4:25-26). When she returns to the city and tells her amazing story, she still questions whether Jesus could be the Messiah, but soon growing numbers of Samaritans believe in Jesus. We can be pretty certain that the Samaritan woman's life—and faith—were changed forever.

Think about it: Had Jesus not gone "there," the ten lepers would not have been cleansed; Zaccheus would have continued to cheat the people; the son of the widow of Nain, the daughter of the Roman official Jairus, and Lazarus would not have been freed from death; perhaps hundreds would never have been healed; the Samaritan woman would have not led a changed life—and our sins would have never been forgiven.

Merciful God, help us to follow Jesus' example of ignoring accepted propriety in order to love all people regardless of racial, economic, and religious boundaries. Amen.

Day 134 / John 15:12-17

What a Friend

You are my friends if you do what I command you. John 15:14

In 1921, a boy living in Boys Town just west of Omaha, Nebraska, wore a leg brace and had difficulty walking. Other boys took turns carrying him on their backs. Someone saw that happening and took a picture that ended up in a magazine. Father Edward Flanagan, the head of Boys Town, saw the picture in this magazine and the caption, "He ain't heavy, he's my brother." The priest, certain that the image and words captured the mission and spirit of the place, had a sculptor create a statue based on the photo and located it near the main entrance to the home. The image and words also were used in the home's fundraising efforts.

True friends often carry one another's burdens and sometimes, as at Boys Town (now Boys and Girls Town), actually carry one another. Jesus established friendships with what in his day was a most unlikely group of followers—tax collectors, fishermen, women, foreigners, and others. He came to save them—and us—from the power of evil that had overcome humanity and the whole creation. On the cross, he gave his life so that new life and salvation could come to all who acknowledge his death and resurrection.

What a privilege it is that Jesus has called us to be his friend. And as the hymn says, "What a friend we have in Jesus, all our sins and griefs to bear!"

Thank you, Jesus, for being our friend, for lifting us up when we are too tired or weak to continue, and for restoring us in fellowship with God. Amen.

Day 135 / Numbers 6:22-27

Blessings

The Lord bless you and keep you. —Numbers 6:24

In today's text, God has shed his blessing on Moses and Aaron and now calls on Aaron to bless the people. He provides him with the words—ones we often hear at the close of services:

The Lord bless you and keep you;
The Lord make his face to shine upon you,
and be gracious to you;
The Lord lift up his countenance upon you,
and give you peace.

Several years ago, I began to pursue my interest in spirituality. As a result, I don't think I've ever felt as closely connected to God and the church as I do now.

In his book *Gospel-Centered Spirituality: An Introduction to Our Spiritual Journey*, Professor Allan H. Sager of Trinity Lutheran Seminary, Columbus, Ohio, describes two approaches we take toward our spiritual lives. One is the "always obey everything, strict letter of the law" method, the other the "reckoned as righteousness, God fills in the blanks" style. If we take the second approach, which emphasizes *our response to God's actions*, we'll say, with Sager: "I . . . shall hold to that Gospel that found and holds me; shall gather regularly with that family of God into which I was first gathered; and shall share and show forth the enlightenings that I have received in the knowledge that I have been blessed to be a blessing."

God, as you have blessed me, let me be that same blessing to your whole creation. And, God, thank you for "filling in the gaps" where my human efforts often fall terribly short, and where I, too, often fail. Amen.

Day 136 / Philippians 4:10-13

He Keeps Me Hangin' On

I can do all things through him who strengthens me.
—Philippians 4:13

I was in the car, running errands, when the station played a song in which Martina McBride sings: "It's hangin' on when your heart has had enough. It's giving more when you feel like giving up." Words I really needed to hear.

It was after midnight as our son left work. Soon he phoned to tell me that his car had died. I picked him up at the garage about 3:30 a.m., returned home for a few hours of sleep, then went to work. By evening we learned the problem was a blown head gasket—serious time and money. It was another in a series of problems that had made life difficult and stressful for me and our family in the past few months.

Through it all, I'd remained fairly calm and confident that God would, as always, be with us to work through the problems—but now that confidence was facing some serious challenges. I'm convinced that God wanted me to hear the words in that song. They reminded me that I didn't need to shoulder all it and that I needed to release it into God's hands.

I wish I could tell you that all the problems have gone away. They haven't. God isn't directly paying the bills, but he is strengthening our hearts and our resolve to deal with them without fear and without as much worry.

Thank you, Lord, for loving me, strengthening me, and giving me your peace—and for watching over me with a Father's eyes. Amen.

Day 137 / Ecclesiastes 4:4-6

Listen, Will You?

Better is a handful with quiet than two handfuls with toil, and a chasing after wind. —Ecclesiastes 4:6

"Blessed is the person who can do two things at once." Is that a beatitude for today's lifestyle? I knew a guy who brushed his teeth and shaved while taking a shower. We see commuters *reading* while driving—and folks doing anything and everything while talking on cell phones. The three *R*s, once "reading, 'riting, and 'rithmetic," now seem to be rushing, running, and resisting. From birth, we've been programmed to hurry.

Karl Marx called religion "the opiate of the people," but today it's speed—and *not* the drug—that's our opiate. Religion often becomes just one more casualty in our drive to do everything and be everywhere. Ben Franklin coined the phrase "Haste makes waste." Did he know that haste comes from an Old English word meaning *violence*?

Countless times in the gospels, Jesus seeks out a quiet place where he can rest, think, and seek out his Father in prayer. Those times of solitude and prayer were vital to Jesus—and they should be equally important to us.

Do yourself a favor. Seek out solitude. Listen to God. Pray. Some of your greatest plans and projects will be conceived and incubated in that womb of prayer and contemplation. Your anxieties and concerns will diminish, and your discerning heart will be better prepared to respond to the needs of others.

Lord God, help us to feast on the words of the psalmist, who wrote: "Be still, and know that I am God." Amen.

Day 138 / Numbers 11:4-6

No More Whine and Cheese

The rabble among them had a strong craving; and the Israelites also wept again, and said, "If only we had meat to eat!" —Numbers 11:4

Peter Deyneka Sr., a great man of God, died in 1987 at the age of eighty-nine. He emigrated from Russia in 1914, founded the Slavic Gospel Association, and spent his life working on behalf of Christians living under oppression in Eastern Europe and the Soviet Union. Many people found ways out of what came to be known as the Iron Curtain countries and never looked back. Not Deyneka. His work brought books, broadcasts, and hope to the believers left behind, including many who today remain thankful for his efforts.

Throughout history, God has chosen heroes to "stand in the gap" on behalf of his people. God used Moses to help free the Israelites from long slavery in Egypt. In the wilderness, God provided the Israelites with manna. Soon, however, they whined, demanding the meat and vegetables they now remembered from the "good old days," when they were slaves.

How could a people upon whom God bestowed so much be such an ungrateful lot? God frees and provides for them—and they hold a "whine and cheese party." But how different are we, in our relative affluence?

Isn't it time we learned from the example of the Israelites of old? God calls us to be thankful people, people who remember his goodness and trust him to provide for our needs. Enough with whining and complaining—let's do more thanking and praising!

Make a mental list of some of the ways God has blessed you, and compose a prayer using some or all of them.

Day 139 / Amos 5: 21-24

Let Justice Roll Down

But let justice roll down like waters, and righteousness like an ever-flowing stream. —Amos 5:24

How many Americans today, I wonder, could identify the Rev. Dr. William Sloane Coffin Jr., who in the 1960s was a household name for his opposition to the Vietnam War and involvement in the civil rights movement? Sloane was chaplain at Yale University and pastor of New York City's Riverside Church. In a 1987 speech, he accused the contemporary church of being unwilling to step beyond its charity work to challenge "unjust structures." Said Coffin: "If you provide food for the hungry you may be considered a saint, but if you ask how come people are going hungry you'll probably be called a Marxist."

The outspoken Coffin was a thorn in the side of churches and the nation's political establishment. So was the prophet Amos, one of my favorite characters in the Bible. Amos described himself as a simple farmer with little to say. In fact, he's one of the most insightful people in either testament—and his audience often found him outspoken and confrontational. Looking at America and the world in the twenty-first century, Amos and Coffin would agree that justice and righteousness are, at best, only trickling in the direction of injustice, hunger, and disease.

Isn't it time for us and for our churches to make Amos's words our battle cry—and for us to be God's water-bearers?

Lord, grant us a willingness to pursue justice on behalf of your poor, oppressed, and forgotten children. Help us to share both the fruits of your creation and the power of your word with all who cry out for your blessings. Amen.

Day 140 / 1 Samuel 17:45-47

Obedience Matters

*But David said to the Philistine, "You come to me with a sword and spear and javelin; but I come to you in the name of the Lord of hosts, the God of the armies of Israel, whom you have defied."
—1 Samuel 17:45*

David—what an incredible guy! He was a simple shepherd boy, sent to the fields to care for the sheep. Later on when his father sent him to an army camp to check on his brothers and bring them food, David volunteered to go out and face the enemy's Goliath.

What I like about David is that he knew what God had sent him to do, and, trusting in God, he did it. I don't think he was especially courageous, but he surely was obedient.

Obedience to God doesn't come naturally. That's especially true when what God tells us to do runs contrary to our wishes. Remember Jonah? It took some extraordinary convincing to get him to obey God's command to go to Ninevah. Without doubt, the ultimate act of obedience was offered by Jesus.

God is calling *us* to obedience. Armed with God's word, we're charged with going out into the world to defeat an enemy whose weapons are deceits, lies, and temptations. The victory will be ours, in the name of our Lord, Jesus Christ, who was himself obedient unto death.

God of all strength and might, empower us, equip us, and send us forth to battle the enemy forces of our world and emerge triumphant in your Holy Name! Amen.

Day 141 / Matthew 6: 31-34

Make a Difference Day

So do not worry about tomorrow, for tomorrow will bring worries of its own. Today's trouble is enough for today. —Matthew 6:34

With all the coverage after the tsunami in South Asia, it was inevitable that we'd get some weird reports in the mix. A London-based scientist warned that a volcano on one of the Canary Islands could collapse in the next few thousand years, sending 100-meter walls of water racing across the Atlantic, perhaps killing millions.

Next few thousand years!? Don't get me wrong: I think governments and other organizations *should* address genuine long-term global issues. But I—and most of us—have enough to worry about *today*! Besides, I'm convinced that God wants us Christ-followers to focus on making a difference in our small worlds, the ones of our workplaces, schools, communities, and neighborhoods. And we can do that by reaching out with the life-changing message of Jesus in what we do and what we say.

Are we making a difference for the people with whom we spend significant parts of our lives? Do they see the love of Christ in us? Do we reach out beyond our self-interest and serve others in ways that help protect, preserve, and enrich their lives? Or do we talk about sharing the gospel, but do that priest-and-Levite thing when we come face to face with real need?

Every year, some organization declares a "Make a Difference Day." Well, fellow Christian, it's today, and tomorrow, and the day after tomorrow, and . . .

Understanding God, help me not to worry, but to trust in you for this day. Thanks for your patience with me and your never-ending love for me—without which, I'd be a real mess. Amen.

Day 142 / Galatians 6:1-6

Beneath the Skin

Bear one another's burdens, and in this way you will fulfill the law of Christ. —Galatians 6:2

Ethel, the cook at our mission, was a dear, sweet woman, but she had a habit of complaining. As I entered the kitchen, she was ranting and raving about the onion she was cutting. It appeared perfect on the outside, but it was rotten inside—and I had purchased it. There was no way to salvage the onion or appease Ethel.

It's often hard to tell from looking at someone what's going on inwardly. We ask, "How are you?"—but how often do we really *want* the true answer if it's other than the usual "I'm fine"?

Many people around us are hurting. As Christ-followers, it's our responsibility to see beyond appearances and carry one another's burdens. It may feel easier and safer to keep relationships shallow, but that's not what God calls us to do. If we take the time and energy to strengthen and deepen relations with people in our lives, we'll be better equipped to see and respond to their needs.

During that year I worked with Ethel, I learned that she was struggling economically and was in constant pain from arthritis and a foot problem. But I'd forget about those things during her rants and only later realized that her problem wasn't really that onion—and that I need to support her with prayer and in other ways.

Who's hurting in your little world today?

Lord, give me eyes that are focused by my heart, so that I am able to see beyond appearances and help bring comfort and healing to another person's hurting heart. Amen.

Day 143 / Matthew 13:24-30

Who Are They Kidding?

Let both of them grow together until the harvest; and at harvest time I will tell the reapers, "Collect the weeds first and bind them in bundles to be burned, but gather the wheat into my barn." —Matthew 13:30

I have more difficulty dealing with *some* people in the church than with other people in my life. I have a high expectation of anyone who professes to be a Christian. We share a faith, biblical standards for living, and we know that God's people are expected to love one another. Doesn't it follow, then, that I should expect from another Christian decency, honesty, justice, and caring behavior—and that I'll be offended when a Christian treats me badly?

I'm bothered—and it affects my worship—when I see a person worshiping whom I know was recently involved in a shady business deal, or when a preacher expounds about the need to care for our brothers and sisters in Christ—and I happen to know that he or she hasn't bothered to check on Mrs. Jones, who's been absent from worship for some weeks.

Luther, considering the parable of the tares (or weeds), offers us two pieces of advice. First, remember that we're far from flawless ourselves and may be a stumbling block to others, perhaps because we overlook or minimize our own flaws. Second, we need to both forgive the tares among us *and* look beyond them to see the true body of Christ and devote ourselves to the important tasks he's given us.

God, help me to be forgiving instead of fussing and to offer grace instead of grumbling. Amen.

Day 144 / Ephesians 6:10-17

Charge!

Therefore take up the whole armor of God, so that you may be able to withstand on that evil day, and having done everything, to stand firm. —Ephesians 6:13

If you're over thirty years old you've probably sung this hymn (*Lutheran Book of Worship*, 509) many times:

> Onward, Christian soldiers, marching as to war,
> With the cross of Jesus going on before.
> Christ, the royal Master, leads against the foe;
> Forward into battle see his banners go!

For years, I hated that hymn—now seldom sung in our congregations—for its apparent glorification of war. My attitude changed as I learned more about "Onward, Christian Soldiers." It was written in 1865 by a teacher in England, Sabine Baring-Gould, for a festival involving students from two schools in neighboring villages. He wrote that he "wanted the children to sing when marching from one village to another." Unable to find suitable music, he one night wrote the hymn "in great haste." He confessed his surprise at its popularity.

The hymn calls us to trust in God's power and wage a *spiritual* war against evil. Its message and imagery are similar to Paul's in today's text. He speaks of the "whole armor of God," the "belt of truth," the "breastplate of righteousness," the "shield of faith," and the "helmet of salvation." The struggle, he emphasizes, "is not against enemies of blood and flesh" but against "the spiritual forces of evil." Notice that these pieces of armor are defensive and that the only offensive weapon is "the sword of the Spirit, which is the word of God."

Lord, equip us for battle and then send us forth with your word of peace. Amen.

Day 145 / Acts 17:1-9

Shake, Rattle, and Roll

When they could not find them, they dragged Jason and some believers before the city authorities, shouting, "These people who have been turning the world upside down have come here also."
—Acts 17:6

I grew up in the 1950s and remember the infancy of "rock and roll." Bill Haley and his Comets was one of the first groups to introduce the style to the general public with "Rock around the Clock" and "Shake, Rattle, and Roll." I recalled that last song recently as the lector at church read: "So I prophesied as I had been commanded; and as I prophesied, suddenly there was a noise, a rattling, and the bones came together, bone to its bone" (Ezek. 37:7).

The title of that song is a fitting description of the way God made his presence known throughout Scripture—and does today. "Shake, Rattle, and Roll" could be God's theme song. God's word, presence, and power have shaken many out of their complacent lives and have shaken up kings and kingdoms. In the sixteenth chapter of Acts, Paul and Silas are in jail and chained when God frees them in an earthquake "so violent that the foundations of the prison were shaken, and immediately all the doors were opened. . . ." (Acts 16:26). God is also a roller: He rolled away the stone at the entrance to Jesus' tomb and Christ conquered death.

We need to trust God's promise that he will empower and protect us as he uses us to shake, rattle, and roll the world in his name.

Loving God, help us to stay the course as we use your word to turn our world upside down so that the hearts of your people may be turned to the right. Amen.

Day 146 / Luke 21:12-19

In That Very Place

By your endurance you will gain your souls. —Luke 21:19

A daily devotional I receive once used the phrase, "Where the rubber of faith meets the runway of life." When was the last time the rubber of your faith hit the road of life? When was the last time your faith in the gospel message of Jesus Christ had a direct impact upon someone else's life?

When I was a teenager, one of the defining moments when you knew you had really joined the "driving crowd" was the first time you "peeled out" or "burned rubber"— when you literally left your mark on the road—and gave testimony to friends and enemies alike that you were "cool." In today's passage, Jesus tells the disciples that the time of their persecution will be the time for the message of the gospel, through both word and action, to reach their persecutors right where they live—to be a living testimony to their adversaries.

The road of life is long, full of unplanned twists and turns; sometimes we're just not sure where it's taking us. But it's on that road where we need to come in contact with others. Have you arrived at that testimonial point in your own life and seized the opportunity to testify to the power and majesty of Jesus Christ? Has the rubber of your faith made its mark on the life of someone else?

God of my open mouth and open heart, lead me to those places where, through me, your words and deeds will be both a positive witness and a significant impact for the sake of the gospel on the life of another. Amen.

Day 147 / Acts 11:23-26

Say, "I'm A Christian"

It was in Antioch that the disciples were first called "Christians."
—Acts 11:26

The word *Christian* is probably one of the most recognized words in the English language. Millions of people around the world have claimed that name as followers of Jesus Christ. But *Christian* is more than a name upon which we can hang our hat or hide behind. The primary dictionary definition for the word is "a believer in Jesus as the Christ, or in the religion based on the teachings of Jesus," but a later definition says, "having the qualities as taught by Jesus: love, kindness, etc."

In the time of the early church, people knew there was a price to pay for calling themselves Christian, including death. As Christians today, we probably don't even think about the great price that comes with claiming Jesus' name, particularly the risk of death. But if we claim the name *Christian*, we better be ready to express Christ's love and kindness at all times. We must be prepared to face being lonely and lost, to admit being flawed, and to face up to our failures. The way of Christ is lined with pain, suffering, and ridicule, but, as Christ said, "It is the only way to the Father." So, are you ready and willing to pay the price? If so, then go ahead, and say it with complete boldness and confidence, "I am a Christian!"

Jesus, help me to proclaim your name and our faith with boldness, both with my lips and with my life, so that all can hear and see my proclamation, "I am a Christian!" Amen.

Day 148 / Matthew 5:43-47

What Does It Mean to Love

For if you love those who love you, what reward do you have? –Matthew 5:46

Webster's Dictionary defines love as "strong affection or liking for someone or something." So what is one to do with Jesus' words? What if we were to substitute the words from Webster's? Our scripture for today would then read: "You have heard that it was said, 'You shall *show strong affection for or like* your neighbor and hate your enemy.' But I say to you, *show strong affection for and like* your enemies and pray for those who persecute you."

Substituting the words "strong affection or liking" for the word *love* in Jesus' words is to gut them of the meaning that Jesus implied.

If we are to be about Jesus' love, then we need to be willing to commit our heart, soul, mind, and strength to that love of others and of God. It can't be some half-hearted effort; it needs to be a complete and selfless love. And it means loving the so-called unlovable—who, if we are truly about God's gospel, should not even exist, for we need to recognize and accept all persons as being deemed lovable because they are all children of God and creatures of his creation.

So, love the Lord your God with all your heart, soul, mind, and strength—and love your neighbor as yourself. Let us love with the love of God because God has first loved us.

God, let your love and compassion work through me, and let me express that love and compassion to all persons according to their needs. Amen.

If You Can Breathe, Then Praise!

Let everything that breathes praise the Lord*! Praise the* Lord*!*
—Psalm 150:6

For me, it's been one of those "Praise the Lord" days. We know that *every* day should be one of those days—but also that there are those days when life is a windshield and you're the bug.

Today our son got his tax refund, money he really needs. At work, I'd dreaded having to deliver some heavy furniture, but it was easier than I'd expected, and the day was beautiful. Tonight at Bible study, when some folks mentioned spiritual problems they're experiencing, I shared how God has worked in my life as I coped with some difficult issues and people—and they seemed to appreciate that.

For me, today, Psalm 150 is the *perfect* psalm. Many of the psalms are about being sorry for sin, asking for help in times of trouble, or offering thanks or intercession. They're great and necessary, but whoever established the order for the psalms should get a medal for making this the last psalm (its final verse appears above). It's a great crescendo of pure praise.

The short psalm doesn't ask questions, but it answers these: *Why* is God to be praised? Because of his mighty deeds, including all creation. *How* is God to be praised? With music and dancing, among other ways. *Where* is God to be praised? In his sanctuary, which means everywhere. *Who* is to praise God? Everything that breathes.

Holy and magnificent God, I need to come to you in praise each day of my life, for without you and your love there would be no days of my life. So I will offer praises to you until the last breath that I draw. Praise the Lord! Amen.

Day 150 / Ephesians 4:29–5:2

Why So Emotional?

Put away from you all bitterness and wrath and anger and wrangling and slander, together with all malice. —Ephesians 4:31

Today's text from Paul's letter to the Ephesians offers some powerful words that are fitting for this Lenten season of self-reflection. The passage is a mix of negative and positive counsel ("Put away" . . . "be kind") and ends: "Therefore be imitators of God, as beloved children, and live in love, as Christ loved us and gave himself up for us. . . ." (Eph. 5:1-2).

When I read these words, I can't help but think about Jesus as he was dying upon the cross. I wonder at his amazing *inner calm* in the face of all that he endured. Without it, how could he have, from the cross, asked forgiveness for those who put him there? Who among us couldn't use a lot more of that quality in the deepest recesses of our beings?

I'm bothered by the anger and bitterness that rears its ugly head through so many people on a daily basis. Why is ours such an angry society? We live in a nation that's affluent relative to the rest of the world, yet we never seem to be satisfied. Most of us have so many reasons to be thankful, but in our interactions we seem far more angry than thankful.

Where is Jesus in the hearts of his people? May God's Holy Spirit help us find the inner peace and calm that our Lord knew.

Loving God, fill me with your peace. Help me to choose carefully the words I share with others, that they may be words used only for the building up of their lives. Create in me clean heart, O God; and renew a right spirit within me. Amen.

Day 151 / Matthew 6:7-13

Yes, You Can Forgive

And forgive us our debts, as we also have forgiven our debtors. —Matthew 6:12

We ended the Monday evening Bible study with the Lord's Prayer, as we always do. This time, though, it had a different impact on us, especially "Forgive us our sins as we forgive those who sin against us." We had just had an animated discussion of two verses in Luke: "Be on your guard! If another disciple sins, you must rebuke the offender, and if there is repentance, you must forgive. And if the same person sins against you seven times a day, and turns back to you seven times and says, 'I repent,' you must forgive" (Luke 17:3-4).

That command can be hard to accept. What if the sinner comes to us and says, "I'm sorry; please forgive me," but gives no hint of repentance? Do we offer forgiveness only if and when the person shows evidence of repentance? I hope not.

Think about Jesus as he hung on the cross. Did he wait for or get any words of repentance from his accusers before he said, "Father, forgive them, for they know not what they do?" Note that he didn't shout, "*I* forgive you." He prayed, "Father, forgive them; for they do not know what they are doing" (Luke 23:34). The scribes had it right for once when they questioned Jesus' healing of the paralytic and asked, "Who can forgive sins but God alone?" (Mark 2:7).

And forgive us our sins, as we forgive those who sin against us. Amen.

Day 152 / *John 14:1-7*

How Can Jesus Say That?

Jesus said to him, "I am the way, and the truth, and the life. No one comes to the Father except through me." —John 14:6

Sugarcoating. It's on doughnuts and the Easter ham. It's also what we call attempts to make bad news sound less bad or even good. Do we do it to the gospel, especially when we don't want to offend?

The words in today's text from John have been described as among the most offensive Jesus uttered, at least to some ears. Tolerance once connoted *allowing* or *enduring* certain beliefs or practices. Now it's often used to mean that truth and value are relative—that no idea or practice is worth more than another.

For those who believe in the living Jesus Christ, scriptural truth is here to stay. We must never be tempted to water down the gospel. But especially among nonbelievers, when we address such matters as Jesus being the "only way," we need to do it humbly, remaining sensitive to feelings and respecting their freedom to believe differently. You could call that sugarcoating. I'd call it staying faithful to the truth of the word without using an evangelistic battering ram.

We've accepted the call to follow Christ, a choice that often doesn't reflect some dominant views of our culture. Buck the trend and stand firm in your faith. Love others and pray for the opportunity to invite them on this fantastic journey of faith.

Lord Jesus, instill in us the power to resist any and all opposition to your word, and to boldly profess you as the only way, the only truth, and the only life that will lead others to your heavenly kingdom. Amen.

Day 153 / John 15:12-15

Dinner with a Friend

I do not call you servants any longer, because the servant does not know what the master is doing; but I have called you friends, because I have made known to you everything that I have heard from my Father. —John 15:15

As I write, it's late. We just returned from an enjoyable dinner with our good friend Daisy. I love the chance to spend an evening with true friends, eating, updating one another on our lives, discussing and debating current events, and just relaxing.

On the night before he died, Jesus gathered with his disciples for dinner. It likely was a time for good food, conversation, and a break from their busy lives. It also was the sharing of the traditional Passover meal—a time to remember and thank God for delivering the Jews from slavery in Egypt. Now, however, Jesus reminded the disciples what lay ahead for him and for them. He used the meal to provide for them, through the sharing of his body and blood, the strength they would need to carry on after his death, resurrection, and ascension.

He calls us, his friends, to join him in that meal—to receive his strength, his power, and forgiveness for our sins. His table is set, and the meal has been prepared. Good friends, come and dine!

Come, good friend, and be my guest. And let the food of my body and blood to you be blest. Amen.

Day 154 / Romans 8:26-27

Intercede Spirit, Intercede

Likewise the Spirit helps us in our weakness; for we do not know how to pray as we ought, but that very Spirit intercedes with sighs too deep for words. —Romans 8:26

We often struggle to find the right words for our prayers. Sometimes we simply can't find them. It's at those times when Romans 8:26 reminds us that the Spirit "intercedes" and connects us with God in ways beyond words.

It was a day I *needed* the counsel and comfort of that verse. I had just learned of the nation's latest school shooting. A student at a school on the Red Lake Indian Reservation in Minnesota shot and killed ten people, including himself, and left seven others injured. People on the reservation long have been victims of unemployment, poverty, and alcoholism. They didn't need this, nor the nation another school shooting.

Oddly, that verse was on my mind. My friend Larry Olson of the Christian group Dakota Road set the words to music some years ago, and I later sang the piece during worship at a Sunday school teachers training event. Now I'd just received an inquiry from somebody interested in the song. It's one of my favorites. The words and music are soothing and meditative; the song is easy to teach and learn; and, most important, the message is solid.

We've all experienced those times in prayer when we can't find the words or thoughts we want to express to God. In those times, it's comforting to know that the Holy Spirit is there to speak on our behalf.

Loving God, be with all of your people whose hearts this day are filled with pain for whatever reason. Bring them comfort, bring them healing, and bring them hope through the power of your presence. Amen.

Day 155 / Matthew 26:31-35

It's Going to Be All Right

Then Jesus said to them, "You will all become deserters because of me this night; for it is written, 'I will strike the shepherd, and the sheep of the flock will be scattered.'" —Matthew 26:31

People leave. It's one of the most difficult realities we face. Fears of abandonment and separation don't disappear with childhood. They hit us square in the face whenever we are confronted by major challenges in our lives.

In today's text, Jesus and the disciples are celebrating the Passover meal—the last meal Jesus would share with his disciples before his death on the cross. For us it became the Lord's Supper, a foretaste of the heavenly meal that all disciples would one day share with Jesus in the heavenly kingdom. First, however, Jesus has to die. He tells the disciples that, as he had twice before, and with the same result—rejection and misunderstanding. Led by Peter, they show false bravado: "Though all become deserters because of you, I will never desert you" (Matt. 26:33). The reality is that the disciples fear being left alone.

In times like that, we need to cling—as the disciples *eventually* did—to Jesus' promise that everything really will be okay because Jesus is always with us.

Gentle Savior, bring us consolation and courage when our lives get turned upside down and fears overtake us. Help us believe in your promise that everything will be okay. Amen.

Day 156 / Luke 24:1-5

God On the Loose!

The women were terrified and bowed their faces to the ground, but the men said to them, "Why do you look for the living among the dead? He is not here, but has risen." —Luke 24:5

I've always liked good Southern gospel music. Sometimes I'll run across one of the Gaither Homecoming shows while channel surfing, and I'll watch and enjoy it for a while. Bill and Gloria Gaither have written many songs through the years, but one of my favorites is "Because He Lives."

> God sent his Son, they called him Jesus;
> He came to love, heal, and forgive.
> He lived and died to buy my pardon,
> An empty grave is there to prove my Savior lives.
>
> Because he lives, I can face tomorrow.
> Because he lives, all fear is gone.
> Because I know he holds the future,
> And life is worth the living just because he lives.

I sometimes imagine what it would have been like to have stood outside the open tomb on the day of our Lord's resurrection and to hear the words proclaimed for the first time, "He is not here, but has risen." What a pronouncement! What a promise!

Pastor Rollie Martinson's phrase "God got loose," is one of the best descriptions of the resurrection I've ever heard. The tomb was no match for God's love. God burst the bonds of sin and death. Our God is on the loose, freely bringing hope, healing, love, and promise to a world in need of Easter every single day.

Dear Lord, you are risen and, because you live, I can face tomorrow without fear. I can anticipate a future in your presence. I can know without question that my life is worth living. Thanks be to God! Amen.

Day 157 / Colossians 1:15-20

Mitakuye Oyasin

He is the head of the body, the church; he is the beginning, the firstborn from the dead, so that he might come to have first place in everything. —Colossians 1:18

I get e-mail devotionals from Pastor Kerry L. Nelson of Covenant Lutheran Church in Houston, Texas. I love this one:

> Yesterday morning, I looked out across a congregation of wonderful people. These are people who went out of their way to come to the feet of Jesus, to make their way to an empty tomb, to be counted among the faithful on the day set aside to worship. These are the hands, legs, and hearts of the risen Jesus. I saw our little gathering in Houston, and I realized that I was just seeing one cell in the body of Christ, which stretches across the world, across time, into eternity. . . .

Mitakuye oyasin is a Lakota Sioux expression that means "we are all connected." In a Lakotan story, a boy asks his grandfather the path to the Creator. Baptists, Methodists, and Catholics come to the reservation, each making exclusive claims. The grandfather says the answer is in the tepee. Over some days and nights, the boy examines a tepee, studying the skin, the painting, and other details. Finally, the grandfather helps him understand that the answer is the poles, which only *together* can support the tepee. Those Christian groups all point to the Creator. Choose which of them you will, but never lose sight of the Creator, advises the grandfather—and the boy begins to understand.

Thank you, Lord, for the shared witness of all believers. Walk with us on our journey of faith and, by your grace, keep us connected to you and to one another. Amen.

Day 158 / Luke 18:1-8

I Want My Maypo!

Then Jesus told them a parable about their need to pray always and not to lose heart. —Luke 18:1

We were starting into the eighteenth chapter of Luke's gospel in our Monday night Bible study group. We quickly found ourselves talking about persistence and the desire for instant gratification. I love this chapter—which begins with today's text—partly because these seemingly unrelated parables and accounts develop an overarching theme.

Jesus uses the parable to help those listening better understand the power of prayer and the importance of being persistent in prayer. The "unjust judge" grants justice to the widow only because he's worn down by her persistence. God, Jesus says, will be faster and more faithful in dispensing justice. But Jesus also asks, "And yet, when the Son of Man comes, will he find faith on earth?" (Luke 18:8).

Jesus lauds the widow's persistence and uses it as an example of how God's people should approach God with their prayers. But persistence must always be coupled with patience. Too often we are more persistent than patient. We want everything fast—fast food, short worship, and instant answers to our prayers. We're like the cartoon character Marky Maypo, who in 1950s commercials screamed at his father, "I want my Maypo!"—a hot cereal that's still around.

Paul wrote: "Love is patient" (1 Cor. 13:4). In our prayers, too, we must be both persistent and patient.

Lord, never let us forget that prayer is a dialogue, and that part of that dialogue needs to be our willingness to listen and patiently await your answer. Quiet us, Lord, so we can hear your voice. Amen.

Day 159 / 2 Corinthians 11:24-28

Be Lifted Higher

And, besides other things, I am under daily pressure because of my anxiety for all the churches. —2 Corinthians 11:28

Mike Williams, a Christian comedian, sings a serious tale of an eagle facing immediate danger as it soars ahead of a storm. He marvels at how the bird uses the storm's updrafts to be lifted above the fury and to fly free and safe. One line in the song got me thinking of Paul's ordeals and my own: "Take that which is coming against you, and let it lift you up higher."

For most of us, our weaknesses and anxieties, whatever they may be, are what hold us back and make us doubt ourselves and our capabilities. But in the early part of the *next* chapter, Paul goes on to describe how his weaknesses have made him a stronger person and witness: "for wherever I am weak, then I am strong" (2 Cor. 12:10).

I've discovered that paradoxical truth for myself and my ministry as I deal with the storms of issues and inconsistencies in the church. I've directed my mind and heart to a more disciplined spiritual life. The storms continue, but I'm much more often able to rise above them and let Christ direct my words and actions.

God, strengthen me in my times of weakness. Empower me when I feel powerless. Sustain me in suffering. God of mercy, I place my faith, my trust, and my very life in you, for in you I find forgiveness and love. Amen.

Day 160 / Psalm 33:10-12

Just Passing Through

Happy is the nation whose God is the LORD, the people whom he has chosen as his heritage. —Psalm 33:12

According to a recent issue of the *CIA World Fact Book*, about 57 million people around the world die every year, of all causes. That's about 1,200 every ten minutes. Those statistics remind us how temporary we are. But our time on earth isn't the entire story. God's story is continually unfolding, and all of us have a role to play.

As Christ's followers, we are charged with being God's ambassadors, responsible for enlarging his place in the hearts and minds of people. With those charges come responsibility and accountability. According to the Scriptures, there really will be a judgment day, when we will have to account for our stewardship.

In God's story, you matter! Yes, sometimes it's hard to see beyond today's chapter of our personal lives. But as Christ-followers, our most important task is to grow in our relationship with Jesus and share with others the unfolding story of what God has done and is doing in the world.

God, let me not only be a part of your ever-unfolding story of creation; but let me also be your instrument to proclaim that salvation story to the world. Amen.

Day 161 / Mark 12:41-44

The Ticket

Truly I tell you, this poor widow has put in more than all those.
—Mark 12:43

The poor widow had only those two coins of little value, but she gave them to help others. This is one of the most powerful teaching moments of Jesus' ministry—and a memorable example of what we are to be about as Christ-followers.

A modern-day example of giving it all away happened after a typhoon hit Japan's west coast in 2004 killing some people, leaving thousands homeless, and destroying homes, other buildings, roads, and bridges. A provincial governor received, from an anonymous donor, a winning lottery ticket worth about $1.8 million. The sender—who apologized for not coming forward in person—expressed condolences to all who had suffered losses from the typhoon and asked that the money be used to assist them. Television commentators speculated: What sort of person would have a once-in-a-lifetime stroke of luck, then let it go?

The widow did it. The anonymous donor did it. What about you and me? It's all about giving—not only money but of your whole self.

Loving God, help us to appreciate your gifts, recognizing them for what they are . . . an outpouring of your love. And then, Lord, help us to humbly surrender all that you have given us for the sake of others. Amen.

Day 162 / Luke 2:46-49

Daddy's Child

[Jesus] said to them, "Why were you searching for me? Did you not know that I must be in my Father's house?" —Luke 2:49

As I do near the start of each day, I reached for my daily devotional book, in this case Brennan Manning's *Reflections for Ragamuffins*. That day's date, I realized, would have been my father's eighty-fourth birthday.

My dad was not a mushy, speak-your-love kind of guy. He had his own way of getting you to learn what he wanted you to know. He was tough, but never mean. He had a quiet gentleness that often would betray his stoic exterior.

I hope I've grown up to be a lot like my dad—and even more like my heavenly Father. I want them both to be proud of me, to be able to say, "That's my child, isn't he something?" I hope I've grown up in the image of both of them, with that quiet gentleness, that caring soul, and a love for those around me. That's what my dad would expect of me, and that's what my heavenly "daddy" would want me to do.

Manning wrote in his devotion for that day that Jesus had an "utter single-mindedness" toward the Father and for God's reign. The Father's will, says Manning, is a river of life, a bloodstream, and all who do the will of the Father become part of that bloodstream and united in the life of Christ Jesus.

Abba, Father, Daddy: Thanks for adopting me as your child, for watching over me, for caring about me, for loving me. What more could a son ask for? Amen.

Day 163 / Colossians 1:24-29

A Carrot, an Egg, or a Coffee Bean?

I am now rejoicing in my sufferings for your sake, and in my flesh I am completing what is lacking in Christ's afflictions for the sake of his body, that is, the church. —Colossians 1:24

The young woman's life had turned into an unending series of problems. She went to her mother and said she was ready to give up. The mother took her to the kitchen, where she filled three pots with water, then put raw carrots in one, eggs in the second, and some ground coffee beans in the third. She let each pot boil for some time, then put the results in separate bowls. "What do you see?" asked the mother.

"Carrots, eggs, and coffee," replied the daughter. The mother explained that the items had faced the same adversity—boiling water—but had reacted differently. The carrot now was soft. The egg, once fragile, now was firm inside. Unlike the other two items, the coffee had changed the water.

The mother asked: "When adversity knocks on your door, which are you, a carrot, an egg, or a coffee bean?"

Today's text reminds us that Paul was happy to rejoice in the suffering he faced. He didn't allow himself to wilt and become soft under adverse conditions. Nor was he like the egg. His heart was soft and loving, and adversity couldn't harden it. Paul was like that ground coffee: Instead of allowing adversity to change him, he used his adversities to make a difference in the lives of those around him.

Which are you in the face of life's adversities?

God, stop my whining and calm my fears so I can bring to others the sweetness of your love and your grace. Amen.

Day 164 / Habakkuk 2:1-3

Need Your Vision Checked?

Then the LORD answered me and said: "Write the vision; make it plain on tablets, so that a runner may read it." —Habakkuk 2:2

Years ago, most people who needed eyeglasses would buy off-the-rack glasses the same way they'd buy flour or soap. Many still do. Unfortunately, the method doesn't do much for many types of failing eyesight.

Without the right glasses, the *nearsighted* person lives in a small world. From a distance, she can't tell who her friends are until she's close enough to touch them. The *farsighted* person, on the other hand, is unsure about things a few inches or feet away. Then there's *astigmatism*, which blurs and bends what we see—and often is combined with near- or farsightedness.

Similar effects can happen with our *vision*—in the broader, much more important sense of that word in today's text. Many of us suffer from nearsighted vision of this type. The only thing that appears real or clear is *me*. Those who suffer from farsighted vision can readily see the speck in the eye of someone else but are unable to see the log in their own. Those with astigmatic vision may perceive wholesome things as evil, help as danger, the important as insignificant—or their opposites.

Fortunately, optometrists and ophthalmologists know how to correct our sight. But only God can correct our vision of the biblical kind, so that we can see and meet the needs of the world around us, both near and far.

Healing God, help us to see more clearly your vulnerable and hurting children. Then by the power of your Holy Spirit, grant us the vision to discover ways to protect and care for them. Amen.

Day 165 / James 2:14-17

Mouth It or Mean It?

So faith by itself, if it has no works, is dead. —*James 2:17*

We had a baptism last Sunday. Little Rachel joined together with us in God's kingdom. The proud parents were asked to make the promises for her, so that she would grow in faith and learn about God and his promises for her. The congregation, along with the family, was asked to profess our faith in the words of the Apostles' Creed.

As we repeated those memorized words one more time, did we *mean* them or merely mouth them? Do we believe in God the Creator? Do we truly believe that Christ was born, lived, died, and rose again—*for us*? Is this one in whom we profess to believe the one we are willing to serve, anywhere, any time, in any way?

Too often we treat our faith as one more thing on our "Things to Do Today" list. We end up sandwiching our religion between our job and our exercise class. Our active and demonstrative service to God and God's kingdom ends up as just one more concern or hassle competing for attention in our busy lives.

That might be okay—*if* Christianity were nothing more than a moral code or a self-help course. But Christianity and our belief in the risen Lord is the central truth from which all our words, actions, and relationships must flow. To be a Christian requires connecting our mouthing with *meaning* and *action*.

God, let the words of our mouths and the meditations of our hearts not only be acceptable to you, but let them be translated and lived out in our actions toward the needs of others. Amen.

Day 166 / Isaiah 41:8-10

Waiting in the Wings

Do not fear, for I am with you, do not be afraid, for I am your God; I will strengthen you, I will help you, I will uphold you with my victorious right hand. —Isaiah 41:10

Native Americans had traditional ways to train young boys to become men. When a boy turned thirteen, he was tested in hunting, fishing, and scouting. Then, as an ultimate test, he was placed in the forest to spend the night alone.

It was one of those nights and so dark the moonlight barely penetrated through the trees. With every twig that snapped, the young brave was certain that some wild animal was ready to pounce and devour him. Finally, the day's first light began to illuminate the forest's interior. To his astonishment, the brave saw his father standing behind a tree, armed with a bow and arrow. We can imagine what was running through his mind: "If I had known my father was there, I wouldn't have been afraid of anything."

Many centuries earlier, Jesus said to the sinking Peter and to the frightened disciples on the Sea of Galilee, "You of little faith, why did you doubt?" In today's text, God speaks through Isaiah, assuring the people of the prophet's time: "Do not fear, for I am with you . . . I will strengthen you, I will help you."

How much braver and more confident we would be if we always remembered that there, never out of touch, is the one who spoke those words to his people through Isaiah. Ours is a 24/7 God. What more could we ask?

God, it feels good to know that, no matter what the situation, you're there with us. That even in the darkest of times, you're always within our reach to hold on to us, to strengthen us, to support us, and to alleviate our fears and calm our hearts. Amen.

Day 167 / John 20:24-27

"Show me" or "Faith"?

Then he said to Thomas, "Put your finger here and see my hands. Reach out your hand and put it in my side. Do not doubt but believe." —John 20:27

I was in St. Louis several years ago and became curious about the origin of "Show Me" on Missouri license plates. According to the leading legend, I was told, a Missouri congressman was speaking at an 1899 naval banquet in Philadelphia and said: "I am from Missouri. You have got to show me."

That's a useful principle in science and many other aspects of life—but not all. You can watch a magician do a trick, but what you see isn't what really happened. Many important things in life can only be seen with a *different* kind of vision, as the once-skeptical Thomas learns in today's text.

Did you ever get a painful sunburn on a cloudy day, the result of invisible ultraviolet light from a sun you couldn't see? When you were a kid, did you ever use one of those dog whistles that emit a high-frequency sound that dogs hear, but you and the neighbors couldn't?

Living strictly by the show-me principle is every bit as dangerous as living life totally as a gamble. For 2,000 years, Christianity has been teaching people like Thomas and us how to know the presence and voice of our invisible God and how to live joyously in our faith. For Christians, in Missouri and elsewhere, those first two words of the Apostles' Creed—I believe—are our counterpart to "show me."

God, without our eyes and without our ears, let us still be able to echo with full confidence those words of Thomas: "My Lord and my God!" Amen.

Day 168 / Psalm 74:1-11

It's About Time

Why do you hold back your hand? —Psalm 74:11

Talk about snail mail! A woman vacationing in New Jersey wrote a postcard and mailed it to her mother in Pennsylvania. It arrived 37 years later, having fallen behind a post-office sorting machine, where it finally was discovered and sent on its way.

That story got me thinking about all the change we've experienced in my lifetime when it comes to how we view time. Today's culture and technology are increasingly focused on *now*. The downside to our instant society is that it fosters the illusion that anything and everything should be ours, well, instantly.

Our impatience spills over into our spirituality. When problems aren't quickly resolved, we get angry with God or become depressed. Others may praise God for fixing *their* lives, but we wonder why God isn't now acting on *our* behalf—as did the people of Israel, whose frustrations are voiced by the psalmist in today's text.

But the simple truth is that following Christ, growing in maturity, building character, resolving most problems, and building strong families and relationships—*all take time*. Let's work to slow down and let God work in our lives. Let's learn to take the longer view of time, remembering always that God's timing is perfect and often very different from ours.

God, why is it that we feel we always have to be in a hurry, and that it all has to get done yesterday? Take my hand and help me to learn to walk more slowly through life. Amen.

Day 169 / Ephesians 5:15-20

Who Am I?

So do not be foolish, but understand what the will of the Lord is. —Ephesians 5:17

Who am I—12601136702 . . .? For the sake of governmental and societal convenience, I've been reduced to a collection of numbers, for the phone company, Social Security, the motor-vehicle bureau, credit-card companies, and so on. We live in a world of "impersonalities." We perpetuate the process by doing the same thing to other people, referring to them by ethnicity, age, economic class, political party, religion, or sexual identity.

I fit neatly into some of those categories. I am religiously affiliated, have a party preference, and am proud of my ethnic heritage. But none of these labels truly defines who I am. I'm Abba's child, and that's the core truth of my existence! Because I'm God's, I live each day in the wisdom of his tenderness. God's love and mercy affects how I perceive reality and the way I respond to the people around me, near and far.

Paul, in today's text, is really saying the same thing, as he urges the Christians at Ephesus to avoid foolish, unwise behavior and instead to understand and do "the will of the Lord." The "days are evil," he cautions them, urging them to make the most of their hours and days, always giving thanks to the Father and "for everything" in the name of Jesus Christ.

God, all praise to you that it's not the question, "Who am I?" but the assurance of, "Whose I am." Amen.

Day 170 / Jonah 1:1-3

Do I Have To?

But Jonah set out to flee to Tarshish from the presence of the LORD.
—Jonah 1:3

For me, it was a surprising and easy victory. About one Sunday a month, my parents would take me to visit my dad's sister and her family, who lived on a farm and raised pigs. I didn't enjoy those visits, but until I was about twelve, I went without much fuss. Then, one Sunday, I said, "Do I *have* to go?" Instead of the "Yes!" I expected, they said I could stay home.

But more often, we've learned, the answer to that question is "Yes"—the task may be difficult, unpleasant, or inconvenient, but we have to do it anyway. That's Jonah's situation in today's text. He doesn't ask, "Do I have to?"—he simply boards a ship headed *away* from Nineveh. Can you blame him? God wants him to go to Nineveh and cry out against the people for their wickedness.

As we know, Jonah eventually did go to Nineveh. He is but one of many figures in the Bible—they include Moses, David, Jeremiah, Joseph, and Peter—whose *first* response to God was to bail out or offer excuses.

We have to do what God calls us to do, but he assures us that he's going help us through it. Whether it's our employment or sharing the gospel, we need to get on with it, trusting God for his presence and strength.

Make your presence known to me, Lord. For it is only in you that I can find the strength, the courage, and the peace to face the large and small challenges that each day brings. Amen.

Day 171 / 1 Peter 4:9-10

Be a Ganderite

Like good stewards of the manifold grace of God, serve one another with whatever gift each of you has received. —1 Peter 4:10

Many international flights from Europe were approaching the United States when the terrorists attacked on September 11, 2001. When U. S. airspace was closed, about three dozen planes carrying some 6,000 passengers landed at Gander, a town of about 10,000 in Canada's province of Newfoundland.

In our times, nobody would have been surprised if the residents of Gander and nearby towns had been overwhelmed by the sheer numbers of stranded travelers. But instead of hiding behind closed doors, residents of the area responded by offering everything from food and shelter to toothpaste, spare underwear (that's sacrifice!), and harbor tours. An Internet search for "Gander" will reveal Web sites honoring the hospitality of the people of Gander.

What a great story! Whether or not people are followers of Christ, whenever love, kindness, generosity, and hospitality are demonstrated, they are without doubt the fingerprints of our Creator upon humankind. If the people of the world can demonstrate such uncommon graces in times of crisis, how much more should the followers of Christ demonstrate these characteristics every day? As children of God, we are called to love one another, love our neighbors, demonstrate kindness, be generous, and practice hospitality, all in the name of Jesus. The words to that old hymn still ring true: "They will know we are Christians by our love."

God, each and every day of our lives, let us be Ganderites! Amen.

Day 172 / Luke 2:13-14

Those Whom God Favors

And suddenly there was with the angel a multitude of the heavenly host, praising God and saying, "Glory to God in the highest heaven, and on earth peace among those whom he favors!" —Luke 2:13-14

We hear those verses as part of the Christmas story, but of course when Luke wrote them there was no Christmas. This was simply the beginning, for Luke, of the *gospel* story.

An older translation put it differently: "peace on earth, good will towards men." The newer translation may be more accurate, but it leaves a peculiar and unsettling impression: "peace among those whom God favors"—but what about others? What about the rest of the human race who don't happen to be "in God's favor" right now—are they consigned to live without peace?

It's too easy to read these words from a self-centered point of view, and with not a little bit of self-congratulation. Of course, we imagine, *we* are the people whom God favors—too bad about the rest! But what if we don't know as much as we think we know? What if, for all our piety and devotion, we're really not any more "favored" by God than the person next to us on the freeway, or in the next cubicle, or at the lunch counter, or in the grocery store?

What if *all* of us were those whom God favors? Wouldn't that mean God's peace was a gift to everyone, all the time, not just the people who think they're "on the inside" with God?

Would it change the way we lived this day?

My soul magnifies your name, O Lord, and my spirit rejoices in you, God my savior! Amen.

Day 173 / 1 John 4:16-21

I Done It for Love

The commandment we have from him is this: those who love God must love their brothers and sisters also. —1 John 4:21

Since she was busy doing other more pressing things, the mother enlisted the help of her seven-year-old son to see that her shoes got shined for church the next morning. Ten minutes later, Richard Ballenger presented a pair of shiny shoes to his mother, who gave him a quarter in payment for his help.

The next morning as she was getting dressed for church, Richard's mother discovered a small paper-wrapped bundle in one of her shoes. She opened it up to find a quarter and a note scrawled in childish letters that said, "I done it for love."

"I done it for love," God whispered at the birth of Jesus. "I done it for love," God wept as Jesus died. "I done it for love," God shouted on that first Easter Sunday morning.

How can we respond to such love? By loving others, of course. We cannot do anything less. "We love because he first loved us," says the writer of 1 John—but he quickly warns that we're "liars" if we say we love God but don't love our sisters and brothers. Thankfully, God—who is Love—will help us in our attempts to do so.

Bless you, Lord, for your gift of unmerited love. Help us to love in word and deed those whom we meet this day. All this we ask in Jesus' name. Amen.

Day 174 / Psalm 40:6-8

Please Lord, Not Tonight

"Sacrifice and offering you do not desire, but you have given me an open ear. Burnt-offering and sin-offering you have not required." —Psalm 40:6

All I wanted was to put on my slippers, settle into my den chair, and vegetate in front of the TV for an hour or so. I hadn't been home five minutes when the phone rang. It was a longtime friend, wondering if we could get together. I sensed he meant *now*. I hesitated, then said yes. "God," I silently prayed, "why are you interrupting my night with *this*?"

For some years, I was one of the "listening ears" at our synod's annual youth event—pastors and lay people who offered their time to listen to youth and adults who wanted to share a problem or concern. It was a vital service that benefited countless numbers of people.

In today's text, David realizes what God desires of him: not material offerings, but that he be attentive to God's call and to the needs of those around him. David tells God that his ear is open to whatever God has to say and that, "I delight to do your will, O my God."

My friend and I got together that night. He's gone through a series of misfortunes over the last several years and recently walked away from a job that wasn't the kind of work for which he's suited. The more I listened, the more I found myself thanking God that I could be there as his "listening ear."

Dear God, forgive me when I allow "my space" and "my time" to take priority over the needs of others. Soften my heart, Lord, and make of me a "listening ear" to all who need a friend this day. Amen.

Day 175 / Isaiah 43:18-19

Reminiscing

Do not remember the former things, or consider the things of old.
—Isaiah 43:18

It's good to spend time with friends and colleagues and to remember not only past things that happened, but also the lessons we learned. Many of the most valuable lessons to be learned come from what we've been through. Yet, if we are to be God's people in our world today, we can't just live in the past.

At the Last Supper, Christ commanded the disciples to take, eat, and drink in remembrance of him, but he also said: "For as often as you eat this bread and drink the cup, you proclaim the Lord's death until he comes" (Cor. 11:26). These words were a directive to the disciples that what was taking place around that table was not a once-and-done act, but something that would strengthen and sustain them as they carried out his ministry in the days to come. It would cause them to remember the past, empower them for the present, and focus their vision on the future.

Isaiah assures God's people that God's message and love are timeless—that God is a God of now, not just of yesterday. So also God promises us now—that God will "do a new thing," and that God intends to do it through us. So, take seriously the lessons the past has taught: Remain faithful, offer yourself to God's service, and then "Go in peace, and serve the Lord!"

God, instill in me the wisdom of old, that I might use it to better the future through your word. Amen.

Day 176 / 1 Samuel 1:9-11

They're Yours to Use, God

Hannah rose and presented herself before the Lord. —1 Samuel 1:9

Hannah's prayers were long and many, as she longed for a child. Finally, while praying in the synagogue at Shiloh she cried out in a desperate vow to God, and her prayers were answered: she became pregnant with Samuel. As she had promised, while he was still very young, she brought Samuel to the temple and dedicated him to God's work, leaving him with Eli. Samuel went on to serve the Lord as a prophet, a priest, and a military leader. But had Hannah not carried through on her promise to God, the history of God's people might have been seriously altered.

Few parents today would be willing to make the sacrifice that Hannah made. In fact, too many parents will not even encourage their children to become active within the life of the church in which they were baptized. Far too many parents are simply unwilling to allow God to use their children to further the kingdom.

God will issue the divine call to serve, even to those, like Samuel, who are very young. Rather than breed reluctance into our children, we need to foster commitment. We need to teach our children to respond to God's call, as did Samuel. We must be ready to say, when God calls: "Speak, Lord, for your servant is listening! She is yours, Lord, use her."

Lord, as so many have discovered, parenting is not an easy job. Remind us that we don't have all the answers, and that we are sometimes wrong. Help us to be patient, understanding, and firm, as we guide our little ones to you, God. Amen.

Day 177 / Ezekiel 34:11-16

Could You Use Some Food?

They shall feed on rich pasture on the mountains of Israel.
—Ezekiel 34:14

Hungry people seem to have a great appreciation for whatever they are given. God, speaking through the prophet Ezekiel, tells the people that they needn't ever worry about being hungry again. God will be their shepherd and they will always have food to eat. Sadly, too many people in this world do not live with such assurances, so when food does appear where once there was none, it can seem miraculous.

Those who work in Christian soup kitchens and food pantries for the poor often report what a joy it is each day to experience the love of the people who help to keep their ministries going. They rejoice each time they pick up the phone and a voice on the other end utters those comforting words, "Could you use some food?" "Yes, yes, we can!" they reply, because they know that the real source of that food is the one who spoke those words of comfort and hope to his people so long ago: "I will seek the lost, and I will bring back the strayed, and I will bind up the injured, and I will strengthen the weak—and I will feed them!" People sometimes say that God works in mysterious ways; but I don't think there's any mystery to God's love, as it is shown through the lives and the generosity of others.

Lord God, thank you not only for the food that feeds us, and for those who have produced it, but also for the opportunity to provide to those in need food and shelter, and the blessing and the comfort of your word and your presence. Amen.

Partake or Pass?

Unless you eat the flesh of the Son of Man and drink his blood, you have no life in you. —John 6:53

Imagine preparing a banquet where the guest of honor, despite being offered all her favorite foods, merely admires the dishes and their aromas, but refuses to eat them. Incredibly, many of us do this very thing, spiritually speaking. We gather around an incredible feast of good things that God has prepared to strengthen and build our lives, such as the Scriptures, prayer, fellowship with other Christians, worship, and serving others through our ministry. But, instead of partaking, we sit there at God's abundant table, passing on one plate after another, without ever taking any of what God has to offer to us.

God's prepared this phenomenal meal just for us! God wants us to do more than just look; God wants us to taste what is there and to know that through this life-giving food we will be able to enrich our lives and become all we have been created to be.

Are there foods of spiritual opportunity that you've passed up recently? Have you taken the time to taste of God's word? Have you allowed yourself the time to sit down at God's table to even see what's been prepared for you? God has prepared an endless spiritual feast just for you and has extended to you a very special invitation. So what are you going to do—partake or pass?

God, maybe we've satisfied the spiritual hunger in our lives with too much "junk food," so we're not hungry enough for your word when called to your table. Steer us away from the "empty calories" of this life, and feed us with the true Bread of Life, your Son. Amen.

Day 179 / 1 Corinthians 12:12-13, 27

Dismembered

Now you are the body of Christ and individually members of it.
—1 Corinthians 12:27

Many congregations are concerned over youth discontinuing their active participation in the church following their confirmation. Add to that the ever-increasing departure of adults from mainline denominations and you have the basis for an answer to the question: If someone leaves the church, are they having an out-of-the-Body experience?

We all need those connections, both to the other members of the Body, and to Christ. I recall a young woman who came one Sunday to the church I served and, during the time for prayer requests, tearfully announced that her father had just been diagnosed with terminal cancer. After the service almost everyone came up to her and just held her and let her cry. Disconnected from the Body, she might have never experienced the love of Christ that surrounded her that day. Another woman, whose son was hospitalized in critical condition following a car accident, might not have experienced Christ's love and support so powerfully if our youth group had not made a point to sit with her, their friend's mother, during worship.

We are the Body of Christ and, as such, that body must remain intact. We are not just a head, or a foot, or a hand, or an ear; we are, together, the Body of Christ. And, being so, none of us should ever have to have an "out-of-the-Body" experience.

Bind us together, Lord, bind us together with cords that cannot be broken. Bind us together, Lord, bind us together; bind us together in love. Gracious God, keep us bound together as one Body, the Body of your Son, Jesus Christ. Amen.

Day 180 / Matthew 8:18-20

A Place to Go

Foxes have holes, and birds of the air have nests; but the Son of Man has nowhere to lay his head. —Matthew 8:20

As a pastor I get many phone calls from people who tell me, "I don't have anywhere to go." I guess homeless people have at least one thing in common with Jesus: he, too, was homeless for the last three years of his life. And anyone who chose to follow him ended up homeless too. They, like Jesus, may have had nowhere to lay their head—but they were not without a place to go; they could always find a place in the loving arms of Christ.

When asked to assist the homeless, I help them find refuge in the form of food, clothing, shelter, and a comfortable bed. But I also pray that they find a refuge for their souls where they will find a sense of peace, a strengthening of their hearts, and a renewal of their energy to reestablish their lives. And I pray they will find a friend in Jesus, a friend who will also provide hope, comfort, and the saving grace that only he can give.

The Son of God may have had no place to lay his head, but we do. Christ calls us to come to him and to lay our weary heads, and our whole bodies, in the shelter of his loving arms, there to receive his love and his protection for the rest of our lives.

God, many in the world are alone, lost, and have no place to go. As they seek shelter for their physical needs, may they turn to you in prayer, where they will find shelter for their souls. Keep all your children in your love and care this night, Lord. Amen.

Day 181 / John 4:7-15

Digging Deeper

Jesus said to her, . . . "Those who drink of the water that I will give them will never be thirsty. The water that I will give will become in them a spring of water gushing up to eternal life." —John 4:13-14

Somewhere in our music collection we have a recording by the Oak Ridge Boys of an old country song written by Lester Flatt and Earl Scruggs called "Dig a Little Deeper in the Well." The words of the chorus go like this:

> Dig a little deeper in the well, boys, dig a little deeper in the well.
> If you want a cool drink of water you gotta dig a little deeper in the well.

The song's directive to dig deeper to find water relates to a process called fracking. Basically, fracking is really the process of hydro-fracturing. This process involves pumping large amounts of highly pressurized water into a seemingly dry well. The water splits apart the shale and opens up new water seams. So, what seems like a destructive process actually creates new water sources for what was once a dried-up well. It's all a matter of digging a little deeper.

In those moments in our lives when the well runs dry, or seems dry, remember Jesus' promise of living water that gushes up to eternal life. The Samaritan women who met Jesus was thrilled at the thought of receiving a drink of Jesus' living water. His is the water that will refresh us in our weariness. His is the water that can gush up through our hardened lives. We may do our part by digging deeper, but it will be God's "fracking" power that breaks through to the life-giving water of Jesus.

God, just as the Samaritan woman sought from your Son the water to end her thirst and to provide eternal life, so let us seek that same water that can only come from the depths of your Son's heart. Amen.

Day 182 / Matthew 25:35-40

Service Issues

Truly I tell you, just as you did it to one of the least of these who are members of my family, you did it to me. —Matthew 25:40

During a lively discussion of this text in our college-age church class, the young teacher asked, "But doesn't Jesus call us to love not just him but *one another*? One of the students, a waitress at a local restaurant, offered her own story:

> Some of the worst customers I end up having to deal with are "visible Christians"—like that table of ten one night who came in after one of the local church's Sunday night services, all happy and bubbly. For over an hour, all they did was run me ragged. "Can you get me this?" or "Can you get me that?" or "My fries are cold," or "Can you get me another slice of tomato? This one's awful green," or "You know my water glass is getting a little low?" And after they finally decided to go home, what did they leave me on the table for all my troubles? A dollar for a combined seventy-seven dollar bill. Many of the people who come into the restaurant and are sporting cross necklaces or WWJD bracelets treat the wait-staff as slaves and not worth their time.

What an eye-opener it would be for us, if only for one day, to see through the eyes of Jesus, all that is *not* being done in his name by the people who so insistently lay claim to being his followers. If only we could come to understand that as we serve others, Jesus himself is being served.

Lord, let us not be simply the bearers of your word but doers of your word for every person and in every place. Amen.

Day 183 / 1 Corinthians 6:17-20

A Heap of Trouble

You are not your own. For you were bought with a price; therefore glorify God in your body. —1 Corinthians 6:19-20

Do you remember the first car you ever owned? I'm willing to bet that, like mine, it wasn't a new car. And I'll bet it wasn't your ideal car either. You probably had some sleek, red, stylish convertible in mind, and, in all likelihood, the closest thing you got to it was maybe the red paint.

If your car was anything like my old Bel-Air, the paint was somewhat faded, it had a few minor dents, its upholstery was stained, and it drifted right every time you took your hands off the steering wheel. But nothing could dampen the excitement you felt whenever you got behind the wheel. It was your car and it gave you freedom! It was worth every dollar you paid for it.

Our physical bodies are a lot like that first car. It was God who gave us life—with slight imperfections!—and who bought us and turned us loose on the world. So what if our feet are too big or we have ears that look like taxicab doors? So what if we're too old or too young, too fat or too skinny? So what if we have trouble doing even simple math? God made us, and God expects us to learn to live with and even love our bodies, to keep them running, and not to let them slip into a condition of disrepair. Glorify God in your body!

Understanding God, let me experience your presence in my life and in my body, with all its joys and faults, redeemed and ever at your service. Amen.

Disaster or Delight?

Then I saw a new heaven and a new earth; for the first heaven and the first earth had passed away, and the sea was no more. —Revelation 21:1

There is so much endtime hype these days! Many people today are intent on using our current crop of natural disasters as sure signs of the end of time. But, as Christians, we know that the great day of the Lord won't come with a series of cataclysmic natural disasters. This type of thinking couldn't be further from the truth or from God's plan.

Instead, John in today's Revelation chapter paints for us an entirely different picture. The end, while still being a time of judgment, is going to be something grand and glorious, like nothing humankind has ever seen. It's going to be a day of shouting and rejoicing, a day to celebrate and give thanks. For the Lord will once again share the world with his people. A new heaven and new earth, free from all the terrible things we now face, will exist, and God's going to make us a part of it.

As people of faith, we look forward to a great homecoming, a festival time when God will "make all things new," when death will be no more and every tear is wiped away. All peoples will rejoice in gladness. I can't wait for the day of the Lord!

Lord, what grand and glorious words of promise! Let us live in hope and gratitude. What a God! What a God! Amen.

Day 185 / Matthew 25:14-23

Everything Matters

His master said to him, "Well done, good and trustworthy slave; you have been trustworthy in a few things, I will put you in charge of many things; enter into the joy of your master." —Matthew 25:21

Jesus' familiar parable of the talents and the slaves spotlights the very different gifts and potentials realized by the three workers. We ourselves are the classic example of how great things can come from the small. In the vastness of all of God's creation, we're nothing more than a speck or one of those grains of sands that God spoke of to Abraham. But in God's plan for creation, each of us was endowed with unique gifts and talents. We are to use these gifts and talents to be all that God has created us to be.

For most of us, that process will require an amazing transformation. Our personal change will entail our own judicious stewardship of our native gifts and talents—and one of God's miracles. In this transformative process, God promises to do what we cannot do for ourselves and commands us to do those things that we can creatively and conscientiously tackle. Like those slaves, we are entrusted by God with his creation, and God continues both to encourage us and to hold us accountable for how we invest our talents and time. Perhaps the surest way to transform our own is by uplifting the lives of others.

The choice is yours. God has created you and gifted you. Will you be one of God's unique servants or one who simply buries talents? Will you grow your gifts, great and small? What will that entail?

Lord God, thank you for your faith in me and for all the blessings and talents you have bestowed upon me. Through your Holy Spirit, empower me to use my gifts to nurture others and to help them flourish. Amen.

Sidestepping Can't Move You Forward

I delight in the law of God in my inmost self, but I see in my members another law at war with the law of my mind, making me captive to the law of sin that dwells in my members. —Romans 7:22-23

Why is it that punt- and kick-return specialists on professional football teams insist on running sideways instead of straight up the field? For some reason, they feel they can gain more yardage running east and west than they can running north and south. I find myself baffled and infuriated when they end up losing yardage.

But then, don't we often do a lot of sidestepping to avoid what sometimes need to be necessary confrontations and responsibilities in our own lives? Much of the time we try to avoid doing what we know is good for us. We run out of our way to avoid things that, however inconvenient, will benefit our lives. How many of us, for example, knowing that we need to be eating more nutritious foods that will benefit our bodies, instead avoid changing our cooking habits to do so? Or fail to find time for the exercise that our bodies crave? Or fail to enter into a daily regimen of prayer, Bible study, and meditating on God's word. Oh, "wretched people that we are"!

As followers of Christ, we need to be doing everything within our power to stand against what can damage our lives—individually and collectively—and to embrace those things that will bring God's blessings and purpose into our lives.

A wise person once said, "The things we avoid are usually the things that we need to embrace." What things have you been sidestepping in your life, in your relationships, in our world?

Loving God, take me by the hand as I run headlong through life, confident that you will guard, strengthen, and protect me as you lead me toward the truth of my life and your kingdom. Amen.

Day 187 / Psalm 147

The One in Charge Cares for Me

Noted Christian author Cheri Fuller encourages her readers, especially those who face overwhelming problems, to pray aloud the last six psalms, Psalms 144–150. One of these, Psalm 147 speaks eloquently of the majesty, generosity, and compassion of God. We are in the hands of a compassionate Creator. The psalmist writes:

> Praise the LORD!
> How good it is to sing praises to our God;
> for he is gracious, and a song of praise is fitting.
> The LORD builds up Jerusalem;
> he gathers the outcasts of Israel.
> He heals the brokenhearted,
> and binds up their wounds.
> He determines the number of the stars;
> he gives to all of them their names.
> Great is our LORD, and abundant in power;
> his understanding is beyond measure.
> The LORD lifts up the downtrodden;
> he casts the wicked to the ground.
>
> Sing to the LORD with thanksgiving;
> make melody to our God on the lyre.
> He covers the heavens with clouds;
> prepares rain for the earth,
> makes grass grow on the hills.
> He gives to the animals their food,
> and to the young ravens when they cry.
> His delight is not in the strength of the horse,
> nor his pleasure in the speed of a runner;
> but the LORD takes pleasure in those who fear him,
> in those who hope in his steadfast love.
>
> Praise the LORD, O Jerusalem!
> Praise your God, O Zion! —Psalm 147:1-12

Day by Day

God called the light Day, and the darkness he called Night. —Genesis 1:5

Reading the account of creation in Genesis, we see that, between the morning and the evening of each day, God accomplished a lot. Having chosen to place us right in the middle of his creation, God expects nothing less of us. God expects us to be good stewards of creation and to use our lives to glorify his name and to improve the lives of those around us, day by day. The 1973 Christian musical *Godspell* captured this imperative as a plea for empowerment, chanting, "Oh, dear Lord, three things I pray."

We seek empowerment:

- *to see God more clearly*—to feel God's presence in the whole of creation, in the beauty and splendor of nature, and in the hearts and souls of people
- *to love God more dearly*—to respond to God's loving touch by touching the lives of others
- *and to follow God more nearly*—not only to be hearers of the word but also doers through our faithfulness and our service.

Minute by minute . . . hour by hour . . . day by day.

On this new day, make us your servants, God. Let us serve you with joy and with the energy that comes through the power of your Holy Spirit. Amen.

Day 189 / 1 Corinthians 1:26-31

Not by the World's Standards

Consider your own call, brothers and sisters: not many of you were wise by human standards, now many were powerful, not many were of noble birth. —1 Corinthians 1:26

While I was out and about the other day, I passed by a roadside stand selling pumpkins. That brought to mind memories of annual outings with my children to choose the perfect pumpkin for jack-o-lantern carving. I admit that I never figured out what qualified as perfection in my children's eyes. More often than not, their perfect pumpkins looked quite misshapen and homely to me.

According to today's Bible text, God's choices don't fit with common convention or meet worldly standards either. To use a pumpkin analogy, God chooses us—misshapen by the ravages of sin—and lifts us up. God scoops out the seeds of doubt within us and washes us clean in the waters of baptism. God gives us a new countenance that is the very image of our creator. And, finally, God places the light of Jesus within us and bids us to let his light shine through us for the whole world to see.

In retrospect, maybe I missed the point of those pumpkin-picking outings altogether. Maybe I was the only one looking for the perfect pumpkin. Perhaps my children were focused more on seeing in each pumpkin the jack-o-lantern it would become. God bless the wisdom of children!

Lord of light, transform our misshapen and sinful selves and use us according to your purpose. Amen.

The Weakest Link

Three times I appealed to the Lord about this, that it would leave me, but he said to me, "My grace is sufficient for you, for power is made perfect in weakness." —2 Corinthians 12:8-9

As I was flipping channels the other night, I happened across game-show host Anne Robinson. You remember her, don't you? Dressed in black, with very short hair and a pouty mouth, she gave the impression of being a real grouch as she shot her favorite line: "You are the weakest link!" I really didn't like the show because of her attitude and because the format encouraged contestants to prey on each others' flaws.

In fact, we are all weak links because we all have weaknesses. We all have either physical defects or character flaws. What's yours? For some of us, it may be something that causes us to feel uncomfortable in social settings. For others, it may be some physical abnormality or chronic disease. Or it may be the lingering effects of past failures.

I'm sure at times you feel trapped by those things that cause people not to see you for who you really are. At those times, like Paul, you need to trust that, even though you may feel like a prisoner to your "weakness," Christ through his victory on the cross has set us free—free from our sins, free from our doubts and fears, free to serve him with confidence and openness in all that we say and do.

Only God is perfect. The rest of us have weaknesses. They make us unique and enable us to rely on God all the more. So rejoice and be glad. God has a lot to accomplish through you—warts, big feet, big ears, and all.

God of the ragamuffins, grant me the serenity to accept the things I cannot change, the courage to change the things I can, and the wisdom to know the difference. Amen.

Day 191 / Psalm 103:6-14

I'd Rather Have Forgiveness

As far as the east is from the west, so far he removes our transgressions from us. —Psalm 103:12

H. G. Wells imagined it, and Hollywood portrayed it: time travel. Popular books and movies have explored what could happen if a person were able to build a time machine and travel either into the future or back to the past.

Don't we all wish we had a time machine, so that we could fix some of the problems we caused or mistakes we made in the past? I'm sure we all would have to admit that we've done some pretty dumb things, missed some opportunities, made errors in judgment, and said or done things that harmed others or hurt their feelings. I'd love to have a time machine so that I could go back ten years and tell my dad how much I love him, something I never got a chance to do before he died.

Well, unfortunately, no such machine exists. But there is such a thing as forgiveness. Christ has told us that all we have to do is come before him and confess our sins, and he will wipe the slate clean. He is willing to accept our sins, forgive us, and clean up our act. Better than time travel, forgiveness is the only thing that can lead to transformation within our hearts and our lives and an indescribable sense of freedom.

I certainly wouldn't mind a few do-overs in my life. But when it comes to choosing between a time machine and God's forgiveness, I'll take forgiveness!

God, I know I've made mistakes in the past, and I'm going to make mistakes and commit sins in the future. As I rejoice in your forgiveness, I long for your guidance. Amen.

Day 192 / Isaiah 61:8-11

Yes, with the Help of God

For as the earth brings forth its shoots, and as a garden causes what is sown in it to grow up, so the Lord God will cause righteousness and praise to spring up before all the nations. —Isaiah 61:11

More than fifteen years ago, my daughter Sunshine said yes to God. On the day of her Affirmation of Baptism, when asked to confirm her faith, she responded with the words, "I do, and I ask God to help and guide me."

Since that affirmation of prayer, proclamation, and service, she's gone on to serve God's church in a variety of ways, most recently as the leader of the church's Monday evening Bible study, for which she spends long hours of preparation. I would hope she's allowed herself to say yes to God in part because she's seen through both her mother and me the importance of doing so by using the gifts God has given her.

Pastor Tom Ehrich described this yes so well in a recent message to me, "It is remarkable when it occurs. And it is quite within our grasp. The prophet's vision isn't some exotic dream. It is what happens when we say yes to God in whatever small or large ways are opened to us." If we just say yes, God will grow what he has planted in us.

Many years ago, Nancy Reagan encouraged the young people in our country to "just say no" to drugs. Today God calls us, just as he has called so many others, to just say yes to him. Listen! Hear the voice of God calling out to you. Then just say yes! You'll be glad you did.

Call out to us, God, in the wildernesses of our lives. Call us to commitment. Call us to service. Call us to faith in you. Amen.

Day 193 / Psalm 139:1-4, 13-16

One in 6,577,415,401

O LORD, you have searched me and known me. You know when I sit down and when I rise up; you discern my thoughts from far away. —Psalm 139:1-2

John's the Baptist's father, as you remember, was Zechariah. Zechariah was a priest, a minister of God who worked in the temple, one of thousands of priests. What were the odds that Zechariah would end up being the one priest selected by lot to enter the Holy of Holies and "minister before God"? That he would be in the temple, in the right place at the right time, so that Gabriel could give him the message that he and his barren wife, Elizabeth, would conceive a child, the very child who would grow up to become John the Baptist?

Coincidence? I think not. Both John's and Jesus' births were ordained by God even before the foundations of the earth were formed.

Your life is the same. Today's passage sheds marvelous light on the intimate way God works in our lives. God knows our names. God knew our parents. God knows us by heart. God has placed us on this earth with an invitation to collaborate in his work. And God knows what he wants each of us to accomplish while we're here.

So today, as you start out with some master plan to "get it all done," don't forget that what you need to get done is really what God has designed for you to do. You are one of God's unique creations. In fact, you are one in 6,577,424,980 (based on one Internet-based population-counter, the world's population has increased by 9,579 people since I titled this devotion . . . about an hour ago). Today, relish that knowledge.

Lord, you've known me even before I was born, and you've chartered a course for me to follow, so that I might serve you to the best of my ability. Fill me, empower me, send me, and use me. Amen.

Day 194 / Psalm 118:23-24, 26-29

Joy to the World

This is the day that the Lord has made, let us rejoice and be glad in it. —Psalm 118:24

When hymn writer Isaac Watts was eighteen years old, he criticized the hymns of the church. His father said, "If you don't like the hymns we sing, then write a better one." To that his son replied, "I have." One of his hymns was shared with the church, and the people asked Watts to write more. For 222 weeks, Isaac Watts prepared a new hymn for each Sunday, single-handedly revolutionizing the congregational singing habits of the English churches.

In 1705, Watts published his first volume of hymns and sacred poems. More followed. In 1719, he published his monumental work, *The Psalms of David, Imitated.* In preparing this work, he focused on Psalm 98, especially verses 4, 6, 8, and 9, when he wrote the hymn that we now know as "Joy to the World." Set to a musical theme adapted by Lowel Mason from "The Messiah" by George Frederick Handel, "Joy to the World" is one of the most beloved hymns of the Christmas season.

The command to "rejoice" can be found more than 500 times in the Bible. The truth behind today's passage runs deep; the joy of Christ's arrival can sustain us for a lifetime. As a great preacher once said, "The surest mark of a Christian is not faith or even love, but joy."

Lord God, let us sing out in joyous praise for the birth of your Son, Jesus Christ, from the first words from out lips each day to our last words each night. Amen.

Day 195 / Matthew 2:1-12

No Need to Reciprocate

Opening their treasure chests, they offered [the baby Jesus] gifts of gold, frankincense, and myrrh. —Matthew 2:11

In his sermon entitled, "The Breaking of Silence," noted Christian author and pastor Frederick Buechner explores three characteristics of childhood that for him define childlike faith. The second characteristic is that "children know how to accept a gift." Children, he says,

- receive gladly and unself-consciously,
- offer no debate as to whether they deserve the gift ,
- have no worries about the etiquette of reciprocating, and
- quickly tear off the wrapping paper, open the gift with gusto, and immediately start to enjoy it.

Children accept the extraordinary as part of their ordinary world. They are excited by gifts but don't spontaneously feel overawed, undeserving, or indebted.

As we hurry and scurry to get it all done before that big day, perhaps we can take a lesson from the children. We are about to celebrate the fact that God has given us the greatest gift we could ever receive. Yet God really doesn't expect anything in return because what he has done he has done out of love. For that matter, there really isn't much we, as human beings, could give back to God that he doesn't already have, except our own love. That will be enough.

God, thank you for the gift of your Son. In return, all we have to offer is ourselves. Accept and use our gifts to you as you choose. Amen.

I Yam

But by the grace of God I am what I am, and his grace towards me has not been in vain. —1 Corinthians 15:10

There used to be a stolid but popular cartoon character, Popeye the Sailor Man, who always and easily proclaimed, "I yam what I yam and that's all what I yam . . . I'm Popeye the Sailor Man." Such enviable self-knowledge doesn't come easily to me. I'm more like the renowned hymn writer John Newton, who wrote, "I am not what I ought to be. I am not what I want to be. I am not what I hope to be. But still, I am not what I used to be. And by the grace of God, I am what I am."

Have you had days when you weren't sure you were being all that you could be, or all that God designed you to be? I have. In fact, it's pretty much that way every day for me. I'm not what I was, but I'm not what I want to be either. The lives I've touched, the things that I've read and heard, my experiences—all have come together to change the way I see myself now, and I stand on the brink of even more changes.

I may not know finally and fully what or who I am. But God's hand has led me through experiences of growth and has left me with the anticipation of even more growth, to the point where I live in faith, never completely satisfied with who I was or am. Each day, God leaves me in a state of dissatisfaction, and that pushes me to new questions, new experiences, new faith in the person I might become.

Loving God, thank you for bringing me as far from my former self as you have. By your grace, I pray that I won't stray too far from my true self, the self you made me to be. Amen.

Day 197 / Luke 2:1-7

The Journey

In those days a decree went out from Emperor Augustus that all the world should be registered. —Luke 2:1

Caesar Augustus required that each of the people under his rule go to register in the town where they were born. This census was being taken so that Rome could effectively levy taxes on its subjects and arrange military conscription.

For Joseph, complying with this government edict meant a difficult journey, not only for him but also for his betrothed, Mary, then in the ninth month of her pregnancy. It would create hardships for the two of them: The several-day journey of nearly seventy miles took them over some very rough roads (probably beset with about the same number of potholes found on any road in Pennsylvania, especially during winter months). As for their mode of transportation, they probably had two rough choices, either on foot or on the back of donkey (Christmas tradition always has Mary riding on a donkey, even though there is no place in scripture that confirms this). The trip also cut off any income from Joseph's carpentry and probably the loss of potential jobs. And then, more poignantly, there was Mary, forced to endure this long journey with the possibility of childbirth any day, and to do so without a comfortable place to stay.

We too are called to journey, to face the obstacles and potholes of life with courage and good cheer. Even when the road is not paved nor the direction certain, we too are meant to bring the savior into the world around us.

God, provide me with the strength and the fortitude to answer your call to service and to follow you wherever and to whomever you may lead me. Amen.

Day 198 / Luke 24:13-16

Present and Accounted For

While they were talking and discussing, Jesus himself came near and went with them, but their eyes were kept from recognizing him. —Luke 24:15-16

Too often we get stuck in the past, or we get fixated on the future. As a consequence, we lose sight of the present. The events and relationships that need our attention right now get overlooked or pushed aside.

Jesus offers us a wonderful example of what it means to be "wholly present" with those whom he encountered during the three years of his ministry. Time and again, Jesus allowed himself to be interrupted by those needing healing. He ate dinner with society's outcast. He attended to the needs of hungry crowds. He walked with his disciples, listened to their questions, met their needs, and taught them to pray. And, while dying on the cross, Jesus heard the confession of the thief beside him and promised him that he would be with him in paradise.

Today, as you go through your day remember the example of Jesus for investing in relationships, for living in the present. Take care to learn from the past and to prepare for the future, but don't miss out on the people and opportunities that God puts in your path this day. When you hear God calling, be sure to be present, and accounted for.

God, sometimes it seems easier to live anywhere but the present with all its demands and responsibilities. But you call us to this moment and to the needs of those whose lives touch ours right now. Keep us focused . . . keep us present for your service. Amen.

Day 199 / John 1:1-3, 14

Is Jesus the Real Deal?

The Word became flesh and made his dwelling among us.
—John 1:14 (NIV)

The Roman writer Tacitus is considered one of our most authentic historical sources, yet only twenty copies of his works exist, the earliest of which is dated thousands of years after his death. The earliest manuscripts we have of Aristotle's work have been dated some fourteen hundred years after he lived. The earliest copies of Julius Caesar's writing have been dated a thousand years after his assassination. The earliest copies of the New Testament, of which there are thousands, have been dated only a few hundred years after Jesus lived. And yet, while they don't deny the existence of Tacitus, Aristotle, or Caesar, religious skeptics argue against the authenticity of Jesus because the New Testament wasn't written until hundreds of years after Jesus had lived, after a whole host of myths and legends had grown up and distorted the original events. Scholars, historians, and archeologists now know, however, that the original writings were written twenty to forty years after Christ's crucifixion and resurrection. Is there any question that the accounts printed from these manuscripts and the things that they describe are real events?

The evidence for Jesus' existence is overwhelming: Jesus came and dwelt among us.

I believe, I do believe, truly I believe it, truly I believe it, truly I believe it! I believe, I do believe, truly I believe it, truly I believe it, truly I believe it! Amen.

Day 200 / 2 Corinthians 12:7-10

God, Handle It for Me?

Therefore I am content with weaknesses, insults, hardships, persecutions, and calamities for the sake of Christ; for whenever I am weak, then I am strong. —2 Corinthians 12:10

Shortly before I left the church where I had worked for so long, we were in the process of trying to do some remodeling of the church's youth room to provide a little more open space. At one point in the church's history, someone had taken what was once large open room and erected several walls to divide it up. One of those short walls came out from the back end of the room for about eight feet into the main room, dividing up that back end into two small offsets. We thought this would be a good wall to remove to provide for a more practical space—that is until we started to demolish the wall, only to discover that it was a load-bearing wall, a necessary wall to keep the ceiling and the floor above from crashing down into the room below it.

God's a lot like that load-bearing wall. God is the main support, something he isn't asking us to do. God is the one primarily responsible to effect healing in others; but it doesn't mean that we need to shy away from contact of and comfort for those who hurt.

What it does mean is that, regardless of our perceived inabilities or innate fear, God's going to work through our weaknesses to make some amazing things happen—things beyond our wildest dreams. But it means that we need to keep tight that relationship with God, so that through it we continue to serve him with both confidence and joy.

Almighty God, let me always be willing to voice my shortcomings and my weakness to you, so that you can use them to empower me in service to you. Amen.

Day 201 / Psalm 24:1-10

Who Is This King?

Who is this King of glory? The LORD of hosts, he is the King of glory. —Psalm 24:10

An ancient legend tells how the devil tried to get into heaven by pretending he was the risen Christ. Approaching the gates of heaven he shouted up, "Lift up your heads, O gates, and be lifted up, O ancient doors, that the King of glory may come in!" The angels in heaven shouted back with joy the psalm refrain, "Who is the King of glory?" Then the devil made a fatal mistake: He opened his arms and shouted back, "I am!" In that act of arrogance he showed the angels his outstretched palms. There were no wounds from the nails, and the angels of heaven refused to let the imposter enter.

Who is your King of glory? Who is the Lord of your life? The one who created and rules the world? The one who is strong and mighty in battle? The one from whom you receive vindication for your transgressions? Or the "sometimes king" to whom you pay homage and offer praise only when things in your life are going okay and you have time or inclination to do so? And when it comes time to open your hands and show your face to the angels in heaven, will they see the marks of the nails on your palms and the image of the cross on your forehead?

Loving God, how fortunate we are to live under the reign of the most compassionate and loving King in all of history. You indeed are powerful and you indeed are just. What a kingdom, and what a King! Amen.

Day 202 / Psalm 118:21-29

The Time Between

This is the day that the Lord has made; let us rejoice and be glad in it. —Psalm 118:24

Ecclesiastes 3 tells us, "For everything there is a season, and a time for every matter under heaven: a time to be born, and a time to die." But what takes place the rest of the time in our lives, between those times of birth and death?

Every year, as I begin a new year's appointment calendar, I look at some of the previous calendar's entries and recall details of certain events or visits. In looking back, I often gain some perspective on how my sharing or my presence may have made a difference to another person. At other times I find myself evaluating my life in general. Even in the midst of uncertainties, anger, and doubt, I realize I was never separated from God's touch, love, and forgiveness.

Only God knows what will take place between today and this day in the year to come. Only God knows what will happen in these times between the times. Much like last year, the year to come will be filled with joys and sorrows, good times and bad. But regardless of what may take place, one fact remains constant: the Lord will provide—for our needs, and for opportunities to share God's presence and power with others. God will fill those times between the times with the divine love so that we might live the days between birth and death in love and service to our Lord.

God, thank you for this day. Help me to use it in service to others in your name. Guide my feet and direct my hands to where you know they will do the most good. Keep me in touch with your word today and all days. Amen.

Day 203 / Exodus 16:1-3

Are We There Yet?

The whole congregation of the Israelites complained against Moses and Aaron in the wilderness. —Exodus 16:2

When I think back on van trips I have taken with church groups I try to focus on the people that were a part of each trip rather than the experiences. Some were cooperative travelers and then there were the "Hebrews," who weren't content unless they were complaining about something or someone.

The Christian life is a lot like one of those van rides. We make that journey with a whole lot of different people: Some make the journey a pleasure by faithfully handling their particular responsibilities along the way. Others are a pain because they either refuse to do what they are asked or just go along for the ride. And, of course, there's always at least one who asks, "Are we there yet?"

The Christian life is a journey that doesn't end until we die and we're received into God's heavenly kingdom. So as to the question, "Are we there yet?"—No! We're not there yet, we're here; and it's here where God is present with us. God's at work in our present world, giving us little glimpses of what the "hereafter" is going to be like, those little "foretastes of the feast to come." To be on that journey with God is to look closely, listen attentively, and walk slowly and patiently so that the Spirit of God can walk with us.

God, as I travel through life with you and those you place around me, help me to make the trip a pleasure by doing the part you have called me to. Help me to focus on what you want to show me here, rather than on where you are taking me. Amen.

Day 204 / Luke 2:41-52

Letting Go

When his parents saw him they were astonished; and his mother said to him, "Child, why have you treated us like this? Look, your father and I have been searching for you in great anxiety," But he said to them, "Why were you searching for me? Did you not know that I must be in my Father's house?" —Luke 2: 48-49

Recently, a nephew graduated, and two nieces were married. Graduations and weddings represent the beginnings of "letting go," something that can be difficult for both parents and children to do.

Today's passage represents for Mary and Joseph the beginnings of their "letting go" process. After having spent time in Jerusalem for the Feast of the Passover, they began the journey back to Nazareth along with hundreds of other friends and relatives. When they finally realized Jesus wasn't with them, they rushed back to Jerusalem where, after a three-day search, they found their twelve-year-old son in the Temple talking with the scribes and elders. Being the typical, caring parent, Mary gave Jesus a tongue lashing for being so disrespectful.

Jesus' reply was calm and measured. No disrespect was intended; his time to begin to fly on his own was beginning. What better place to start than in his "Father's house"?

We all face times when it is especially hard to let go. For those who live by faith, letting go doesn't mean abandonment; it means entrusting those we love to the care of God, who never lets us go. It is a comfort that Mary must have felt as she treasured all these things in her heart; and it's the same comfort we can know as we say our goodbyes.

Loving God, be with those who are letting go and with those who are about to begin life anew. May these new lives ever be centered and grounded in your love and mercy. Amen.

Day 205 / Jeremiah 31:7-9

Where's Your Babylon?

With weeping they shall come, and with consolations I will lead them back. —Jeremiah 31:9

A homeless man once told me that his primary goal in life was a better relationship with God, explaining, "A job and a home are my goals, but I know until I reestablish my relationship with God, those will never happen."

Confused priorities are exactly what got the Israelites into the predicament from which God had to rescue them. Over many years, Israel moved farther from its loyalty to the God who had rescued them from slavery in Egypt and instead made money and power their primary gods. The result? Babylon. There they lived for years as a nation scattered, yet with the promise that one day God would gather and return them together to that land of milk and honey.

Where is the Babylon to which you've been scattered? Most likely, it is where your heart and your interests lie. What is the treasure that you hold nearest and dearest? If it isn't God—then welcome to Babylon!

The minute anything takes preeminence over God, you'd best start packing your bags and change your name to Joseph, because you've sold yourself into slavery and are about to begin a long journey. But there's always a way back from Babylon—God never lets go of our hearts, even in our deepest despair, way down in Babylon. God will bring us back from wherever we have wandered.

Thanks, Lord, for bringing me home, kicking and screaming, when I prefer to wander away. Help me put you first in my life, so that the choices I make will be easier. Thank you for loving me, even when it isn't easy to do so. Amen.

Day 206 / Psalm 19

May the Words of My Mouth . . .

Let the words of my mouth . . . be acceptable to you, O Lord.
—Psalm 19:14

We've all heard the words, "looks can be deceiving." Can you easily be spotted as a Christian? Would someone looking at you be able to tell that God has chosen you as a messenger of God's word?

God placed the divine word into the mouth of a reluctant Jeremiah. God took this young boy—probably only a teenager—and appointed him as a prophet to the nations to spread the word of God. And what words they would be! Words of condemnation and words of hope; words of imminent danger and words of promise; words describing a horrible time of captivity and words proclaiming freedom. All these words would come from the mouth of one of the least likely sources of God's word.

Just as crossword puzzles are a great exercise for expanding one's vocabulary, so daily reading of God's word is a great spiritual exercise for expanding one's understanding of God. So let the word of God fill your mouth. Take it into your heart and meditate upon it. And then, let those words flow from your mouth; that others may be blessed by its message, and that the loving arms of God, your rock and your redeemer, may welcome you into God's kingdom, holy and acceptable.

Loving Lord, let me be filled with your "God vocabulary." Place into my mouth those words of comfort and promise, those words of power and strength, those words of love and salvation for all your people. Amen.

Day 207 / Exodus 4:10-12

A Fool's Tale

I will be with your mouth and teach you what you are to speak.
—Exodus 4:12

If you're like me, all too often while reading newspapers, watching newscasts, or even hearing sermons, the words of the famous soliloquy from Shakespeare's *Macbeth* come to mind: "A tale told by an idiot, full of sound and fury, signifying nothing." So many words, so little content!"

Moses, on the other hand, doesn't want God to put the words in his mouth, and doesn't want to speak them. He comes up with all sorts of excuses to avoid being God's spokesperson. God's got words of wisdom, direction, and good news for the Lord's people, and Moses just doesn't want to be the messenger.

Christians are given the opportunity to say much, and yet say virtually nothing. We get so hung up on the words that we want to say that we don't speak the words that God wants to place in our mouths. We tend to focus more on our own needs than the needs and lives of those around us, which makes it easier to not share with others our own faith story and beliefs, the words that tell of God's love.

Let God's words enter you; then let them flow from your tongue—full of sound, full of fury, signifying the most precious gift ever given to humanity—the gift of eternal life in our risen Lord and Savior, Jesus Christ.

Lord God, let the words of the hymn "I love to tell the story" be not only the motto for all Christianity, but our covenant with God, as well. Amen.

Day 208 / Psalm 61:1-4

Under God's Wings

Let me . . . find refuge under the shelter of your wings. —Psalm 61:4

Several years ago, when a massive fire destroyed large areas of Yellowstone National Park, forest rangers discovered a dead mother bird underneath whose wings emerged three tiny chicks, still living. She could have easily flown to safety herself, but she refused to abandon her babies. Because she had been willing to die, those under the cover of her wings lived.

We, too, can be comforted in the knowledge that, sheltered by the wings of God, we can have protection from the firestorms of life. We can rejoice knowing that God, through Jesus Christ, has shielded us from the fires of hell, to the point of giving his life for us so that we might live and grow.

The psalmist pictures God as a refuge, a fortress, a place of safety and protection, who hears our cries above the noises of the city streets, above the sounds of the weapons of war, and even from the deepest depths of our despair. In the same way, the apostle Matthew portrays God as a mother hen who gathers her brood under her wings to keep them safe. We are those chicks and God is our mother hen. It is there we find warmth, we find shelter, and we find protection—under the wings of God.

Raise us up on eagle's wings, bear us on your breath, O God; make us to shine like the sun, and hold us in the palm of your hand. Amen.

Day 209 / 1 Thessalonians 5:12-21

Every Moment a God Moment

Rejoice always, pray without ceasing, give thanks in all circumstances. —1 Thessalonians 5:16-18

Being a Christian doesn't make one different from others in this world because we all sport the black-and-blue marks where life has bumped into us. One of the most important parts of the human anatomy is the nervous system, which allows us to sense differences in objects simply by touch, to distinguish between hot and cold, and to experience both pleasure and pain. It also affects the way we feel toward and about God's creation and the people in it. The nervous system allows us to experience the physical, psychological, and emotional pains and joys of life—all of which are "God moments."

Paul's words to the church at Thessalonica make clear that every moment must be a "God moment," a moment for which we should rejoice. Every moment represents an opportunity for us to worship God, to offer prayer, and to give thanks, both for the good times as well as for God's sustaining and strengthening power during life's more difficult times.

Worship, be it public or private, should always be a time when we can not only offer our prayers and our praises but also a time when we can be quiet and listen for God's word to us. As the psalmist wrote, "Be still, and know that I am God" (Ps. 46:10). Whenever possible during your day, find those quiet moments and worship God.

Awesome and ever-present God, you are my hope, you are my rock and my salvation, my fortress. On you rests my deliverance, my salvation and my life. God of love, you are and always will be my refuge and my strength. Amen.

Day 210 / Luke 7:11-17

A "Don't Touch Me" Church

Then [Jesus]came forward and touched the bier. . . . And he said, "Young man, I say to you, rise!" The dead man sat up and began to speak, and Jesus gave him to his mother. —Luke 7:14-15

I always look forward to the time during worship when we can make physical contact with others in the congregation, either during the passing of the peace or just a time of simple greeting. It's amazing how uncomfortable people can be just during a simple handshake. Lutherans are, for the most part, a "don't touch me" church.

When was the last time you left the church feeling untouched? I wonder how many of us leave the church on a Sunday morning not just untouched by those around us, but also by the presence and the power of the living Christ. How many of us go from that place still dead? Christ touched that funeral bier and brought life to one who was dead. What miracles might come about by the touch of your hand?

Christ wants to touch us, just as he did the widow's son at Nain. He wants to restore life to our bodies and life to our souls, so that we may, through both the passing of the peace and simple handshake and good morning, bring new life in Christ Jesus to others. In the words of the old gospel hymn, "He touched me, oh, he touched me; and oh what joy now fills my soul. Something happened, and now I know; he touched me and made me whole."

Lord, touch the lives of others through my touch, that they may know healing, that they may be whole! Amen.

Day 211 / Matthew 8:1-4

What If Jesus Had Said, "No"?

Lord, if you choose, you can make me clean. —Matthew 8:2

What if, when the leper called out to him, Jesus had responded, "Guess what? I don't want to." What if Jesus told any of us, "I don't feel like listening to your whiny prayers. I don't want to be bothered by any of you. Why don't you just all go away?" And what if he told God, "Father, take this cup away right now. I don't want to spill my blood or give up my body. I don't want to die for any of them; they're just not worth it!"

Sometimes we're convinced that, because we don't get the answer to our prayers we wanted, Jesus has said "no." We need to understand that Jesus will answer our prayers, but he will do it God's way. God has never, and will never turn a deaf ear to our pleas. Christ is alive and active in our lives every hour of every day. His answer to our prayers is never, "No way"; it's always, "*My* way."

So, go ahead, put your faith in God. Trust God with your life. Offer God your all, and then sit back and watch God tell you, "Thank you. I do want to use your life, to share my word and to share my love!"

God, thanks for the "yesses" in my life. Thanks for trusting in me to be your disciple and your messenger, for those times when others would question whether I'm yours and if you love me. Loving God, thanks for letting them hear you say, "Yes!" Amen.

Day 212 / Romans 12:1-2

A Simple Letter Change

Present your bodies as a living sacrifice, holy and acceptable to God. —Romans 12:1

I once saw a message outside a church that read: *All Life Is Sacred*. I thought about how true those words *should* be for our world but often aren't. Many people really don't value life—their own or anyone else's—unless there is some personal benefit involved.

But what if someone reversed the letters in the word "Sacred" so that it read "*Scared*"? Sadly, that might be a more accurate commentary of our society. Because we devalue life, many people live in fear of their survival and practice some form of isolationism. People now feel the need to "set themselves apart" from the world, to live out their lives in their own protected space.

Ironically, the root of the word "sacred" connotes something or someone to be "set apart," or to be made holy. Just as Paul called upon God's people to set themselves apart, holy and acceptable, for the work of the kingdom, God also calls us to set ourselves apart from this world, even as we live and serve in the world. So God calls us to be "in, but not of" this world. To be "set apart" by God can be scary, but we don't have to live in fear in our service to God, who changes us from being scared to being sacred, so that we can serve in truth and love.

Understanding God, I know I shouldn't be afraid to serve you, but I admit, I am scared sometimes. I don't want to face the sting of rejection from someone who doesn't want to know you. Help me to "do all things through Christ who gives me his strength." Amen.

Day 213 / Exodus 3:1-6

Lose the Shoes

Remove the sandals from your feet, for the place on which you are standing is holy ground. —Exodus 3:5

In the story of the burning bush, God calls Moses to make a decision, to figure out what he's going to do with his life, and with God's people. Everyday God calls us to holy ground, to those places where we must make decisions on how we're going to handle this life with God, and live it out in the context of our everyday existence.

When we decide to turn away from our selfishness and pride, we're standing on holy ground. Moses tried every lame excuse in the book to get out of what God told him to do. Whether he chose to accept it or not, Moses had been blessed by God and chosen to be the leader and the liberator of God's people. When we surrender to the best that is in us, and give it for the work of God's kingdom, then we die and are reborn on holy ground.

God has gifted and empowered each of us. Sometimes we have to trust God and let God lead us to use those gifts for others. But we have to set aside our fears and doubts and surrender to the best that is in us—the presence and the power of God. Only then does God allow us to die to ourselves and become reborn right there on God's holy ground.

Help me, God, to bare my feet and my heart in your presence. I'm ready to make decisions, lose my selfishness, take risks, lose my fears, and surrender all that I am to you. Help me place my feet on your holy ground. Amen.

Day 214 / Exodus 3:10-15

Please Don't Talk to Me, God

God said to Moses, "I AM WHO I AM." —Exodus 3:14

The cartoon character Popeye used to sing, "I am what I am, and that's all what I am, I'm Popeye the sailor man," as a way of saying, "What you see is what you get." In a sense, that's what God is trying to help Moses to understand about God's identity and person: God is the Almighty, the same God worshiped by Abraham, Isaac, and Jacob.

Many Christians practice their prayer life solely as a monologue. They don't talk "with" God; they talk "to" God. As long as those prayers remain monologues, most people are comfortable. But to say that God talks to humans tends to rattle more than a few cages. It seems irrational to say that the God who speaks to us is the God of Abraham, Isaac, and Jacob. So what do we tell those who ask us, "What is this God's name?" We can tell them that God is the God of comfort for those who suffer; the God of consolation for those who mourn; the God of promise for those who are without hope; and the God of grace for the unloved, the lost, and the sinful. We can tell them that God is the God who was, who is, and who always will be, the one to whom we can go with our greatest joys and deepest sorrows.

Loving God, speak to us, for we are listening, hanging on your every word, rejoicing in your presence in our lives. Direct our feet, and focus our eyes and hearts so we can share with your people the message that I AM is with them, now and for eternity. Amen.

Day 215 / Job 31:5-8

Why Doesn't It Add Up?

Let me be weighed in a just balance! —Job 31:6

My job involves a complicated accounting system that has to be balanced at the end of the year. Sometimes the numbers don't add up right and, despite my attempts to figure out the error, something stays out of balance.

Similarly, Job can't figure out why his relationship with God is so far out of balance. In his mind everything adds up: He's been faithful in his devotion to God, he's led a good life, taken care of his family, and been helpful to those in need. What's wrong here?

Have you checked out your relationship with God lately? If God were to take an accounting of the books, would your page be in balance? Have you dispensed the same measure of grace to others that God gives to you? Have you forgiven the sins of others as readily as God has forgiven yours?

Sometimes the problem is obvious and easily resolved, but we're just too close to the situation to see it, so we need to go back with a changed mind-set and gain a different perspective on our life and relationship with God. Whatever it is that's throwing your relationship with God out of whack, step back and let God work with you to bring the balance into your life that God desires for all creation.

God, pull me closer to you and give me your guidance and your love so that I can lead a full and balanced life as I joyfully serve you. Amen.

Does It Really Matter?

But who do you say that I am? —Matthew 16:13

Mel Gibson's *The Passion of the Christ* was one of the most controversial films of recent years for many reasons, not least for its graphically violent portrayal of Christ's trial and torture, and the bloody horror of his death on the cross. Regardless of aesthetic considerations or feelings about movie violence in general, or even historical accuracy, it is worth asking why that violence should bother us, especially we who claim to be Christ's followers. Are we ashamed by it? Does it appall us? Or are we afraid to face that what possibly took place may be a truth much uglier than what we learned in Sunday school? If nothing else, this movie has caused many to consider their own answer to Christ's question, "Who do you say that I am?"

Whether one sees the movie or not, it's worth asking ourselves who this Christ is who endured such suffering, who would love us so unconditionally, who would take the burden of our sins upon himself, and who would forgive those sins without reservation. And after honestly answering all those questions for ourselves, hopefully we can each answer Christ's question with the same bold conviction of Peter: You are the Messiah, the Son of the living God. And it shouldn't take any Hollywood production to bring us to that statement of faith.

God, instill in us faith and trust so that, in thankful response to Jesus' sacrifice, we can boldly proclaim that the one who gave his life for us is the Christ, the Son of the living God. Amen.

Day 217 / Isaiah 53:3-10

The Beauty of the Crucifixion

As one from whom others hide their faces he was despised, and we held him of no account. —Isaiah 53:3

For the people of Israel waiting for God's promise to come true—the promise of a savior that would lead them out of despair—what kind of hope could they put in a savior such as the one Isaiah describes? This servant is a tragic figure, almost a wimp. He is an object of horror; but in that suffering, he is also the beauty of God.

Just as the people of Israel had a hard time seeing the Messiah in the suffering servant, so is it difficult for Christians to look past the blood and the gore of Jesus' body as it hung on the cross and see our Savior. We need to see beyond what is only an external tragedy—a naked, helpless victim nailed to a piece of wood. There is much more to the death of Jesus than that. Within that shattered body is the soul of God that, in the face of all that suffering, displays a level of dignity that is immeasurable. Within that broken and bleeding figure is a love that knows no end, that offers forgiveness to all. Most assuredly, Christ's crucifixion was brutal and dehumanizing; but it was, at the same time, beautiful because of his example to us of unwavering obedience to the glory of God, and in his display of love for all humanity.

Merciful God, how can we ever offer enough thanks to you for the price paid for our sins? As we direct our eyes to the specter of the cross, let us see not only a symbol of pain and suffering, but also a sign of victory, freedom, and love. Amen.

Day 218 / Luke 1:26-33

3.14159265358979 . . .

He will reign over the house of Jacob forever, and of his kingdom there will be no end. —Luke 1:33

Pi is a transcendental number, one whose ratio cannot be calculated precisely; nor does it have any emerging or obvious pattern of numbers. Its ratio is an endless parade of numbers that goes on infinitely. Simply put, it has no end, though mathematicians continue to seek one.

We live in a world that is becoming increasingly quantifiable. We aren't satisfied unless we can arrive at a definite solution to every problem: Everything must be definable in terms of yes or no, black or white, good or bad, existent or nonexistent. It must have verifiable characteristics and allow us to make a decision. Maybe that's why we continue to seek after both pi and God—because we can neither define nor determine an end to either one.

Like pi, the kingdom and the will of God are infinite. John tells us in Revelation that God is the Alpha and the Omega, the beginning and the end of time and space. And we can no more see to the end of the universe than we can see the end of God's reign. Something lies beyond those billions of digits of pi—something new, nonrepetitive, mysterious, and exciting. And much lies beyond our current, very limited understanding of God's nature and being. God's presence in our lives continues to evoke endless questions—the answers to which will always be the same.

God, continue to challenge us to seek more and more knowledge about you and about your will for our lives. Like a good performer, always leave us wanting more. Amen.

Day 219 / Ecclesiastes 9:1-4

One Bellybutton

Whoever is joined with all the living has hope, for a living dog is better than a dead lion. —Ecclesiastes 9:4

An old Yiddish blessing translates, "Good health to your belly-button!" Everyone has a bellybutton, which serves as a reminder that life comes from life: people are conceived inside people and are cut free to become persons.

Yet those who have given birth to another living being have a connection that transcends the physical. Parents never really let go; that connection of love and concern for their children's well-being and success remains. Even without the physical attachment, our bellybuttons remind us that love never ends.

But thank God we only have one bellybutton. God, the almighty and loving parent has not, and never will sever a connection with us. God's love goes with us wherever we go. God is there in those times when we feel like we've been disconnected from the world, those times of pain and suffering, doubt and defeat, agony and loss. There is no mark of separation because God has not cut us loose. Yet we each bear the mark of connection—that of the cross, placed upon our head at baptism, which reminds us that our very life is from God, and that God will never let us go. That mark challenges us to live in the joy of life, starting from the very center of our being in which God must dwell to give us life.

God, there are those who may accuse us of "navel gazing," and that's okay. You call us to direct our thoughts inward, to examine closely what lies within us—our belief and our obedience and servant response to your call. God, keep us connected and give us life. Amen.

Day 220 / 1 Corinthians 15:51-56

Death In My Rearview Mirror

Where, O death, is your victory? Where, O death, is your sting? —1 Corinthians 15:55

Once, while driving, I saw in my rearview mirror a group of motorcycles coming up behind me. One of the bikers was dressed in the usual black leather jacket and helmet, but a skeleton hood covered his face. As I stared at this black-clothed skeleton, all I could think was that death was right behind me.

As I get older, and each morning I read in the obituaries of people my age and even younger who have died, that specter of death does enter my mind. I see death lurking in the rearview mirror. Yet I don't fear death; rather, I fear more what anguish my death might bring to those I leave behind. But as for death itself, the words of Paul provide all the comfort and assurance we need. The death and resurrection of Christ has taken away any worries we might have about death because we know death can't win. Paul's words serve to remind us that Christ has paid the price for our sins. Christ has beaten sin, death, and the devil—and as his disciples, that victory is one that we can also claim.

So don't panic if you see death in your rearview mirror, focus your eyes toward the final victory that lies ahead.

God, we offer our thanks to you for the sacrifice you've made for us. We rejoice to know that death can't claim us because our life is in your hands. What a comfort—what a peace! Amen.

Day 221 / Acts 11:25-26

Who Are We?

It was in Antioch that the disciples were first called "Christians." —Acts 11:26

I once read a church newsletter containing this statement: "We know God calls us to serve and bear witness to God's love and to support and encourage others in that effort. We are praying for you this month and hope this reflects God's love and our intent to bond in the Spirit with your efforts to bear light in an often dark world." How does the world outside the church see the church, we who are Christ's body?

The top religion news stories every year are dominated by denominations fighting over: sexuality, war, and leadership struggles; scandals about child sexual abuse; even where church members can pray and with whom. Is it possible that the world outside the Christian church knows it only by the fighting that takes place within it?

How do you suppose the people of Antioch viewed these first "Christians"? Were they known by their love and mercy or by their discord? Where they known by their caring and generosity or by their rituals and self-absorbed behavior? Were they known by their openness and receptivity or by their closed, cliquish society? Can we be confident today that, in the words of the gospel chorus, "They'll know we are Christians by our love"?

People of God's church in today's age, as the world looks upon us—will they know? God, let them always see you in us. Amen.

Day 222 / Luke 10:30-35

Owe the Debt

Take care of him; and when I come back, I will repay you whatever more you spend. —Luke 10:35

What do you suppose were the thoughts and memories the beaten man carried with him after his recuperation? Did the Samaritan's charity have any bearing on the way he dealt with others later in life? Do you think he remembered the cruelty of the robbers and subsequently shaped his life and behavior toward others in that same way? Or do you think he shaped his life remembering the generosity of that nameless Samaritan, and offered similar kindness to others?

For some people, being indebted to someone for some random act of kindness can be difficult and unnerving. Why do we feel we always have to "pay someone back" for something nice that they've done for us? Why isn't it possible to just accept their kindness and say thank you? First John tells us, "We love because he first loved us" (4:19). Our love for others should not only be in response to God's initial love for us, but also a way of expressing our thanks for the debt Jesus paid to free us from our sins.

So, bruised and battered traveler along this journey of life, your wounds have been tended and dressed, not by some anonymous Samaritan, but by the Great Physician. What will you choose to do—simply go on with your life, or pay forward the debt you owe? The choice is yours.

God, thank you for taking the time to stop, bend down, ease my pain, help me up, and send me on my way—no, on your way. Let me be that Samaritan to others whom life has beaten down and left for dead. Amen.

Day 223 / 1 Peter 1:13-16

You Gotta Have Hope

Set all your hope on the grace that Jesus will bring you when he is revealed. —1 Peter 1:13

Checking out the headlines on any given day can be a depressing experience—life at times looks pretty hopeless. But if you keep your eyes focused on Jesus Christ, you can be assured of hope even in the most difficult circumstances. Consider these reasons you can remain hopeful even when everything seems to be falling apart:

1. *Jesus is going to win the final victory.* How comfortable are you in your relationship with Jesus? Are you certain that Jesus will win in the end?

2. *Jesus is going to set you free.* Because Christ has set you free from your sins, you can be all that God wants you to be without worrying about all your past baggage.

3. *By believing in Christ, no one in this world can condemn you.* Being in Christ, you're a new creation because through God's love we receive new beginnings and eternal life in Jesus Christ.

4. *God's love goes beyond any human understanding.* Never forget that God loves you and wants the best for you all the time. Even in the bleakest of times, there's always going to be a light shining.

Remember Paul's words in Romans: "If God is for us, who can be against us?"(8:13).You can rejoice loud and long because God is for you and through God's love you can find hope!

God, what a comfort to know that my faith, trust, life, and hope rest in the blood and righteousness of your Son. To know that he gave it all on the cross for me is all the hope I need to face the ugliness of this world. Amen.

Day 224 / Psalm 4:1-4

Sit Still and Be Quiet!

When you are disturbed, do not sin; ponder it on your beds, and be silent. —Psalm 4:4

How many parents have yelled at their kids, "SIT STILL AND BE QUIET!" over the years? And how many children have actually done that in response? It's hard for a child to sit still, but, to be honest, we adults don't do much better.

That's a shame; because sitting still, for even a brief period of time, can be incredibly powerful. In the stillness and the quietness of the Garden of Gethsemane Jesus received the power from God to withstand one of the most horrendous ordeals ever experienced by a human being. If we're too busy to be still and listen, how will we ever know what it is that God wants us to do, to hear the cries for justice from God's people, to enjoy the beauty and majesty of God's creation?

When David wrote today's psalm, he was troubled by the threat of enemies that surrounded him. Who or what are the enemies that surround and threaten us today, that make us anxious and fearful? Is that anxiousness, anger, or worry really worth it? Probably not. There is a time for action, but there is also a time to heed some of the most valuable words God has ever given us: "Be still, and know that I am God" (Ps. 46:10).

Lord, when I become too busy for my own good, too busy to see and hear the needs of those around me, please tell me to "Sit still and be quiet!" so that I take time to listen to the cries of the world and the sound of your voice. Amen.

Day 225 / 2 Thessalonians 1:5

Reckless, Raging Confidence

This is . . . intended to make you worthy of the kingdom of God.
—2 Thessalonians 1:5

Why is it that so many people feel they have to have their lives perfectly right before they can come before God in church? Moses wasn't perfect, nor were David and Noah and Abraham, and certainly not Adam and Eve. All of the disciples and apostles had their faults, too. God accepted and worked with and through them, so why not us? Isn't the reason we come into Christ's presence so that God can make us righteous?

Too many people feel their lives are such a grave disappointment that they aren't worthy to be in God's presence or to receive God's trust. But if you're willing to exercise a reckless, radical confidence in Christ's love, you'll find yourself wrapped up in God's big, loving arms for life.

Christ never said, "Come to me, all you who have cleaned up your act, or have never sinned, and I will give you rest," but, "Come to me, *all who labor and are heavy-laden,* and I will give you rest." Jesus knows we've got burdens and problems, that we're sinners, and it's okay with him. He loves us even when we're tired, beaten down, discouraged, and ready to quit.

Stop trying to be something you're not. None of us is perfect—and certainly not God's church—but all are welcome! So bag the excuses, and I'll see you in church!

Lord, it boggles the mind that, even with all our faults and weird thoughts and ideas, you still love us. Until we can be that loving, accepting, and forgiving, we can only give you the best we have to offer, and leave it to you to do the rest. Amen.

Day 226 / Matthew 6:1-4

The Heart of a Servant

Beware of practicing your piety before others in order to be seen by them. —Matthew 6:1

In pediatric oncology units, where many children face a terminal diagnosis, nurses strive to create a warm and child-friendly environment. Day after day these children cry out for some small measure of relief and these nurses hear their cries and serve them unselfishly.

The willingness of these nurses to go above and beyond the call of duty is not their way of seeking glory, or of feeling good about themselves. Rather, it is the act of the humble servant who is simply serving out of love. They remind us that what we do for others needs to be done with a pure heart, not for gain, but for God. It's easy to serve when it's done for some personal benefit; but Jesus has called us to serve in his name simply for the sake of others. Christ wants our motives always to be heavenly ones.

So, when you wake up tomorrow morning, approach your entire day with a servant's heart. You won't have to look far to find opportunities to express and to share it. Just go ahead and do it—but do it for Christ and for his kingdom. And after you've served, don't go tooting your horn about it. It's not necessary—since you've been promised God's reward, what else do you need?

God, why do we think we always need to have someone see or know about the good things we do? Why can't we just act in anonymity? Please God, take us by the hand and lead us to service in your name. Amen.

Day 227 / Isaiah 53:4-6

It's Part of the Gift

Upon him was the punishment that made us whole, and by his bruises we are healed. —Isaiah 53:5

It can be extremely easy to just gloss over the suffering of Jesus, even if we truly believe in his sacrificial death on our behalf. Even for those who maintain strong ties to their church and are adamant and sincere about their faith, there still remains that tendency to become desensitized to the words of the Gospels as they describe what Jesus went through. It's as if we simply want to move past the suffering and go straight to the resurrection. We just want to experience the "feel good" part of the story. Maybe it's because we know the ending is happy that we don't feel the need to emphasize the "ugly" part. But without Good Friday there is no Easter. And if we are to be alive in the risen Christ, then we must be willing to allow ourselves, and who we are, to die with him.

We should never forget nor ever take for granted Jesus' suffering. His long walk is part of the gift. As the prophet Isaiah foretold in today's passage: "By his wounds we are healed." The walk that Christ made, the pain and humiliation he endured along the way, were all part of the gift that he gave for us, the gift of his body and blood on the cross—and the gift of his life for our sins.

God, we need to be jolted out of our complacency and out of our "comfortable Christianity." Thank you, God, for doing what it takes, both now and on the cross. Amen.

Day 228 / Philippians 1:27-29

Live the Life

Live your life in a manner worthy of the gospel of Christ. —Philippians 1:27

Some sportspersons are content to stay on the bench and watch the game, but to be their best they need to push the coach to let them actually play. In the same way, serving Christ is not something we can do from the sidelines. We need to be living examples, not "vicarious Christians" who sit back and watch the work of others. Rather than just encourage or criticize others, we've got to get down in the mud and get our own hands dirty.

Neither can we live the life of a Christian through others. Like riding a roller coaster, until you climb in that car yourself, you'll never know the thrill or the terror or the joy of the ride. We can't fully understand Christ's love for us if we don't offer ourselves for his service. We can't live the Christian life if all we're content to do is just try to understand what he's done for us.

God is not looking for perfection. We're not going to score every time. All we're asked to do is serve God by fully and fearlessly using the abilities and the gifts with which we've been blessed in all that we do and say. There are no benchwarmers in God's game of life. We're all starters, and we can all make a difference.

Lord, you've blessed us with the skills to play the game, so put us in the game; we're ready to play! Amen.

Day 229 / Psalm 55

Lumps

Cast your burden on the L*ORD. —Psalm 55:22*

Some wise person once said that "into every life a little rain must fall." I would expand that to include that "into every life a few lumps will arise." No one is able to make the journey through life without having to deal with some lumps. Those lumps may take the form of obstacles that crop up as we travel; or they may be the lumps that accompany the bumps that life itself inflicts upon us.

You can't avoid life's lumps by trying to get around them; that may leave you wandering aimlessly in the wilderness, like Moses and the Israelites. Picking and choosing only the lumps we think we can conquer only takes up much of life's precious time. If you suspend the journey, you will never get to enjoy the rewards that await you. And taking an attitude of reckless abandonment will subject us to eventual, and discouraging, pain and injury.

No, the only way to deal with life's lumps is to let God safely help us navigate them. That doesn't mean we won't feel the lumps, or that we won't be injured by them. But Jesus made the same journey with the help of his Father, and he's there to take us by the hand and do the same for us.

God, help us to travel with you so that we can safely navigate the lumps of life. Amen.

Day 230 / Colossians 4:2-4

Fall Off Your Knees

Devote yourselves to prayer, keeping alert in it with thanksgiving.
—Colossians 4:2

At an international soccer match, one of the teams scored while the goalkeeper was still kneeling in the goal finishing his pre-match prayers. That should remind us of the need to maintain a strong balance between prayer and action. Prayer is the foundation of our recognizing God's place in our lives, but if Christians are to have maximum impact upon our world, we can't simply pray, or who knows what will sail by our ears while we kneel!

God does not primarily work the divine will in the world without our participation. Yet many of us struggle with the tension between prayer and action. In the face of crisis, some people seem content to be solely focused on prayer and its power, while others are more inclined to take action. Neither of these approaches will ever be the complete answer when it comes to responding to a crisis.

In some circumstances, it's easier and safer to pray for God to take whatever action is necessary. But for each situation in our lives, we need to find a balance between the time we spend on our knees and that time we need to be moving our feet and hands. If you truly want to serve God, by all means, go to God in prayer, but then "fall off your knees" and make a difference.

God, it's hard to lead another along that walk with Christ when we stay on our knees. Loving and compassionate God, open doors for us so that we can walk out into the world with your message of love and mercy for everyone. Amen.

Day 231 / Colossians 3:12-14

Grace and Mercy Hand In Hand

Just as the Lord has forgiven you, so you also must forgive. —Colossians 3:13

Grace and mercy are marvelous gifts we should be willing to offer freely to others but often don't. It may be that we don't feel we can offer what we don't fully understand. In short, grace is receiving something beneficial that we don't deserve, and mercy is not receiving some negative consequences that we do deserve.

There's no question that through our sin we deserve God's wrath, not God's love. But through the mercy and grace demonstrated on our behalf through Jesus' death and resurrection, we've been forgiven, and we've been freed from the penalty of sin. And what does God ask of us in return for that grace and mercy? Only that we extend that same grace and mercy to others.

As Christians, we can talk a good talk about grace and mercy. But in truth, when it comes to putting these two concepts into practice in our lives, most of us tend to fail miserably. Has someone you know mistreated you? Have you been the victim of some injustice by someone or some institution in our society? If you can answer "yes" to one or both of these questions, then I urge you, as difficult as it may be, to extend God's mercy and grace to them by offering them forgiveness, just as our Lord has forgiven you.

Loving and forgiving God, melt the ice away from our hearts, and remove the stubbornness from our characters. Show us the way of tenderness and love, so that we can offer to all your mercy, your grace, and your forgiveness. Amen.

Day 232 / Mark 15:6-15

Which Jesus?

Pilate, wishing to satisfy the crowd, released Barabbas for them. —Mark 15:15

An ancient manuscript refers to Barabbas as having the first name Jesus. Moreover, Barabbas means "son of Abbas," that is, "God." If all this is true, then he was, literally, "Jesus, Son of God"!

Barabbas joined a band of religious terrorists called Zealots who sought to remove their fellow Jews from the oppression of Roman rule. But this activity, which included robbery and murder, placed him alongside the other Jesus on the balcony of Pilate's praetorian. As a gesture of good will toward the Jews on the Passover, Pilate agreed to release one prisoner of their choice. Which Jesus would they choose—the Jesus of power or the Jesus of peace?

Christ came into this world so that it would be a place of justice, but he did it without coercion or games. He made it clear that no one would be forced to be a part of his kingdom. Barabbas, on the other hand, chose to use the way of power, thinking the only way to deal with those who wielded power unjustly was to destroy them.

The same choice faces us today: How will we handle our lives and the forces that attack us from day to day—with power or with peace? Many still cry out for Barabbas. With power they sense security; with love, vulnerability.

So—which Jesus will it be for you?

God, the right choice isn't always easy. It's difficult to be understanding when we're feeling kicked around. It's hard to love when we feel we've been wronged. Lord, speak to us and help us to hear your words of peace and reconciliation. Amen.

Day 233 / John 11:38-44

From Death . . . Life

Did I not tell you that if you believed, you would see the glory of God? —John 11:40

It must have been scary for those who were standing at Lazarus's tomb; it's not every day you see life come out of death. Can you imagine the range of emotions that must have existed in the crowd that day?

During World War II it is reported that, during bombing raids, Jewish families would go to the nearest cemetery and hide out in unfilled, open graves for protection. On more than one occasion, while in these graves, some expectant mother would give birth. As awful as life seemed at the time, when the words "A child is born!" were passed among them, for at least a brief moment, hope existed. In the midst of their despair and fear, they kept hoping that someday God would send to them the promised Messiah, even if he were born in a graveyard—each birth was a reason for God's people to celebrate and hope.

Christ calls us out of death and into newness of life, life in his risen presence and power. So, it is time the stone was rolled away from the tomb that is our life, so that when Jesus calls to us, "Christian, come out!" we can step out into the light, freed from the death of sin, freed to once again live out our lives in service to Christ.

Lord, let us be willing to die to our sinful self, that we might be raised anew to serve you throughout all the days of our lives. Amen.

Day 234 / Matthew 28:19-20

Take My Life, and Shove It!

Go therefore and make disciples of all nations. —Matthew 28:19

Have you ever found yourself in a situation where you felt like you were being shoved, pushed, or forced into going somewhere or having to do something? To be forced into something or somewhere unleashes a whole gambit of emotions—anger, fear, distrust, uncertainty, revenge, reluctance, and a host of other unpleasant feelings toward the place or toward the person responsible for our being there.

But when it comes to God, we get a nudge, a word of encouragement, or a promise. God did it to Noah and to Abraham. He did it to David, to Jeremiah, to Job and to a host of others in the Old Testament. God did it to many through the words of Jesus, and continues to do it today. God pushes us—not necessarily to the ground, but, at times, to our knees in prayer; and at other times into service. God sends us out to baptize, to teach and to make disciples of all nations in God's name. God knows what we need to succeed in life and he knows the importance of the word and the divine presence in our lives so our success can be assured.

Sometimes that's all we need: for God to take our life, and shove it!

Give me a push, Lord, when I begin to get lazy or disinterested. Give me a push when I fail to recognize the needs of those around me. And give me a push, Lord, when I "wimp out" on expressing my faith in you and my love for you. Amen.

Day 235 / Micah 3:5-8

A Bad Connection

But as for me, I am filled with power. —Micah 3:8

Recently I missed an important appointment because my car battery was dead. It didn't take the mechanic long to diagnose the problem: a bad connection from the energy source to the battery. I couldn't do my job because of a bad connection.

Unfortunately, the Lord's power wasn't there that day to start my car. And neither will we be able to give voice to the gospel, if we lack the power of God simply because there is a bad connection. God's power is somewhat like electricity in a car. If the starter doesn't receive power from the battery because it isn't connected to the source of that power you're going nowhere. There's got to be a connection or nothing works—and we must stay connected.

So take a little time every now and then to check your connection to God. Are you reading God's word daily? Are you in conversation with God through prayer every day? If so, then there is no end to what you will be able to do for the good of the kingdom. So, get wired, get empowered, and get working. With the power of God in you, there's no end to what you will be able to do.

Fill me with your power, Lord, and send me on my way so I can bring life to the dead batteries in the hearts of your people. Amen.

Day 236 / Isaiah 55:4-5

The Good News Man

Nations that do not know you shall run to you. —Isaiah 55:5

As a child, I grew up in an idyllic neighborhood, where every summer night you could hear the bells tinkling, and you knew the Good Humor Man was coming. He was like the Pied Piper of our neighborhood: We ran to him, because he had something we wanted—ice cream!

Isaiah's words conjure up this scene from my childhood. The man driving that truck didn't know us, but with his bell he called us to him, and we came running because he had something with which to feed us. In our eyes, he was glorified. But it also conjures another image from Luke of children going to another man, to be in Jesus' presence. God gave him the glory and he couldn't wait to share it. He was the Good News Man. He had not only what the children wanted, but what they needed: lots of love and God's word. Jesus was the kind of person that people just came running to.

So, what kind of person are you? Do God's children come running to you? And if they do, what do you have to offer them? With what do you have to feed them to satisfy their souls, to ease their pain, to bring them joy, to teach them? Are you a good news franchise? Do you have what they want and need?

God, let me be the bearer of your good news; so that when people come to me, I can dispense to them endless scoops of your word and your love. Amen.

Day 237 / Numbers 6:22-26

Does God Make Faces?

The Lord make his face to shine upon you. —Numbers 6:25

People use "looks" all the time to communicate. Often the message that can be read on our faces speaks far more about who we are and how we feel than what we can voice with our words.

Moses calls upon the face of God to remind the people of just who God is: the one who blesses, the one who keeps, the one who is gracious, the only one who can bring peace to their lives, and the one whose face shines upon them because they are God's chosen people. But the face of God has not always shone with satisfaction and happiness. Imagine the face of God just before flooding the earth, or think how God's face must have been one of sadness, mixed with anger, as God's Son hung suffering on the cross.

What kinds of faces do you suppose God makes at us? Certainly we do things that displease, sadden, and anger God. But because God is so loving and forgiving, more often than not God's face beams as it "shines upon us." The words to Moses' benediction are powerful ones because they describe perfectly the God who created us and who loves us, despite our faults, the God who blesses us, keeps us, and makes God's face always to shine upon us.

God, forgive me for the faces I've made—not only at others, but at you—faces of doubt, anger, and disbelief. Let my face always beam with thanks, praise, joy, and pure wonderment, knowing that it's you who loves me and will always be there for me. Amen.

Day 238 / Genesis 9:12-17

God's "Bow"

I have set my bow in the clouds, and it shall be a sign of the covenant between me and the earth. —Genesis 9:13

God's bow signified a new start and a sense of hope for Noah and for all who had survived the flood. Witnessing the incredible beauty of that covenant sign gave them an understanding both of God's power and of God's "soft side." Only an all-powerful God could create something so overwhelming; and only a God with a "soft side" could put aside anger and allow them to start over again.

Next time you see a rainbow, think about the new beginnings it signifies. Listen for God speaking to you, saying, "I was there for you through your tough times. I sheltered you, and I kept you and your family and friends safe through all the storms that hit you. And now, look up and see my sign for you, my promise—not that the tough times are ended because they will always be there—but instead a promise of a new beginning because you've answered my call to you and you've gone where I've sent you. You're my Noah in this place, so welcome those I send you, prepare them for the end of their life's storm, and send them on their way. This rainbow is a sign of hope for you and for everyone who trusts in me to calm their storms. Go in peace and serve me, now and always."

God, sometimes it takes a rainbow to remind us that you love us, and that we need never fear anything in this world again. Let us know that everything will be all right because you are with us, riding out all of life's storms, and bringing us home safely. Amen.

Day 239 / Matthew 13:1-9

From Adversity to Fertilizer

Other seeds fell on good soil and brought forth grain, some a hundredfold, some sixty, some thirty. —Matthew 13:9

Christians might see themselves as any of these seeds at one time or another. But most often we are like those seeds that end up landing among the thorns, which Jesus explains are like "the one who hears the word, but the cares of the world and the lure of wealth choke the word, and it yields nothing" (Matt. 13:22).

What are some of the thorns that attempt to choke out your spiritual growth? Do you ever feel like the various issues that cause suffering and stress in your life make you doubt your belief in God? What steps could you take to improve the soil of your spiritual life?

If a seed is to grow to its potential it must land on good quality soil and it must be properly cared for. It must be watered and it must be fed the proper nutrients. The same is true of the seeds of God's word that God has planted in our lives—not only must they be nourished by the baptismal waters, they also must receive the proper fertilization to promote growth. So I urge you to turn life's adverse circumstances into fertilizer and use them to help your spiritual life to grow to its fullest as you seek out ways to serve God through those in your midst.

God, we know there are nutrients in life's troubles. Help us to see and hear what is contained in those, and learn to see our own shortcomings and what we can do to grow in your grace and in our commitment to the work of your kingdom. Amen.

Day 240 / 1 Peter 5:6-11

Like a Rock

Humble yourselves therefore under the mighty hand of God, so that he may exalt you in due time. —1 Peter 5:6

Good old Peter was a unique character, and he stands out in the Gospels like a sore thumb. He was loud, assertive, and, at times, a "blow-hard." But he also had a heart of gold and unlimited enthusiasm. No wonder Jesus liked him so much! Except for some rough edges and a less-than-polished character, he was the type of person Jesus wanted as one of his disciples—bold, brazen, and unafraid.

But Christ's death and resurrection changed Peter. In those years following Christ's ascension, the once loud, often obnoxious Peter underwent even more changes. In a much more subdued and focused way, Peter finally became the rock that Jesus had once called him. He became that stone upon which the followers of Christ built their church.

But Peter knew that the real rock was the one that nothing could move, that would last forever and remain sturdy and strong—the risen Christ. Peter stood firm as the earthly example of just who that risen Christ was and what he expected his followers to be: messengers to the poor and persecuted, hope for the down and out, and promise and direction for the lost.

So who are you? What would be the nickname that Christ would give to you? Can he depend upon you to be "like a rock?"

Christ, often we are more like shifting sand than the rock you want us to be. The tides of temptation and the winds of change too easily move us where we hadn't planned on going. Anchor us in your word and your love. Like Peter, make us your rocks. Amen.

Day 241 / Luke 24:45-53

Good-bye and Godspeed

Lifting up his hands, he blessed them. —Luke 24:50

Saying good-bye is rarely easy. It's hard to do it without getting mushy and melancholy, or letting our emotions get the best of us. When we get involved in others' lives, we come to care about them and want to see the best of life happen for them.

Luke writes, in describing Christ's ascension, that Jesus leaves the disciples not only with the promise of the Holy Spirit's power, but he also blesses them before sending them on their way to continue to carry out his ministry to their world. He sends them on their way, filled to overflowing with his knowledge and the power of the Spirit, and raising his hands, he wishes them Godspeed—that God would always be with them throughout their journeys.

As people come and go from our lives, that's all we can do as well—pray that some of our words and deeds remain with them and help them, and then wish them Godspeed, that they would forever remain in the mercy and love of Jesus. Even when our emotions get the best of us, it's a comfort to know that we've done all that God has led us to do for them, and that we've left them in far more capable hands than our own. Saying good-bye isn't easy—but to say Godspeed is to allow one's soul to rejoice.

God, into your hands I place my life and my hope and the lives of all whose lives I touch each day, knowing that in your hands all of us will find comfort, peace, and the promise of your sustaining grace, now and forever. Amen.

Day 242 / Matthew 26:47-50

We Can Only Try

Jesus said to him, "Friend, do what you are here to do."
—Matthew 26:50

I wonder if Jesus felt like a failure that night. For three years he had loved these twelve who had stayed so close to him and given them all that he had to offer. He had fed them with his word all along the way and, in the end, he had broken himself, and fed them with his own body and blood. His ultimate goal was to teach and to prepare them for their own journeys that lay ahead, to guide them and help them, so that they wouldn't fail.

But, in the end, Jesus' relationship with Judas ended in betrayal, symbolized by one of the most loving acts that can be shared between two people, a kiss. In his only response to Judas that night Christ said, "Friend, do what you are here to do." With these words, he places the burden of failure back on Judas, who had made the conscious decision to allow his feelings to lead him and become the betrayer. It was Judas who was the failure; he was the one who had failed Christ, and failed himself.

Jesus had not failed Judas because Jesus had loved him with a love that no kiss of betrayal could destroy. Jesus never stopped trying. We don't fail when we try; we only fail when we stop trying.

God, help us to never stop trying with those you place in our care, even when we're faced with the risk of the kiss of betrayal. And hold us close to your heart, so that we do not give you that kiss either. Amen.

Day 243 / Ruth 2:11-13

The Shelter of His Wings

May you have a full reward from the LORD, the God of Israel, under whose wings you have come for refuge! —Ruth 2:12

I love the image and the promise Boaz expresses here. Ruth did receive her reward, because God had led her to a people who both accepted and cared for her. They knew how to welcome the stranger in their midst. We, God's church, could learn a great lesson from these words. We come in contact with strangers each day, and, as the people of God, God's disciples, we need to be ready to extend the hospitality of God's kingdom to them. It needs to be our mission and ministry to lead these strangers to a place of refuge, safe under the wings of God.

The old Swedish hymn "His Holy Wings" is almost a continuation of those words of Boaz. Its words would make a great prayer anytime, but especially at the end of a day:

Thy holy wings, O Savior, spread gently over me
And let me rest securely, through good and ill in thee.
Oh, be my strength and portion, my rock and hiding place
And let my every moment be lived within thy grace.

Oh, let me nestle near thee, within thy downy breast,
Where I will find sweet comfort and peace within thy nest.
Oh, close thy wings around me and keep me safely there,
For I am but a newborn and need thy tender care.

Oh, wash me in the waters of Noah's cleansing flood.
Give me a willing spirit, a heart both clean and good.
Oh, take into thy keeping thy children great and small,
And while we sweetly slumber, enfold us one and all. Amen.

Day 244 / 2 Corinthians 4:8-10

Standing

We are afflicted in every way, but not crushed. —2 Corinthians 4:8

Very often, the greatest expression of one's faith, and the truest expression of God's love, can be found within the context of a funeral service. I am a firm believer that a funeral should not be about mourning the death of a friend or loved one, but should be about the celebration of a life lived for the sake of Christ.

I recently said goodbye to a wonderful servant of God who had lost both his legs to diabetes; for the last several years of his life he stood and walked on artificial legs. Sometimes he wavered on those artificial legs, but I knew that his faith in Christ never wavered. At his funeral, in tribute to his steadfast spirit in the face of such a challenge, we sang these words:

> "Standing on the promises I cannot fall
> Listening every moment to the Spirit's call.
> Resting on my Savior as my all in all,
> Standing on the promises of God."

As Christians, we can always stand on the promises of God. We may sometimes waver, but God will never let us fall; for we are able to rest in the strength of God's powerful arms that will forever support and sustain us throughout all our days on this earth.

Lord of life, thank you for your promises on which we can stand, sometimes firmly, sometimes wavering, but always held firmly in your loving arms of rest and assurance. Amen.

Day 245 / John 20:26-29

Jesus Is My Homeboy?

Thomas answered him, "My Lord and my God!" —John 20:28

Jesus has suddenly become "big business," from the box office records for the movie *The Passion of the Christ* to the huge sales of contemporary Christian music. There's even a T-shirt featuring a friendly-looking Christ with the caption, "Jesus is my homeboy," slang for he's my best friend, my buddy. This "homey" Jesus is obviously more mainstream and more palatable than a "crown of thorns"-wearing Jesus, especially to Christians on the fringe. But it may also represent a move away from organized religion and toward a more personal and spiritual view of Christ, which can be both good and bad.

Those who only think of Jesus in terms of a friend or a buddy have perhaps lost the sense of awe and majesty that Jesus deserves. The Jesus who invited Thomas to place his fingers in the nail holes and place his hand in Jesus' side wasn't Thomas's buddy, as is obvious when he said, "My Lord and my God!"

Christ is not some pop icon, he's not some still picture from a movie, and he's certainly not anyone's "homeboy"; he is and always will be the Christ, the Son of the living God. He is to be worshiped, exalted, praised, and revered, so that at the sound of his name every knee should bow and every tongue confess that Jesus Christ is Lord!

God, may we be ready to proclaim those words of Thomas at all times, and not just some peppy catchphrases. Help us to make you number one in our lives and not just another pop icon. Amen.

Words to Live By

But surely, God is my helper; the Lord is the upholder of my life.
—Psalm 54:4

Every time the composer Johann Sebastian Bach wrote any music composition he always included at the beginning of each piece the letters "jj," which stands for the Latin phrase *Jesu Juva*—"Help, O Jesus." So it seems that when he began to create any of his music, Bach would always request divine help. At the end he wrote the letters SDG, which stood for *Soli Deo Gloria*—"To God alone glory." Bach concluded any piece of music by thanking God and giving God all the praise.

Bach's asking for God's help as he began his work, and then giving thanks and credit to God when finished, should serve as the impetus for each of us to be more intentional about including God in all that we do during the course of each day. If a person of Bach's talent and giftedness made it a habit to ask for God's help and to give God thanks, how much more should we do the same?

We are all dependent upon the Lord for everything. The words of the psalmist remind us we really do need God's help, far more than we care to admit! And giving thanks to God gives us needed perspective to understand that all we accomplish is from God's gracious hand.

God, the giver of all gifts, may we also live our lives by first asking, "Help, O Jesus," and in the end giving all the praise to you as we pray, "To God alone glory!" Amen.

Day 247 / Psalm 150

The Buck Can't Stop Here

Let everything that breathes praise the Lord! —Psalm 150:6

These words of the psalmist remind us that the "buck" of God's word cannot stop here, with us. The bounty and the blessings of God's word must be paid forward by each of us.

How many of us who attended church this past Sunday listened only for soothing words of comfort? How many of us got caught up in the emotionality of singing hymns? How many of us dutifully attended a Sunday school class or Bible study to help us feel good about ourselves? How many of us felt comfortable tucked away safe and sound in God's sanctuary?

God does not want us to avoid taking up the challenge of ministry. We're not supposed to be "couch potatoes for Christ." I will always remember the words I saw carved into the arch above one church door, "The Word of the Lord must not be bound." God's word cannot stop inside the walls of our sanctuaries or our closed lips. God's word must be taken into the world and shared with all who will open their ears and their hearts to its message, and it is up to us to make that happen. God has blessed us with riches beyond our wildest imagination: God's love, mercy, grace, and the word. The "buck" cannot stop here!

God, you've filled us with your word and you have commanded us to spread that word to all the world. Open the doors of our churches and open the mouths of your people, that the joy of your good news might be spread throughout this world. Amen.

Day 248 / John 8:6-11

Will You Drop the Stone?

Let anyone among you who is without sin be the first to throw a stone at her. —John 8:7

What did Jesus write when he squatted in the street as this woman awaited the impact of the first stone? Scripture never records any specifics, and biblical scholars through the ages have debated it. St. Augustine speculated that what Jesus scratched in the dust before these men was a list of their own sins and indiscretions. And, having done so, he stood up, looked into their eyes and issued his challenge: "Let any one among you who is without sin be the first to throw a stone at her."

They couldn't, and neither should we. Who was that woman to Jesus? What made her worth saving and forgiving? Who are we, that this same loving Christ should care about us and forgive us? And what about those who move in and out of our lives each day? Who are they? Do they deserve God's saving grace, or are they simply a target for the stones that we hold?

Before we get ready to throw that stone of condemnation at another, perhaps we should first stand up straight and look that person in the eye to see who they really are. We just may see that, deep within that person, Jesus lives in their heart. And if we find him there, then we need to drop the stone we're holding and just walk away.

Lord, forgive us our sins, as we forgive those who have sinned against us. Amen.

Day 249 / Acts 2:43-47

What Is the Church?

Day by day the Lord added to their number those who were being saved. —Acts 2:47

What is the church? A building? A body of believers? If so, in what or whom do they believe? What is the church's purpose for existence? What is its task?

Some of today's churches have, in some aspects of their worship and ministry life, caved in to society's demand to become more enticing by using high-tech worship methods like multimedia presentations or clever marketing techniques to lure people to the worship and programs. They're "feel good" churches." And by so doing, these churches too often forfeit their ability to proclaim effectively the truth of the gospel and lose their ability to disciple and discipline their members. They are churches that have gotten off-task.

We need to keep in mind that the real task of the church is not to make men and women happy; it is to make them holy. The true task of the church is to prepare its membership to be the body of Christ. And if one is to be the body, then that body cannot be made out of mortar, bricks, and boards. The real church lies within the hearts of its people. Where that message is preached pure and holy is where one will find the true church.

God, let your church live in the hearts of your people. Let your church be your people. Amen.

Day 250 / Matthew 7:15-20

Uglifruits

Thus you will know them by their fruits. —Matthew 7:20

An uglifruit lives up to its name: rather shriveled, with a leathery, green and yellow skin that feels almost mushy, as if turning rotten. Inside, however, it has a delicious, sweet flavor and is filled with nutrients. Outward appearances are not always a true indicator of what may be hiding inside.

Jesus warns the people of false prophets who, by all outward appearance and behavior, give the impression that they possess valuable knowledge and insight and should be believed. But he calls them "wolves in sheep's clothing" who don't always "practice what they preach."

Jesus teaches them what we have come to call "The Golden Rule": If we wish to have others not treat us as "uglifruit," then we must treat others with respect and expect the good from others. Simply put, we cannot appear to others to live one way while acting the opposite toward them.

Jesus told the people, "You will know them by their fruits." How will the world know you—by what they see on the outside or by what lies within? Are we Christians really "uglifruit"? Do we need to go deeper within the ugly exteriors of society to taste what is hidden within? After all, the "uglifruits" of our world may just be worth their expensive price that has already been paid by Christ.

Lord, let me be slow to judge and willing to taste. Amen.

Day 251 / Ecclesiastes 9:7-10

Seize Life!

God takes pleasure in your pleasure!
—Ecclesiastes 9:7 (The Message)

Every spring I embark on what I call my annual "spiritual pilgrimage," but it's of a different nature than you might expect. It involves doing something that I love, and, like most pilgrimages, I always feel renewed and reconnected afterward. My pilgrimage is to go watch the NCAA basketball finals with some of the guys with whom I used to play morning basketball. It has sort of become a time of ritual for us.

I believe that these words from Ecclesiastes are some of the most valuable in all of Scripture. We who spend our days worrying so much about this aspect and that concern of life really need to take the words of the writer seriously and "seize life!" We all need to laugh more and worry less, to let loose and enjoy the joy that God has packed into each of life's days. We all need to find that part of our life that, second only to the worship of almighty God, is that sacred thing, that spiritual journey that brings immense joy to our life and uplifts our heart—even a college basketball game! So, eat, drink, and be merry, and enjoy today, for an even greater joy awaits you in the kingdom of God!

God of joy and laughter, thank you for placing me in a world that is so filled with the wonders of your hand. Fill me with your Holy Spirit so that my senses are alive and alert to those wonders, that I may always be ready to seize life! Amen.

Day 252 / Romans 1:16-17

The Three-Foot Wall

The one who is righteous will live by faith. —Romans 1:17

The impala is capable of jumping to a vertical height of ten feet, yet it can easily be restrained behind a wall that is no more than three feet high. Why? Because an impala will not jump without first being able to see where it will land.

It seems that many Christians live like impalas when it comes to exercising their faith. Those three-foot walls of worry, fear, or even common sense keep us from exercising God's gift of faith. When we insist on living out our Christian lives purely by sight, and try to determine the outcome before we act, we short-circuit faith and cut off God's power. Our spiritual lives begin to shrivel; we live at a lesser level of satisfaction; and our ability to influence the world for God is seriously compromised.

The mind-set and inbred instincts of the impala will always prevent it from leaping into the unknown. But we can place our complete trust in the Word of the risen Christ. When we make the choice to trust God enough to walk by faith rather than by sight, we exercise our faith, which causes it to grow. With our spiritual lives strengthened, we are able to live out our lives to their fullest potential. Today's the day to start living life by faith and not by sight.

Lord, help me let go of things that prevent me from leaping over the wall because of my fear of what's on the other side. Help me to trust that you are waiting there with open arms to catch me. Help me to take that flying leap of faith. Amen.

Day 253 / Matthew 23:1-7

Pseudo-Pietism

Do not do what they do, for they do not practice what they teach. —Matthew 23:3

Seventeen centuries after the time of Jesus, a document called the Code of Connecticut appeared, which prohibited such Sabbath Day activities as running, traveling, cooking "victuals," making beds, sweeping, cutting hair, shaving, or even kissing one's spouse, lest "the party in fault . . . be punished at the direction of the court of magistrates." Can you imagine that Code being enforced today? These laws would not only seem archaic, but stupid, as everything stopped for a day.

Today's text is a powerful reminder that religious people aren't always willing to "practice what they preach." Instead, we often create our own interpretation of God's laws, either for one's own convenience or the power to control. And it is this sense of control that we, as God's church, must strive to avoid, lest we use the church to "hammer" home the message of the gospel, instead of presenting it with love. We cannot allow ourselves to become so self-righteous that we dispense that gospel with an air of judgmentalism, or to believe that we are so devout that we are above repentance. For the church to be the true purveyors of God's word, we must be able to deal with others by using an equal portion of law and gospel; and we must value and sanctify all of God's creation.

God, there's a self-righteous person hiding deep within me, and I need your help in dealing with that person. Help me not to be so proud of your love for me that I begin to become haughty and judgmental. God, let me serve you humbly and faithfully. Amen.

Day 254 / Galatians 6:9-10

Straight Journey

Let us not grow weary in doing what is right. —Galatians 6:9

In 1994, at age 73, Alvin Straight decided to travel from northwest Iowa to western Wisconsin to visit his estranged brother, who had recently suffered a debilitating stroke, and to "mend fences." Amazingly, he successfully made this trip after six weeks on a riding lawn mower going five miles per hour. His persistence, commitment, and devotion paid off!

In several of his parables, Jesus talks about being persistent, especially in our prayer life. He invites us to come to God, to bring our problems, our concerns, and our very lives to God, and to do so persistently. God expects our persistence in our service in Christ's name as well.

What if every Christian everywhere demonstrated Alvin Straight's kind of persistence, commitment, and devotion in their service to Christ? Have you ever dreamed of giving your life in service to the Lord, but then, for some reason, you abandoned your dream? How many lives could be influenced for Christ if we worried less about the practicalities of our dreams and the impossibilities of our journeys and instead relied upon God's support, direction, and guidance? God wants us to spend more time acting on our dreams and journeys with courage, conviction, and faith. May God give you the courage and desire to serve the Lord with persistence, commitment, and devotion.

God, sometimes the journey of life is tiring and filled with obstacles, and we are inclined to quit. Fill us with your patience and persistence, so that we might continue our journey in service to you, even if it's only at five miles per hour. Amen.

Day 255 / Psalm 139

God Who Knows All

O LORD, you have searched me and known me . . . You knit me together in my mother's womb. —Psalm 139:1, 13

We have lots of questions about God, and we have lots of questions that perhaps only God can answer. But long before we thought about asking questions about God—or even realized there was a God who would entertain our questions—God was already questioning us, subjecting us to God's most intensive and searching knowledge.

In calling the prophet Jeremiah, God said, "Before I formed you in the womb I knew you, and before you were born I consecrated you" (1:5). Like Jeremiah, God has always known us—even before we were born. And on the day of our baptism, God blessed us, having already filled us with God's goodness and with talents and abilities to be used to spread the word of the kingdom and God's love.

From the time of that baptism God has prepared us to serve the Lord—to be God's hands and God's heart in this world. So, rejoice in God's knowledge of you. Rejoice in the fact that Jesus loves you and has given his life for you. Rejoice that God has chosen you to be God's servant, to be God's messenger, and to be God's child.

Lord, you've claimed me to be yours even before my birth. God, I want to always be your child and to love and serve you every day of my life. Fill me with your Word, empower me by your Spirit, and lead me by your hand. Amen.

God's War

The weapons of our warfare are not merely human, but they have divine power to destroy strongholds. —2 Corinthians 10:4

The persistence of war reminds us that despite all that God has given us, we remain unsatisfied. We allow our lust for power and possessions to overshadow the reason for which God has both called us and empowered us—to carry out the divine will.

God called Jeremiah to fight a different type of war, a spiritual war in which we also have been drafted to be God's soldiers. God is waging a spiritual war with all of creation, an all-out moral battle. Our world is filled with superstition and ignorance, with brutality and pain. God has called us into a continuous and energetic battle against all of it. God is for life and against death. God is for love and against hate. God is for hope and against despair. God is for heaven and against hell. There can be no neutral ground here.

God hasn't given us a few years or even a few days in which to look around and make up our minds as to which side we want to be on, or even whether we want to join a side at all. God's already made that choice for us. We have been empowered, equipped, and sent forth into a war for the souls and lives of God's children.

And in God's war there are no casualties—only victors!

God, prepare me for the battle, and send me off to march behind the cross of Christ, to fight for justice, freedom, and for the souls of your people. Amen.

Day 257 / Luke 7:44-50

Splangchnizomai

"Your faith has saved you; go in peace." —Luke 7:50

Jesus is fine-tuned to all our hates and loves, disappointments and delights, brokenness and togetherness, and the fears, joys, and sorrows. He knows what hurts each human heart.

The Greek verb *splangchnizomai* is usually translated, "to be moved with compassion." But it's derived from the Greek noun, *splangchna*, which means intestines, bowels, the inward parts of the body, which we often call the source of our strongest emotions, such as when we talk about our "*gut* reactions" or "being *moved* with pity."

But even these expressions fail to capture the true essence or meaning of *splangchnizomai.* The compassion that Jesus showed throughout his ministry is far different from any superficial emotions, pity, or sympathy that we might express. His heart was torn; his gut wrenched; and the most vulnerable parts of his body laid bare before those who saw him. His is a love and compassion that erupts from the very bowels of his being and operates on a level that no human will ever be able to match.

Jesus is able to resonate with our hopes and fears, to rejoice in our celebrations and weep with us during our times of desolation. He is the human manifestation of the compassion of God. He holds on to us with a compassion that knows no frontiers or boundaries, which he extends to both saint and sinner.

God, may we always be able to come to you, knowing that there, in your tender and loving arms, we will find comfort for our bodies and peace for our souls. Amen.

Day 258 / Matthew 16:13-15

Asleep Or Awake?

He said to them, "But who do you say that I am?" —Matthew 16:15

A woman began to awake from surgery to remove a possibly cancerous breast lump. As she was being wheeled away, the young woman clearly asked anyone in the room who was listening, "Does this mean I don't have cancer?" The busy surgeons stopped and smiled toward her, and one said kindly, "That's right, you don't have cancer. The lump was benign."

With that simple, pointed question, this woman reminded them all of an anonymous, unconscious patient's worry and fear, of the purpose of their activity, and of their common humanity. Not only did this patient wake up, she woke up the rest of the room.

So, how awake are we? Has the message of the good news that God has placed within us become like that young woman, unconscious and anonymous? We must always ask ourselves Christ's question: "Who do you say that I am?" To answer that question honestly and offer others the good news of God's saving grace, we need to be firm within our own hearts and minds about who we know God to be and why Christ gave his life for us. Our message needs to be about a God who loves us despite our faults and about his Son Jesus who took our faults and sins to the cross, and who rose again triumphantly, declaring victory over death for all.

Lord, rouse us from our slumber to joyfully proclaim your name and the message of your love to all the world. Amen.

Day 259 / Philippians 2:3-8

His Story, His Mission

Do nothing from selfish ambition or conceit. —Philippians 2:3

Storytelling can be a particularly effective method for sharing the gospel, and also a way to draw others into a fuller appreciation for the gospel story. One especially valuable part of the storytelling process is sharing our own stories as an example of how the message of God's word has had an impact on our own lives.

Paul stresses the importance of leading our lives by Christ's example, that we be willing to humble ourselves so that we might place the needs of others before our own needs. When we focus on ourselves and our own problems and circumstances, we can become inwardly paralyzed, which then prevents us from being everything that God intends us to be, including serving others effectively.

Following Christ is more than an exercise in introspection; it really needs to become a reaching out to others, to lovingly serve them in *Jesus*' name. So today, if you're finding yourself feeling "paralyzed" by the weight of your own personal concerns, I would encourage you to shift your focus from yourself to the Son, and find someone you can serve in his name. Let your story and their story combine to become his story, and you will find that the weight will become lighter and the "paralysis" will disappear.

Loving God, send us forth in peace to serve others in your name. Amen.

Day 260 / Romans 5:1-5

Invest Wisely

We also boast in our sufferings, knowing that suffering produces endurance. —Romans 5:3

Those who invest in the stock market know of the benefits that may come to the investor, the company that is invested in, and the public that company serves. Although predicting the impact one's investments may produce is impossible, in order for any impact to take place, an initial investment must be made.

Most Americans know of Anne Sullivan's investment of her time and energy in helping the blind, deaf, and incorrigible Helen Keller. Despite criticism from her family and friends, Anne remained faithful to her call from God, knowing that all of the pain, inconvenience, and suffering would be worth it. Having received the benefits of Sullivan's investment, Keller went on to invest her own time and skills in teaching other deaf and blind individuals to become productive members of society.

Paul's words remind us of the importance of persistence, that through our suffering we come to know the value of endurance, which in turn produces character, which in turn produces hope—a hope in the presence and power of Jesus Christ who will never disappoint us.

What is God calling you to be persistent about? To whom or to what is God calling you to invest your life? Whatever or whomever it may be, invest wisely, and the benefits to you and to others will come back to you more bountifully than you ever imagined.

Loving God, you've invested so much into my life: your word, your love, and your only Son. Work through me so that your investment may produce a bountiful harvest that will enrich the lives of those around me. Work through me, that I might work for you. Amen.

Day 261 / Revelation 3:20

Open House

I am standing at the door, knocking. —Revelation 3:20

If you looked out the window and saw Jesus coming toward your house would you begin to run around frantically, trying to hide all the inappropriate videos? Would you put the Bible on the coffee table and put away the *National Enquirer*? Would you turn on a Christian radio station?

What about your behavior? Would you treat your family any differently? Would you say grace at mealtime? Would you invite your friends and relatives over to meet him? How much would you have to clean up your language? If you had plans to go out, would you be willing to take him with you, no matter where it was? Where would he see you spend your time, and what would he see you doing?

And when his visit came to an end and he left, would you be sad or relieved? Jesus' presence should never be in the form a visit for which we have to prepare; it should be the way we live our life every day, as he told us in Matthew, "And remember, I am with you always, to the end of the age" (28:20). Or, as a man named Jimmy Brown once wrote: "So today as you go about your life, consider what you would do if Jesus came to your house to spend some time with you."

There are times in life when we are asked to entertain many important people, but you are by far the most important guest. Keep me patient and calm as I welcome you into my home. Amen.

Day 262/ Matthew 5:43-45

Snake-Bitten

Love your enemies and pray for those who persecute you. —Matthew 5:44

Imagine Jesus trying to free a rattlesnake that had become hopelessly wedged between two boulders only to have the snake repeatedly strike at him, even after he was successful. Why would he take such a risk? Jesus might respond, "That snake was attempting to strike because that's what his nature told him to do. My nature is to love and provide freedom for all my Father's creatures. So, should I forgo my nature because the snake chose to exercise his?"

Snakes run rampant throughout our world, and they have the tendency to want to impose their nature on ours. But in the midst of their attempts to "bite" us—even if we're attempting to free them from the mess they're in—we must be willing to risk our life to set that person free from what has captured them.

As "Christ-followers," we are called to follow Jesus' example to not grow weary in our efforts or to become "snake-bitten." The snakes may hiss at us, they may rattle their tails, and they may even strike out at us because it's their nature. But, like Jesus, it must be our nature to love and provide freedom for all of God's creatures. So, what's your nature?

Lord God, confident that you're always there to love and protect me, help me to free those who are trapped and in pain. Without fear of being bitten, let me reach out to touch them so that they might be set free to serve you with a joyous heart. Amen.

Day 263 / 2 Corinthians 5:1-7

I'm Home?

We have a building from God, a house not made with hands, eternal in the heavens. —2 Corinthians 5:1

An old gospel hymn goes:

> This world is not my home, I'm just a-passin' through.
> My treasures are laid up somewhere beyond the blue.
> The angels beckon me from heaven's distant shore,
> And I can't feel at home in the world anymore.

Paul is trying to assure the Corinthian church that they, like God's people of the Old Testament, will always have their home in God's kingdom. None of us can even begin to imagine what it must have been like for the Hebrew people who, already without a home, and being held captive in Egypt, were then sent on a forty-year journey, wandering without a true home until God brought them to the home (land) that had been promised them.

Those who are sent to shelters after natural disasters know it not as their real home, but only as a location out of which their life takes place and through which they are only passing. In the same way, this world is not our home, and all of us are just passing through. The real treasures for us are somewhere far beyond the boundaries of this world. And, someday, the angels of God will call to us to come home to live with God, there in God's heavenly place; so that we will no longer feel "at home" in this world anymore.

God, continue to remind me that "home" isn't a place on this earth; but that "home is where the heart is," and that my heart and my being is alive, well, and serving you in your kingdom. Amen.

Day 264 / Numbers 21:4-5, 16-18

Dammed Up

Gather the people together, and I will give them water.
—Numbers 21:16

One chilly morning our kitchen sink pipes froze and burst. Unfortunately, the plumber shut off the wrong feeder line to fix them, and water wound up gushing out all over him! Similarly, the Israelites are complaining because they think that God has shut off their water supply and left them to wander around in the wilderness. They are convinced that God has turned off the valve and stopped their flow of the life-sustaining water they so desperately need.

But God hasn't shut off the valve. Rather, their water has been frozen by their faithlessness and lack of trust in God's saving power. So God leads them to the well at Beer and turns the warmth of God's heart upon them, unfreezing their faith, thus letting the waters once again flow.

How often have we frozen the flow of God's daily waters of baptism to our lives? Yet there is no "shut-off valve" that will stop the flow of God's love and mercy; we cannot divert or stop the flow from that baptismal fountain into our lives. We may interrupt it temporarily, but God will find a way to unfreeze the flow so those waters may again bless and cleanse us. And when they do, we too will shout, "Spring up, O well! Spring up, refresh us, soothe our thirst, and wash us clean!"

God, let your waters of life flow over us each day, washing us clean, so that we may serve you in truth and purity. Amen.

Day 265 / Matthew 3:11-12

Shhh! It's a Surprise!

One who is more powerful than I is coming after me. —Matthew 3:11

Everyone needs a surprise in their life; they can be fun and exciting, especially those that come with absolutely no forewarning or expectation, just BAM!—there it is! Sometimes God lets us know ahead of time what's coming, just as Noah was warned of the flood, or Mary is told of the one to whom she would give birth.

But God is also the God of surprises who continues to come to us in ever-surprising ways. God is constantly entering our world in a myriad of disguises. God is hiding in those we have yet to forgive, concealed in the hearts of those whom we despise and reject. God is hiding behind the face of the unacceptable and the unloved, those whom we criticize and ignore. God is the prisoner, the prostitute, and the AIDS patient—the lost and the lonely.

But to experience the surprise of God's presence, we need to look beyond the packaging, to look past what we only see with our eyes. We need to do more than expect and wait; we need to allow God to surprise us anew each day with God's love, power, and with God's Son. And then we need to be today's John the Baptist and shout to the world, "One more powerful than I is coming—get ready because here comes God, the great surpriser!"

Come on, God, shake us out of our shoes! Fill us with the power of your Holy Spirit, so much so that we can't keep quiet about it. Replace our whispers with a shout that tells the world that you are King of Kings and Lord of Lords! Amen.

Day 266 / James 1:2-4

Farewell and Forward March

Let endurance have its full effect. —James 1:4

Caught up in our own little worlds, we often are convinced that whatever happens to us, good or bad, can and does only happen to us. We claim that the good things happen because of our skills and savvy, while we blame our woes on God and God's seeming and abandonment.

For instance, parishioners often feel abandoned when a pastor resigns, as if they aren't cared about, that they won't be able to go on, and things will never be the same. No matter how much the pastor tries to assure them that it isn't anything personal, there are those who cannot be convinced otherwise, and must be committed to the pastor's prayer.

One key life lesson is that life goes on—with you, without you, and regardless of you. Change, sometimes subtle, sometimes dramatic, is inevitable. Our concerns should not be so much with the changes, but rather with the opportunity they give us to grow and learn, to envision a larger world beyond ourselves. God didn't fill us with all the things we'll ever need to know and then let us become couch potatoes. God's work is dynamic—a call to experience something new each day about God, the world, and our place in it. And, most important, we are not abandoned—God will always be there to go along with us on this adventure.

May our ever-present God of steadfastness be with each of you as you continue on your spiritual journey. May God fill each day of your life with new thoughts, new visions, and new adventures as you go in peace and serve in Christ's name. Amen.

Keep the Change

Jesus Christ . . . will transform our earthly bodies into glorious bodies like his own. —Philippians 3:21 (The Message)

When was the last time you heard or even said the words, "keep the change"? During tight economic times, many people are inclined to keep a rather firm grasp on their money. Even as some charities report record donations in the face of natural disasters, "compassion fatigue" can set in with too many needs to be met at once.

God, however, makes a point of telling us to "keep the change" each day. Paul tells the Philippians that one day Christ will come and change our earthly bodies. Gone will be the crippling effects of deforming maladies like arthritis, disabilities like blindness, as well as diseases like AIDS. Why? Because Jesus Christ has paid the price, and has told us to keep the change.

We who follow Christ have been changed by his death and resurrection and called to use the gifts with which he has blessed us. He has directed us not only to be hearers of the word, but doers. He wants us to see and hear the needs of others, and then, with that same love and compassion that he has shown to us, touch the lives of the hurting and lost in whatever way we can. For, you see, Christ has not only told us to "keep the change," but to also give that change away, both literally and figuratively.

God, thank you for the price you've paid for me and for giving me the change. Open my heart that I might invest that change to bring about that same change in others, so that they might turn to you and receive your gifts of your love and forgiveness. Amen.

Day 268 / Ephesians 6:10-18

Game-Form

Put on the whole armor of God. —Ephesians 6:10

Anyone who's ever spent any time around competitive sports, at any level, knows that an athlete just doesn't show up the day of a game and compete. Long before that time there's a lot of preparation, conditioning, and practice that has to take place.

Paul talks to the Ephesians about being properly equipped for a battle for their very lives against the most dangerous foe they could face: the evil of the devil. Paul exhorts them to be ready and dressed for the battle, for if they're ready, then the devil can't harm them and they are assured of certain victory.

If we are going to win our own battle with the evil one and claim victory, then we also need to prepare. We can't go into this contest without training or we risk injury. The Gospels tell us that Jesus studied the word, fasted, and prayed. For us to be Christ's followers, we too must fill ourselves with his word and pray for his presence. Every day of our lives we run the risk of being accosted by the evil one, so we need to have our complete selves ready at all times. God calls us to be alert, to be prayerful and to be strong in our faith. If we're not prepared, sin's going to win.

God, the great coach of life, push us to the limit of our abilities, abilities that you have given us, so that we might stand firm against the forces of evil, and that we might become victorious in your name over sin, death, and the devil. Amen.

Day 269 / Colossians 1:15-20

Immortal, Invisible, God Only Wise

He is the image of the invisible God. —Colossians 1:15

A complacent atmosphere seems to permeate many churches, with God's people taking God and God's church for granted. Some even go to the extreme of treating God as their own private possession. As God's total and complete body, the church of the risen Christ, we cannot go allow ourselves to go through life thinking that, even though we can't see God, God is there, "walking and talking with me." Has God become nothing more than that for us, like the air, necessary, but invisible?

Life for all of us has gotten so busy, but hopefully not so much that we take for granted the beauty and the majesty that is the God of all creation. Slow down, take the time to just enjoy it all. Spend time with your family, walk in, breathe in, and take in God's creation—both the splendor of God's creation and the joy of those who surround you each day. Do this, and there should be no doubt in your mind that God is anything but invisible. We can see God in all creation but we must be willing to look beyond ourselves, and we must be willing to think beyond the "Jesus and me walking hand in hand" mind-set. God is immortal; God is awesome; and God lives in, with, and through all of us.

God, even as we ask you to take us by the hand and walk with us, let us never take our eyes from your creation and those you place around us, and there see your face. Amen.

Day 270 / Acts 16:25-34

Magnitude Immeasurable

Immediately all the doors were opened and everyone's chains were unfastened. —Acts 16:26

Millions of people who live in earthquake zones face the prospect—and sometimes the reality—of disaster, a prospect that fills many with fear. Fear also gripped the very soul of the jailer in Acts—not regarding the power of the earthquake that opened the prison doors, but that his own life was in jeopardy because he thought that the prisoners had escaped, and that he would be blamed. But instead of a physical death, he experienced death to his old life of sin, and a rebirth, through baptism, into a life with Jesus Christ. Even though scripture implies that he never even realized a quake had taken place, it shook his life down to its very soul with a force so powerful that no Richter scale could measure the magnitude of its impact.

That's the power of God: a force that defies measurement; a force so powerful that nothing can survive its fury, and not be changed. The power that sprung open those prison doors to free Paul and his colleagues is the same force that God has used to set us free—free to love and serve God. And that's the holy earthquake that's going to shake up your life—so, hold on tight, because God's about to create a "whole lot of shakin" in your life. And what an experience it's going to be!

Go ahead, God, rattle our cages, right down to the very depths of our being. Shake us up and fill us up with your word and your love, so that we can bring a "heavenquake" into the lives of those around us. Amen.

Day 271 / 1 Corinthians 3:11-14

It's Your House

The fire will test what sort of work each has done. —1 Corinthians 3:13

A respected carpenter was about to retire, but a wealthy client coaxed him into building one last home. Anxious to put his working days behind him, he decided to cut corners by using inferior materials and being less particular about his workmanship. Imagine the carpenter's shock when, upon completion, he discovered this house was a retirement gift from his client! If he had known beforehand that this was to be his home, he would have built it with the finest of materials and workmanship. But now, it was too late.

We all build our lives, much like a carpenter builds a house. The materials we use to build that "house" are the things with which we build our lives—faith, love, grace, mercy, forgiveness, and kindness (or their opposites). Are we using the best materials? Are we living our lives with a purpose? Are we pursuing excellence as we work in the name of Jesus Christ? Are we building it for his glory? Or, has shoddy workmanship been the story of our lives? How many corners have we cut? What kind of inferior materials have we used to construct it?

If you need to do some remodeling or some home improvements, I suggest that you start with that firm foundation of Jesus Christ. Build your house well, and live a long and happy life with Christ.

God, you depend upon me to do your work, and to use the skills you've given me to do a quality job. Never let me fail you, Lord. Let me always be willing to give my best effort as I help to build your kingdom here on earth. Amen.

Day 272 / Philippians 4:6-7

Lighten Up!

Do not worry about anything. —Philippians 4:6

An essay sometimes attributed to a monk named Brother Jeremiah, from the Graystone Monastery in Nebraska, has brought calm to many souls. It reads, in part, "If I had my life to live over again, I'd try to make more mistakes next time. I would relax. I would limber up. I would be sillier than I've been this trip. I know of very few things I would take seriously. . . . I would have more actual troubles and fewer imaginary ones. . . . If I had my life to live over, I would start barefooted earlier in the spring and stay that way later in the fall. I would play more. I would ride more merry-go-rounds. I'd pick more daisies."

Those words recall Jesus' promise when he said, "I came that they may have life, and have it abundantly" (John 10:10). So, what are you waiting for? Go ahead, live that abundant life. Go ride a merry-go-round or a roller coaster, climb a mountain, or just take a walk in the woods. Have some ice cream. Go on a trip. Pick a daisy. Walk bare-footed with God. It's never too late to lighten up and live your life over again. Try it, you'll like it!

Go ahead, God, make me giggle. Slow me down, so that I can look around and appreciate the world you've made and all the people in it. Nothing in life is ever worth the worry to which we're prone. Take my hand and fill me with your peace. Amen.

Day 273 / John 17:17-19

Christian Paradox

Sanctify them in the truth; your word is truth. —John 17:17

Webster's defines the word "paradox" as "a person, situation, act, or set of objects that seem to have contradictory or inconsistent qualities." Christians are often bundles of paradoxes: We profess to believe, and yet we doubt. We claim to be hopeful, but we are easily discouraged. We preach the love of Christ, but we harbor hate deep within. We profess to live by grace, but are often unwilling to offer it to others.

If we are both to live by and to offer grace, then we need to acknowledge those paradoxes that are a part of our life as Christ's followers. Our inward selves are in constant turmoil as our desires wrestle with God's will, while on the outside the world often sees a life played out in inconsistencies. We must be willing to recognize both the light and dark sides of our existence so that we can learn who and whose we really are and thus be brought to a better understanding of God's grace.

Christ offers us a paradoxical message of hope: "For their sakes I sanctify myself, so that they also may be sanctified in truth" (John 17:19). Because he was willing to die, he has given us life. Because he lives, we need not ever fear death. Because Christ has beaten death, we can be that great paradox: simultaneously both saint and sinner.

God, you know my good and you know my bad, and yet you love me all the same. Thank you, God, not just for loving me for who I am, but often times in spite of it. I love you! Amen.

Day 274 / Daniel 10:10-14

I Don't Understand, God

From the first day that you set your mind to gain understanding and to humble yourself before your God, your words have been heard. —Daniel 10:12

Who among us can understand the mysteries of God? On a clear night, look up at the stars. Take a few minutes to observe an infant's movements and behaviors. Stop, and place your hand on your chest and feel the beating of your heart. What you see or feel or hear or touch are only a few of the multitude of mysteries of God's creation.

Yet it's also a mystery why God often seems blind or deaf or helpless. How can this God's eyes and ears and hands be closed in our greatest need? Why is it so hard for us to understand God's mysterious ways?

During those times in my life when I've voiced these very questions, I remember Paul's words, "For we know only in part, . . . but when the complete comes, the partial will come to an end. . . . For now we see in a mirror, dimly, but then we will see face to face. Now I know only in part; then I will know fully, even as I have been fully known" (1Cor. 13:9-10, 12).

God promises that we shall know, and understand, by believing in God's love and grace and trusting in the promises of God's hope, forgiveness, mercy, and in the truth of God's word.

God, your ways remain a mystery. Let me always live in the amazement of your power and gentleness. I place in your hands, with full confidence, my cares and worries, trusting in your mercy, strength, and love to sustain me all my days. Amen.

Day 275 / Malachi 3:16-18

You Will Always Be . . .

They shall be mine, says the Lord *of Hosts. —Malachi 3:17*

Being the creatures of habit that most of us are, we all have difficulty adapting to changes that affect our lives. But we also know that life is such that everything changes from day to day—save one thing for we who place our lives in the hands of Jesus Christ: No matter what else in our lives may change, we are, and always will be, God's.

Every day, any variety of circumstances not only may make our tomorrows different, but may alter our entire lives. When the Hebrew people began their return from exile—what was for them, a different tomorrow—God reminded Jeremiah, "At that time . . . I will be the God of all the families of Israel, and they shall be my people. . . . The people who survived the sword found grace in the wilderness; when Israel sought for rest, the Lord appeared to him from far away. I have loved you with an everlasting love; therefore I have continued my faithfulness to you" (31:1-3).

In this world in which we live, there are no guarantees. Each of us faces our own new day, with all its goods and bads; but in the midst of all that may change we need to remember God's promise of faithfulness to Jeremiah. So, never forget: Tomorrow will be different—but you will always be God's.

God, be with us all in the coming day and in each day that will follow. Help us to have confidence that, no matter how gray and lonely the day may be, your Son is there, ready to warm our lives and bring to us his guiding light. Amen.

Day 276 / 1 Thessalonians 1:7-10

Sandwich Board for Jesus

. . . in every place . . . your faith in God has become known, so that we have no need to speak about it. —1 Thessalonians 1:8

A once popular advertising venue involved wearing an advertiser's message rather than announcing it verbally. People wearing sandwich boards—two printed panels held together by shoulder straps—would walk the streets promoting businesses or products.

In his letter to the church in Thessalonica, the apostle Paul commends the believers for their spirit and their convictions. He praises them for living lives in faithful witness to Jesus. He tells them that good messages are getting back to him from nonbelievers who have witnessed how these young Christians openly and joyfully serve God. The believers in Thessalonia had become living for the kingdom of God. They had become the message, Paul tells them.

God doesn't ask us to wear sandwich boards, but God does ask us to shoulder the responsibility of proclaiming that the kingdom of God is at hand. We do that best through the testimony of lives lived according to Jesus' example of humble servanthood and faithful obedience.

God, let my life declare the glory of your kingdom and the promise of your love for all. Let me be a living witness to you. Amen.

No Jumping To Conclusions

Live in harmony with one another . . . —Romans 12:16

Perhaps you've heard the story of the traveler who purchased a bag of cookies and took a seat in the terminal to await her flight. Within minutes, a gentleman sitting in the seat to her right reached into the bag and helped himself to a cookie. The woman was flabbergasted, but rather than say anything, she took a cookie from the bag and made quite a show of eating it. She was absolutely nonplussed a few moments later when the man helped himself to a second cookie. So she ate another as well. They were down to the last cookie when the announcement came to begin boarding. The man plucked the cookie from the bag, broke it in two, gave half to her and headed for the plane. Wishing that she had given the man a piece of her mind, the woman furiously gathered up her belongings. In the process she discovered her own unopened bag of cookies on the seat to the left of where she had been sitting!

Imagine how embarrassed the women must have felt upon discovering her mistake! But just think how much worse the situation would have been if she had said something. There's a lesson to be learned here about not jumping to conclusions. But, more importantly, this scenario and others like it in our own experience provide opportunity for us to practice living in harmony with others and to be compassionate and humble according to Jesus' example.

After all, people are far more important than cookies!

God, help me engage my brain before my mouth so I always address others in a manner befitting my relationship with you. Amen.

Day 278 / Proverbs 25:2

Hidden In Plain View

It is the glory of God to conceal things . . . —Proverbs 25:2

While on location in Somalia some years ago, a reporter gave a grapefruit to a young boy whose emaciated body bore the distended belly and dry, wrinkled skin of someone dying of starvation. To the reporter's surprise, the desperately hungry child quietly thanked him but then turned and began to walk in the direction of a nearby village. The reporter followed the boy as he painfully made his way along the dusty road cradling the precious fruit.

On the edge of town, the newsman saw the boy kneel beside the prone body of a small child lying off to the side of the road. The younger child's eyes were glazed over and he wasn't moving. The reporter assumed, wrongly, that he was dead. Only later did he learn that the two children were brothers.

The newsman watched while the older boy bit off a piece of the grapefruit and chewed it. But rather than swallow the fruit, the boy gently opened the younger boy's mouth and spit the fruit into it. Then he manually worked the boy's jaws up and down until the boy was able to swallow the bit of fruit.

The reporter learned from a local missionary that the older boy had been providing for his brother in this manner for several weeks. Only a few days later, the older boy died of severe malnutrition, while the younger brother clung to life.

The tragedy of this event cannot be overestimated, but hidden within it is a reminder of another sacrifice—that of a loving God who gave the life of his son to save us from sin and death.

Lord Jesus, reveal yourself to us in various ways in every moment of our lives. Amen.

Lord, I Hope So

Rejoice in hope, be patient in suffering, persevere in prayer.
—Romans 12:12

Hope fuels the human heart and allows our spirits to soar. Hope abounds when a couple stands before a congregation and promises, "I do." Hope is why we continue to bring children into this crazy, fallen world. It's why there are hospitals and universities—and why the Chicago Cubs keep going to spring training.

We can survive extraordinary losses, but not the loss of hope. That's why we Christians need to daily stay focused on the presence and the power of God in our lives.You know the story of Peter's attempt to walk on water. He did fine until he turned from Jesus, lost his focus, panicked, and nearly drowned. When we focus more on our storms than on the presence of God, we're in trouble.

When we focus on Christ, these are the kinds of thoughts he will cause us to think. So, even in the severest of storms, put your mind in a place that will lead you to think hope-producing thoughts.

This morning prayer by St. Patrick offers nourishing food for our hearts and minds:

I arise today with God's strength to pilot me,
God's might to uphold me, God's wisdom to guide me,
God's eye to look before me, God's ear to hear me,
God's word to speak for me, God's hand to guard me.
Christ with me, Christ before me, Christ behind me,
Christ in me, Christ beneath me, Christ above me,
Christ on my right side, Christ on my left,
Christ when I lie down, Christ when I sit down, Christ when I arise.
Christ in the heart of everyone who thinks of me,
Christ in the mouth of everyone who speaks of me,
Christ in every eye that sees me, Christ in every ear that hears me.
I arise today through a mighty strength, the invocation of the Trinity.
Amen.

It's No Contest

I will grant peace in the land, and you shall lie down, and no one shall make you afraid. —Leviticus 26:6

Come election day, most of us are glad that, at long last, there will be no more negative political ads on TV for awhile. We look forward to a resolution to all the political maneuvering that, hopefully, will be the best for our country.

Imagine if our political candidates' platforms would include the sorts of promises God made to the priests of the Hebrew peoples: victory over our enemies and plentiful harvests. Yet we all know that many of the promises politicians make to us will never materialize. We can only pray that those who win will open their hearts and minds to God's wisdom in making any decision.

But God makes promises that no politician ever could: a promise to live among God's people and be in direct contact with them, and, best of all, the words, "I shall not abhor you. . . . I will walk among you, and will be your God, and you shall be my people." What a promise—and no flip-flopping! We can be confident that the ultimate leader of our life is that same God who faithfully executes those promises for the good of all. So, no matter who wins the election, we can rest assured that we are the beneficiaries of the only victory that ever counts—Christ's victory over sin and death. Hallelujah! We all win!

Thanks, God, for keeping your promises to us! May those elected to public office be guided by your wisdom and strengthened through your Holy Spirit, so that they will lead us with the same compassion, understanding, and love with which you lead us. Amen.

Day 281 / Exodus 20:17

Give Me What's Within You

You shall not covet . . . anything that belongs to your neighbor. —Exodus 20:17

How often we've been told how wrong it is to covet what someone else has. Yet all the media we encounter daily constantly throws countless enticing objects for us to covet—God's commandment is easier said than done! Webster's *New World Dictionary* defines the word *covet* as wanting ardently something someone else has, and to long for it with envy. And to "envy" means "to feel ill will, jealousy, or discontent about a person's possessions, and to desire to achieve them; to even begrudge that this person would even enjoy this possession."

But, as Christians, we possess within us the tender, giving heart of Christ. And it should be a heart that can easily be seen by others in both the random and purposeful acts of kindness that we show. That heart should be a gift that is so precious that everyone we come into contact with will want it; not out of jealousy or envy, but out of the sheer desire to also experience and to be able to express the love of Christ in his or her own life.

God has given us a gift far more precious than any gemstone—our Lord has given us the gift of God's Son and his love. So, open yourself up and share with others the most precious gift in God's kingdom.

God of love, help us to share with all the gift of your love. Let us be so ready and willing to give that gift that no one will have a reason to covet it. As someone once said, "Love isn't love until you give it away." Amen.

Bad Day on Planet Earth

Who will separate us from the love of Christ? —Romans 8:35

Some days, positive optimism just isn't part of the game plan. We get angry at everyone and everything; we experience feelings of hopelessness, worthlessness, and doubt. What could separate us from the love of Christ, given how we feel on those days? Just about everything!

So many things go on in this world and in our lives that make even devout believers ask themselves whether they can maintain their faith in God in the face of life's adversities and tragedies. Probably every Christian has uttered the words, "Why me, God?" at one time or another. Some people respond with a flat-out denial of faith: "How can a loving God stand by, inactive, and allow it to happen?" Others try to "faith it all away," and convince themselves that if they simply close their eyes and pray extra hard, all the bad things in life will be gone when they open their eyes, only to discover that they can't just be willed away.

In those difficult times in life God hurts right along with us as we struggle. But God also values our struggles because they force us to put aside our "fantasy faith" for a true faith that helps us to face honestly the ugly facts of our lives. Only then can we believe God's promise that nothing can separate us from Christ's love.

I'm sorry, God, for not trusting you. Things are really rough right now, and I'm not sure about what might happen, but please help me to always be sure about one thing, that "nothing will ever separate me from the love of Christ Jesus my Lord"! Amen.

Day 283 / Luke 12:41-48

What a Waste

Blessed is that slave whom his master will find at work when he arrives. —Luke 12:43

God is in the business of reclaiming and recreating waste. In God's eyes, no one is so far gone that God is unable to rebuild them to a meaningful, purposeful life. It's never too late to recognize waste in our own lives and ask God for forgiveness and grace. Once we've done that, God is there to take us by the hand and get us back on the track of real life, so that we can offer ourselves up for God's use.

Now could be a good time to take a self-inventory. Are you being responsible and a good steward of the gifts God has given you, or are you allowing yourself to waste away? If so, you need to take the action necessary to make some changes and offer yourself through prayer to God. Ask God to be a part of your total life so that you can put your God-given talents to work for the good of the kingdom and for the cause of Christ!

In so doing, think about two questions: What gifts, abilities, and/or talents do you possess that are not being fully used in service to Jesus? What are the decisions you need to make that will allow God to do the divine work of re-creation with your life, so that you may be used to effect God's purpose?

God, thankfully, you're not in the trash business! Instead, you're the ultimate recycler! Thanks for being an understanding and loving master! Amen.

Day 284 / John 1:5-9

The Greatest Thing

If we confess our sins, he who is faithful and just will forgive us our sins and cleanse us from all unrighteousness. —1 John 1:9

Several years ago at a political meeting, someone asked the question, "What is the greatest thing in the world?" None of the stunned politicians attempted an answer, but finally a young aide said, "The greatest thing in the world is that we can walk away from yesterday."

Those words summarize the essence of the gospel of Jesus Christ: The good news of the Christian faith is that we can walk away from our yesterdays. Paul was able to walk away from his persecution of Christians and answer Christ's call. The prodigal son was able to walk away from the moral failures of his life and back into the loving, forgiving arms of his father.

Being able to walk away from the failures and the guilt of yesterday doesn't mean escaping responsibility for one's actions. Instead, it is a liberating message that tells us that no one is tied to a past from which there is no release. We are only in "bondage to sin" if we are unwilling to allow God to forgive us. Only when we acknowledge our sins before God and seek forgiveness will God tell us to "take a walk." And to be able to take that walk, hand in hand with God who loves us for who we are, leaving behind our yesterdays, is truly the greatest thing in the world.

God, there's no reason why you have to forgive us when you know full well that we eventually will do something else wrong—but you forgive us anyway. Thanks for being the greatest thing, not only in this world, but in all of eternity. Amen.

Day 285 / Matthew 5:11-12

Gotta Love a God Who Loves the "Odd"

Blessed are you when people revile you and persecute you and utter all kinds of evil against you falsely on my account.
—Matthew 5:11

I've seen many odd roadside attractions in my travels. There's the World's Largest Buffalo at the edge of Jamestown, North Dakota. Bemidji and Brainerd, in Minnesota, have statues of Paul Bunyan. Hallam, Pennsylvania has a house shaped like a shoe, built by the founder of a shoe company. Oddities aren't limited to statues and buildings. The showman P. T. Barnum was a master of finding and displaying, among other things, so-called "odd" people, including General Tom Thumb, a midget.

The most prolific collector of odd people is God. Consider this list of some of the people he's called to carry out the work of his kingdom: a ninety-year-old man and his equally old wife, who gave birth to a child . . . a long-haired strong man . . . an adulterous king . . . a prophet-farmer . . . an adolescent girl who conceived a child through a spirit . . . a ragtag collection of fishermen, a tax collector, and a religious zealot . . . a persecutor of Christians. All must have been regarded as odd balls, but each heard God's call and responded.

When Jesus spoke the words of today's text on that hillside, he offered words of hope and encouragement to all of us odd people who claim to be his disciples.

God, thanks for loving me and for standing with me, despite my odd behaviors and imperfections. Amen.

Day 286 / Luke 18:18-25

Change My Heart

[Jesus] said to him, "There is still one thing lacking. Sell all that you own and distribute the money to the poor" . . . But when he heard this, he became sad; for he was very rich. —Luke 18:22-23

How does what you truly believe and how you act on those beliefs compare to what is God's will for your life? For instance, how closely do you and God agree on the subject of generous giving? It's a question I struggle with daily.

Theologian Richard Foster claims that the quickest way to determine if you have a selfish heart is by giving something away. Imagine taking all of your assets—your pension, checking account, stock funds, and equity in a house—converting them to their cash value, and then giving that money away. That's exactly what Jesus asked the rich ruler to do in our text for today. Are you surprised that upon hearing Jesus' command the man became sad and, according to the writers of the gospels of Matthew and Mark, turned and walked away? I suspect that in the same situation I would have responded in like fashion.

We can try as hard as we like to minimize what Jesus asks of us, or to rationalize what he really means by "all that [we] own." But the better way to deal with this very, very difficult command is to fall to our knees and ask God to change our selfish hearts, trusting that in God all things are possible.

Generous and loving God, instill in us that same desire to be generous with our material goods and our lives . . . and to always do so in the name of your Son, Jesus Christ our Lord. Amen.

Day 287 / Mark 15:39

God's Son

"Truly this man was God's Son!" —Mark 15:39

I love the statement by the centurion who was standing at the foot of the cross when all "heaven" broke lose at the moment of Jesus' death. "Truly this man was God's Son!" I think that statement is one of the most powerful and revealing confessions in all of scripture. It speaks volumes about the man who said it.

Here he was, a Roman centurion, possibly even one of those who mocked and beat Jesus before his crucifixion. He was required to remain loyal to Rome, and to his emperor. But in that one statement by him, his allegiance went out the window. In his confession of faith, we are provided a powerful example of the radical affect Jesus had on those around him, even in death. The centurion recognized that Jesus was, in every physiological way, a man . . . a human . . . a living, earthly being. But "Caesar's man" also recognized Jesus to be much, much more. The centurion realized that this man Jesus who was "obedient to the point of death, even death on a cross" (Phil. 2:8) was, in fact, the beloved Son of God. Imagine the impact of this realization on the rest of the centurion's life.

Are you able to stand at the foot of his cross and confess, "Truly this man is God's Son!"

Dear God, help me follow the example of the centurion and boldly proclaim Jesus the Christ and him alone. Amen.

Forever Is More Than an Hour

I will dwell in the house of the Lord forever. —Psalm 23:6 (NIV)

I remember a discussion way back in my junior high Sunday school class about what it means to "dwell in the house of the Lord forever." At the time, I interpreted the psalmist's words to mean that after I died I would live forever in heaven with Jesus.

That certainly is accurate, but it's not adequate. As an adult, I've come to understand that the kingdom of God is present now. Christ's promise to his disciples, "Remember, I am with you always" (Matt. 28:20) means that Christ dwells in us and we in him now and forever.

What does this mean for our lives today? It means that we are never separated from God's love, which is revealed to us in this one named Jesus. I am reminded of a phrase from a beautiful song by Michael W. Smith, "And a friend's a friend forever if the Lord's the Lord of life." Forever with God is more than an hour, or a day, or a year. Forever is a lifetime with a friend . . . that same friend who, in the fifteenth chapter of John's gospel told his disciples (and us), "You are my friends" (v. 14). Forever is a relationship with the one who has called us his friends.

I was glad when they said, "Let us go into the house of the Lord," for it is in that house—in that eternal relationship with my Lord—that I seek to dwell forever. Thank you for making that possible, Lord Jesus. Amen.

Day 289 / Romans 5:6-8

Stop, Look, and Worship

But God proves his love for us in that while we still were sinners Christ died for us. —Romans 5:8

The writer of the Gospel of John leaves no doubt as to the sacrificial nature of God's love for us. He tells us that, "God so loved the world that he gave his only Son, so that everyone who believes in him may not perish but may have eternal life" (3:16).

What an incredible God! How can we help but fall on our knees in worship before such unfathomable love?

On many Sunday mornings we can be found worshipping God. It's also worth noting that we frequently begin our meals with a reverential moment of prayer. And daily devotions certainly count as worship. But, if I am truly honest, I have to admit that more often than not I worship God when it's convenient or in times of crisis. How about you?

It's probably not convenient for God to forgive us over and over and over again. And yet, I have no doubt that God is willing to be inconvenienced if it means saving even one wayward lamb. Why? Because, unlike you and me, God isn't concerned about being inconvenienced. God is concerned about being faithful, faithful to the promise made through Jesus' death to love us no matter the cost.

The cross is a reminder of God's willingness to be inconvenienced out of love for us. May it be a reminder to us to stop, look, and fall to our knees in worship of our incredible God!

God, turn our eyes to the cross and accept our praise and thanks for your Son who died there for all of us. Amen.

Day 290 / 2 Corinthians 5:16-17

Extreme Makeover

So if anyone is in Christ, there is a new creation: everything old has passed away; see, everything has become new!
—2 Corinthians 5:17

I was watching a TV show recently where three people from the audience were given head-to-toe makeovers. The changes wrought by these extreme makeovers were truly amazing. What I found particularly interesting was that the transformations went deeper than their appearances. Their attitudes also changed. They seemed more confident and more content with themselves.

Would you be enthusiastic about undergoing an extreme makeover of your life? I'm not sure I would be. To tell the truth, I'm not all that comfortable with change. I'm generally satisfied with how things are. I'm also threatened by the idea that there may be things in my life, or in me, that need to change.

The apostle Paul knew first-hand what it meant to undergo an extreme makeover. After meeting Christ on the road to Damascus, Paul was transformed from being a persecutor of Christians to a proclaimer of Christ. In that moment, Paul's old self—right down to his name—passed away, and he became a new person in Christ Jesus.

Day in and day out Christ accomplishes the same thing in us. Through the power of the Holy Spirit, our sinful self-serving lives are transformed. We become new creations through which God's love is poured out upon a world desperately in need of an extreme makeover. Change is always difficult. But in Christ, all things are possible.

Heavenly God, Martin Luther once called us "little Christs." Come into our lives Jesus . . . make us new . . . make us you. Amen.

Take Nothing!?

These twelve Jesus sent out . . . —Matthew 10:5

They couldn't take any gold, silver, or copper along with them, nor a bag to carry anything in. They could take only one tunic, no sandals and no staff. According to Jesus' command, they were to cure the sick, cleanse the lepers they encountered, cast out the demons, and even raise the dead. But that wasn't all. Jesus also made it clear that they were not to accept payment of any kind for what they were doing! Can you believe it? These novice disciples, after less than a year of living in Jesus' presence, were now expected to live only on faith. Scary!

I can't help but think that the disciples probably set out with a great deal of uncertainty, perhaps even wondering aloud to one another whether or not they would be up to the difficult tasks Jesus had given them. It seems to me that they might have been strongly tempted to lay low and avoid getting into situations where their faith and their faithfulness would be tested.

How willing are you to live by faith? Are you a risk-taker for Christ, or are you satisfied with playing it safe in your willingness to follow him? There is no getting around the fact that Jesus expects great things of us. But what is equally true is that he promises to provide all that we need to follow him faithfully in spite of our fears.

Stretch me, Lord, beyond my desire to play it safe in my service to you. Equip me, empower me, and send me forth in faithfulness to your command. Amen.

Day 292 / 2 Corinthians 4:1-6

Do Not Lose Heart

Therefore, since through God's mercy we have this ministry, we do not lose heart. —2 Corinthians 4:1 (NIV)

There is a disease for which medical science has no cure. It's called spiritual burnout or "losing heart." Do you understand what I mean? It's when you feel like you're wearing a sign that reads "City Dump . . . Feel Free." It's when you feel like the world is crashing down on you and God is off somewhere else totally disinterested in what's happening to you. It's when you feel like the whole "God thing" just isn't worth it anymore.

On the basis of today's text, we can assume that the apostle Paul was acquainted with the malady of spiritual burnout. And he responds by reminding all who suffer from this disease that the ministry we have been given comes from a <u>*merciful*</u> God. In other words, God hasn't abandoned us. God knows our weakness. God is faithful. God will sustain us even when our faith falters.

We do lose heart much more often than we're willing to admit to others or even to ourselves. In those times, how can we avail ourselves of God's power? We can pray. Even when words fail us, from the deepest depths of our despair, God hears our cries for help. When we haven't the heart to reach out to God, God reaches out to us, whispering, "Trust me and trust in my mercy. It will be all right."

Merciful God, you know there are times when I feel so burdened by life that I fear I cannot go on. At those time especially, and at all times, help me feel the firm grip of your hand in mine assuring me that you are with me always just as you promised to be. Amen.

Day 293 / Romans 5:6-8

No Gold Stars Needed

But God proves his love for us in that while we still were sinners Christ died for us. —Romans 5:8

As Sunday school children, we were assigned a weekly Bible verse to memorize. On Sunday mornings, we would take turns reciting the verse aloud from memory. If we were successful, gold stars were placed next to our names on the bulletin board. Trust me, there was stiff competition to see who could earn the most gold stars.

I believe it's important to learn Scripture, but doing so in this manner inadvertently taught me that Jesus loves good people who follow the rules and get more gold stars than anyone else. It was a hard lesson to unlearn. Only many years later did I come to understand that, while obedience to Christ is important, thank goodness his love for me isn't dependent upon whether or not I obey him. I've come to know that Jesus' love for me never fades or falters. He loves me on my best days, and he loves me just as much on my worst days. Why? Not because I am lovable, but because I am his. Jesus died for me. He literally saved me from sin and death by his blood.

So, while the world may tell us that our value is tied to our performance, we know better. We find comfort in the knowledge that there is one whose love and acceptance is not based on what we do or don't do. Jesus loves us for "whose" we are. And that's the most important lesson we need to learn in life!

God, thanks for loving me thanks for dying and thanks for rising and living and accepting me just as I am. Amen.

Day 294 / Isaiah 48:17

The Leader of the Band

Thus says the LORD, your Redeemer, the Holy One of Israel: "I am the LORD your God, who teaches you for your own good, who leads you in the way you should go." —Isaiah 48:17

I read something the other day about the "little band of people that followed Jesus," and it brought back memories of my days as a trumpet player in the school band. I remember my band years fondly as some of the most meaningful and enjoyable times of my life. Friendships begun in school band continue today. In fact, just last fall at my fortieth high school reunion, I spent a great evening with the six other band members who made up the trumpet section during our senior year.

Throughout the evening, we reminisced about our band experiences and about its director. His name was Mr. Rothenberger, but we all called him "Dutch." Several times over the years I've been asked to name people other than my parents who were influential in my upbringing. Dutch always gets included on my list because, in addition to teaching me the joys of music, Dutch taught me to care about others and to share life with them.

There are two others who also make my list of very important people. Rev. Myers, my pastor during my growing up years, taught me about God and God's love for me. And my high school Sunday school teacher, Don Newcomer, helped me understand the importance of integrating my faith and my life

Together I learned from this trio of very important people what it means to follow a leader. Under their leadership, I grew in faith, knowledge, and love.

Christ our Leader, direct us, teach us, and lead us, as we, your instruments, your living legacies, attempt to perform your songs of love and forgiveness to all of your creation. Amen.

Day 295 / Luke 10:38-42

Out of Control

". . . there is need of only one thing." —Luke 10:42

I love to ride roller coasters . . . the faster and higher, the better. I thrill to the twists, the turns, the upside downs, and the loops. But I cannot tolerate rides that involve any kind of spinning or swinging motion. I become agitated and nauseous, knowing that things are out of my control.

Sometimes life seems like a spinning carnival ride. We twirl from one activity to the next at a breakneck speed that leaves our heads spinning and our bodies crying for it all to stop.

In 1961, Anthony Newly and Leslie Bricusse wrote and produced a musical for the London stage called, "Stop the World, I Want to Get Off." It's the story of a circus performer named Littlechap, who marries another performer and has a child. Eventually the pressures of circus life and family responsibilities overwhelm Littlechap and he pleads for the world to stop so he can get off and walk away from it all

Ever feel like your life is out of control? It's especially then that we need to re-center ourselves in God. It's especially then that we need to remember that only one thing is needed. His name is Jesus. Follow Mary's example and place yourself at Jesus' feet to listen and learn.

Help me, Lord, to find my center in you. Keep me from becoming so consumed with the concerns of my life that I fail to notice the concerns of others. Grant me strength to face what this day brings, knowing that in you I have all that I need. Amen.

Day 296 / Exodus 3:1-11

Holy Ground

Then he said, "Come no closer! Remove the sandals from your feet, for the place on which you are standing is holy ground" —Exodus 3:5

God's call comes to us in many ways, sometimes cajoling us to act, at other times prodding us to move. God's call can comfort, but it can also pester us to a "holy discontent" that can be salved only through obedience to the one who calls us.

It was on Mount Horeb that Moses heard God's call, but he could hardly believe what he was hearing! Did God really intend Moses to lead the people out of slavery in Egypt? Even when God assured Moses saying, "I will be with you," Moses wondered as to the validity of the call. And so God gave Moses a sign by which he would know that it truly was God who was calling Moses. The sign was this: God promised that once Moses obeyed the call and delivered the people out of Egypt, he would return to worship God on the very mountain on which he was called.

The sign that Moses was sent only came as Moses went. The same is true for us. It is in the process of obeying God's call that we come to know God. We set forth in faith. It is in the course of the journey that we come to know the whos, whats, whens, wheres and whys of the life to which God has called us, and realize that all of life is lived in God's presence. All of life is "holy ground."

Lord, help me to trust that along with your call comes your presence and your power. Lead me, O Lord, won't you lead me? Amen.

Day 297 / 1 Corinthians 15:51-57

Easter Is to Dye For

"For the trumpet will sound, and the dead will be raised imperishable, and we will be changed." —1 Corinthians 15:52

I borrowed the title above from a church sign I spotted on my way to work. That line got me thinking about Hinkle's Pharmacy in my Pennsylvania hometown. Still there, it had a great lunch counter, and at Easter they made their own chocolate eggs. They made and sold their own egg dyes, which my mother and I used to transform eggs into multicolored things of beauty.

In today's text, Paul talks about another kind of dying—or, more precisely, transformation from death to a new kind of life. Paul writes: "For this perishable body must put on imperishability, and this mortal body must put on immortality" (v. 53).

Remember the raising of Lazarus? Jesus uses that miracle to help the disciples and others mourning Lazarus's death understand what must happen to *him*. "But even now," Martha tells Jesus, "I know that God will give you whatever you ask of him." When Jesus says, "Your brother will rise again," she replies: "I know that he will rise again in the resurrection on the last day." Jesus assures her: "Those who believe in me, even though they die, will live, and everyone who lives and believes in me will never die" (John 11:21-26).

What happens next—Lazarus now lives!—is a foreshadowing of the greatest miracle of all: the Easter fulfillment of God's promise that we will all be raised imperishable and immortal.

God of love, let me die to self that I might be transformed to love you. Amen.

Spring Has Sprung

There is a time for everything, and a season for every activity under heaven. —Ecclesiastes 3:1 (NIV)

I love spring! The return of songbirds, the burst of color from tulips and daffodils, and the tinge of green on trees inspire hope within me and fill me with renewed energy. Spring is a glorious time of year, but every season is special and has unique blessings to offer.

The writer of Ecclesiastes recognized the uniqueness of the seasons. But the seasons of which he writes aren't determined by the calendar year, but by the very patterns of our lives.

Aren't you thankful that spring returns every year? How dull, hopeless, and dreary life would become if not for the promise of the return of spring each March. A life without spring reminds me of the fantasy city of Narnia in C. S. Lewis's *The Lion, the Witch and the Wardrobe*. The Witch has taken over the land of Narnia and has turned the land into perpetual winter. Life is frozen in time and the promise of new life is gone. Fortunately for us, we have the hope of new life and each spring we get a glimpse of just how beautiful that new life is.

And we have an even deeper awareness of this time of year when things "spring forth." On Easter morning, God sprung Jesus from the grave and, in doing so, freed a frozen world from sin and death. In Jesus' resurrection we've been given the gift of eternal spring.

For the gift of new life found in your creation and in your Son, we offer our thanks, God! Amen.

Day 299 / Hebrews 12:26

A Voice Is Silenced

At that time his voice shook the earth; but now he has promised, "Yet once more I will shake not only the earth, but also the heavens." —Hebrews 12:26

I don't know that his voice (through his writings) ever shook the earth, but for those who have had any opportunity to read *Heartsongs* or any of the other four volumes of his incredible poetry, you can't help but be moved by his thoughts and his words. The name of the writer is Mattie Stepanek. He was a young boy from Maryland who had a very rare gift for writing, which began at the age of three. Mattie also had a rare form of muscular dystrophy that ended his all-too-short life on June 22, 2004, at the age of only thirteen.

Mattie's writings, along with the courage he displayed throughout his battle with this deadly disease, became an inspiration to millions of people around the world. His zest for life and his undying faith are powerful examples of what our Christian life and witness can be.

How can you shake your own world and perhaps a bit of the world beyond your immediate sphere of influence? We seldom think of ourselves as movers and shakers, but all things are possible with God. Life in Christ is to be more than a mere game of survival. It is filled with undiscovered possibilities and an abundance of opportunities for serving. So, what are you waiting for? Get shaking!

Gracious God, help us to hear you speaking in our world today. Bless the writers and poets who sing your truth to those with the ears to hear. Shake us out of our comfort zones and present us with opportunities for serving you. In Jesus' name. Amen.

Day 300 / Galatians 5:13-15

The Gift of Freedom

For you were called to freedom, brothers and sisters; only do not use your freedom as an opportunity for self-indulgence, but through love become slaves to one another. For the whole law is summed up in a single commandment, "You shall love your neighbor as yourself." If, however, you bite and devour one another, take care that you are not consumed by one another. —Galatians 5:13-15

The Declaration of Independence pronounced the colonies free from British rule on July 4, 1776. But freedom never comes without a price. Our country's freedom was paid for through the blood and the sacrifice of those men and women who fought for a dream, a dream that would become the United States of America.

The message of the gospel preaches a similar tune. Through Christ's death, we've been given another freedom, freedom from sin and death. It was also paid for by a great price. God sent his only Son to shed his blood and die for us. He fought the battle against sin and death and overcame them for us. Although the cost was high, Jesus' death and resurrection purchased freedom for anyone who trusts in him and calls him Savior. By faith, we become children of God and co-heirs with Christ to God's kingdom.

With this freedom comes a tremendous responsibility. Just as our nation's freedom is not a license to do whatever we please, so our freedom in Christ is not an invitation to live without restrictions or without regard for the needs of others. Our freedom is given in order that we unselfishly respect and care for all people. Our Christian freedom rings when we choose not to indulge all our desires, but choose a life that both praises and honors God.

We thank you, O God, with hearts and hands and voices for all the wondrous things you have done. Help us to honor your gift of freedom in gospel by living lives that freely display your love. Amen.

Day 301 / Luke 8:42b-48

Touching with Faith

He said to her, "Daughter, your faith has made you well; go in peace." —Luke 8:48

Today's passage from Luke's Gospel is both a healing story and a story of faith. A woman who had endured a flow of blood for twelve years fought her way through the jostling crowd to touch the hem of Jesus' robe. Why did she not try to face Jesus directly? Did she fear he would not pay attention to her because she was a woman? Did she think he might avoid her because of her hemorrhage, which according to Levitical Laws made her unclean?

We don't know for sure why she approached Jesus the way she did. We do know that Jesus felt power go out from him, and that when the women was "found out," Jesus pronounced her well. Why? Because she had faith.

Have you ever stopped to think about how fortunate you are to be in relationship with Jesus? By virtue of our own baptism into the death and resurrection of Christ, we have already been "found out." We are in touch with the Great Healer. We are invited to come to Jesus face to face. His healing, forgiving hands are forever outstretched and ready to embrace. There is nothing to fear. Come forward. Trust him and expect a miracle.

Dear Jesus, may your Spirit draw me forward into your arms without fear. Touch me and heal my brokenness. Restore in me the hope of your salvation. Amen.

Day 302 / Jeremiah 29:11-14

Seek and You Will Find

When you search for me, you will find me. —Jeremiah 29:13

Have you ever noticed that whenever you look for something you've lost, it seems you end up finding it in the last place you look? Not so with God. Our God, in the words of theologian Gerhard Frost, is a "down-to-earth God" who has come seeking us and has found us. Jesus appeared in the flesh and continues to be present for us in word and sacrament. In this way God keeps coming to us.

So what is this talk of seeking God, and why do we sometimes feel as though we are lost? We don't need to climb some ladder or go on some expedition to find God. We already know exactly where God can be found. But we have a hard time believing the good news of the gospel, that our searching is over. We were lost, and now we are found.

We also know that we are prone to turning away from God and searching for satisfaction or peace or well-being in ungodly things. When we search for life in the wrong places, we come up empty. But when we return to God ("seek" God, perhaps), we find ourselves "found" once more.

God's not the one who's lost. We are. But now we also know where to find God.

Gracious God, thank you for searching me out. When I get lost or stray from your presence, gently turn me around and guide me back to your loving arms. Amen.

Day 303 / Psalm 61:1-4

Calling Mobile Crisis

Hear my cry, O God; listen to my prayer. —Psalm 61:1

One day a young man was referred to me through a local nursing home. He had wandered into their facility confused, anxious, angry with his family, and homeless. The nursing home staff brought him over to the mission so I could talk with him before admitting him. During our conversation, it became very obvious that his needs were far greater and more complex than anything we could offer at the mission. To get him the help I felt he needed, I called in mobile crisis, the mental health services in our county. They respond to situations where an individual requires immediate crisis intervention.

The people from mobile crisis delivered as I hoped they would. They offered the young man comfort, support, and a "safe place" where he could take some time to sort out his problems and talk with others about them.

God's a lot like that mobile crisis person for our lives. God's "heavenly crisis hotline" is open and available twenty-four hours a day, three-hundred-sixty-five days a year. God hears our cries, comes to us, and meets with us where we are. In God we find that "safe place" where we can take time to work things out, where we can bring our suffering and our most challenging questions. You don't need a referral. Just begin with the words of the psalmist: "O God, listen to my prayer."

Compassionate God, hear our cries, not only of sorrow and desperation, but also our cries of joy—joy in the knowledge and certainty that you are and will always be with us, even to the end of the age. Amen.

The Bag on the Side of the Road

They came to Jericho. As he and his disciples and a large crowd were leaving Jericho, Bartimaeus son of Timaeus, a blind beggar, was sitting by the roadside. —Mark 10:46

One day as I was driving from one side of town to the other on the bypass that runs around the outskirts of Greensburg, I noticed a large black garbage bag lying beside the road with debris or garbage hanging out of it. Obviously, someone just decided to dump their garbage.

It reminded me of old blind Bartimaeus who sat beside the road. By the standards of society in his day, he was like a bag of garbage. Like so many others discarded because of some physical condition, he sat waiting to be reclaimed.

Unlike the garbage bag I saw, Bartimaeus was able to speak for himself. He cried out, "Jesus, Son of David, have mercy on me!" He could not see Jesus, but he trusted that Jesus would hear him and answer his prayer. And answer it Jesus did. In fact, Jesus restored the man's sight. The man responded by following Jesus on the way.

We follow a God who loves us all—criminal and victim, healthy and infirm, rich and poor. Someone once manufactured a T-shirt that read, "God don't make no junk!" How true that is. As God's people, we are called to reach out to the "throw-aways" of our world. Everyone has value in the eyes of God.

O God, when we are tempted to treat people like garbage or toss them because they are flawed, remind us of our own imperfections and that you love us all just as we are. Grant us compassion for all your children. Amen.

Day 305 / 1 Thessalonians 5:6-11

Reject reject reject

For God has destined us not for wrath but for obtaining salvation through our Lord Jesus Christ, who died for us, so that whether we are awake or asleep we may live with him. —1 Thessalonians 5:9-10

In today's passage from the first letter to the Thessalonians we read: ". . . Through our Lord Jesus Christ, who died for us, so that whether we are awake or asleep we may live with him."

Those words *"our Lord Jesus Christ, who died for us,"* are words that we often forget about, or that tend to get buried in the more joyous rhetoric that comes out of the mouths of the "faithful." We sometimes get so caught up in the joy and the euphoria of Christ's victory, that we often times forget about his sacrifice.

It's a basic fact of Christianity, and probably the single most important fact of our faith . . . Christ died for us. He let his body be hung on that cross, endured unbelievable suffering and death. To put it very simply . . . he took our place. We don't have to suffer. We don't have to endure the pain or try to handle the ridicule and embarrassment . . . he did it for us . . . he took our place.

I remember several years ago a relatively new attender at the church coming to me and telling me that some long-time member actually came up to her before the service started, and instead of welcoming her to worship, told (not asked) her to move because she had "taken her place."

I was furious when I heard it, not so much that it happened to a visitor who just happened to be a friend of mine . . . but that it happened at all . . . right there in church in the presence of God. Just who do we think we are? We're gathered in that place of worship at the grace and generosity of Almighty God! That sanctuary, just like our individual lives, is God's dwelling place. It exists to continually remind us that we need to gather together on a regular basis to give thanks to the one "who took our place." They are words that each of need to internalize and never utter . . ."I took your place."

Thank you Lord, for sacrificing your life for mine! Amen.

His Peace Still Reigns

And the peace of God, which surpasses all understanding, will guard your hearts and your minds in Christ Jesus.
—Philippians 4:7

The tranquility of my overnight work, the joy of the movies we watched, and the contentment we experienced when the client at the house at last was able to sleep through the night were all suddenly shattered with the "breaking news" of the terrorist bombings in London.

As the images of the damage and loss of life began to play themselves out on the TV screen, I sat stunned by the fact that once again unknown numbers of lives had been ended, and the lives of countless others permanently scarred, both physically and mentally. And as I sat there, watching it all unfold, within me I felt the stirring of those same emotions that were a part of September 11, 2001.

I felt anger toward those who perpetrated these acts against innocent people. I felt fear, uncertainty, and insecurity for my safety and for that of my family. Fear and uncertainty have become the terrorists' most effective weapon. I also felt the sadness for those families who have lost loved ones, for the injured whose lives have been forever affected, and for a world that seems bent on destroying itself.

But I am a person of faith, so I did not dwell on anger, fear, and sadness. I recalled that God is a peacemaker, and God is the source of true peace. On this extremely difficult and disturbing day, I was moved again and again to pray for "the peace of God, which surpasses all understanding," including my own.

May your surpassing peace, O God, keep our hearts and our minds in Christ Jesus our Lord at all times, but especially when uncertainty and fear come knocking on the doors of our lives. Amen.

Day 307 / Ephesians 6:1-4

Are We Family?

Children, obey your parents in the Lord, for this is right. And fathers, do not provoke your children to anger, but bring them up in the discipline and instruction of the Lord. —Ephesians 6:1, 4

In my work I encounter a significant number of men who have a common story: they are products of dysfunctional, non-harmonious, and unloving families. As I listen, ask questions, and offer input, my mind often jumps to this passage from Ephesians. It is difficult for children to obey and respect parents who are abusive, neglectful, or needlessly harsh. Children try the patience of even the best parents when they are disobedient, rude, or nasty.

How have we strayed so far from the advice given here? Reflecting on the commandment to honor father and mother, Alvin Rogness says:

> We have much power over each other in the family. Children have frightening power. They more than anyone else can make their parents glad or sad. Parents have awesome power. By their love and wise counsel they can encourage love for God and become God's agents, giving their children a sense of worth and security, compassion for others, and courage for the future. (*Living in the Kingdom,* Augsburg Fortress)

Very simply, it all boils down to the command of Christ to all of us, "You ought to love one another as I have loved you." If we can practice this kind of love in our families, we can change the world—for the better.

God, may your presence and your love guide my family and all the families of our world. Teach all family members to respect, love, and forgive one another. Amen.

Day 308 / 1 Peter 2: 9-10

You Need Not Fear the Darkness

But you are a chosen race, a royal priesthood, a holy nation, God's own people, in order that you may proclaim the mighty acts of him who called you out of darkness into his marvelous light. —1 Peter 2:9

In two of his novels, *Bleak House* and *A Christmas Carol*, Charles Dickens makes reference to a very important person in the life of a town or city near the turn of the century—the lamplighter. As the sun was about to set, the lamplighter ran through the streets of the town with a long taper and a ladder, lighting the gas lamps that lined the streets, so that people wouldn't have to wander through those streets in the dark. Just before sunrise the next day, he would once again make his rounds, using the cup end of his taper to extinguish all the lights.

I don't know of too many children who don't, at some point in their young lives, experience a fear of the dark. Some children carry the fear of darkness with them into adulthood. But most of us, when we become adult, replace a fear of the dark with other fears—failure, rejection, loss, pain, loneliness, and disappointment. All of us, at one point in our adult lives, wrestle with such fears, which do seem to intensify at night. Daybreak often brings some relief.

The writer of First Peter reminds us that we are called out of darkness into the marvelous light of Christ. He has overcome the darkness of sin and death. His light brings hope to the darkest situations. And even when our earthly lamp is extinguished, we have the promise of a new and eternal dawn.

Lord God, as you guided your people Israel through the wilderness with a pillar of fire, light our way by the light of Christ. In our times of darkness, illumine our lives with the light of hope. Amen.

Day 309 / 1 John 3:17-18

Integrity

Little children, let us love, not in word or speech, but in truth and action. —1 John 3:18

As the children of God and followers of the risen Christ, we are called to a life of integrity, moral uprightness, and honesty. We are called, as Christ's followers, to have the mind of Christ in all that we say and do. That's a tall, if not impossible, order. How can we love as Christ loved? How can we faithfully follow the lead of the one who revealed the essence of love?

Put very simply, for us Christians, talking the talk isn't enough. Saying "God loves you" a thousand times isn't going to fill a child's empty belly or shelter him or her from the heat and the rain. The writer of James put if very succinctly when he wrote that "Faith without works is dead" (2:26). If we're not willing to do it, then we shouldn't say it.

The world will see our Christian faith when they see it in action. Then our words and our actions will align with those of Jesus. If we are to really be his followers, then we can't say one thing and do another. Martin Luther King Jr. said, "The time is always right to do what is right." Every time and every place is the right time and place for speaking the truth in love and doing the loving thing.

God, call us to faithfulness, call us to honesty, and call us, through both word and deed, into complete service in your name. Amen.

It's the Little Things

O give thanks to the LORD, for he is good; for his steadfast love endures forever. —1 Chronicles 16:34

How often we overlook the little things in life. How seldom do we pause to give thanks for the mundane and routine things that grace our days. A note from a friend telling me he's been praying that my life's schedule would soon return to normal prompted me to think about some other things. . .the daily food lovingly prepared for the men I work with by my seventy year old cook . . . a container of Swedish meatballs that only cost me a dollar. . . a bowl of orange Jello (my favorite). . . the gift of a favorite CD from my sister-in-law whom I haven't seen in several years . . . the cleansing and refreshing rains of this past week.

When I stop to think of all of these "little things" of life, I realize that I have had yet another blessed week. I realize that God's love and care endure in my life each day. Insignificant acts, maybe when viewed from other eyes, have a profound impact on my life. Acts carried out by one of God's creations—each done out of the love of Christ—are a huge expression of God's love for us all.

There are no "little things" in our lives, for all are gifts from our good God. That means that nothing we do for another is a "little thing" either. God's love endures through you and me. That is certainly something for which to give thanks!

God, fill me with that endless love, and open my eyes to all that you've created, both big and small. For all of it, I give you thanks. Amen.

Pea Pickin'

It shall not return to me empty, but it shall accomplish that which I purpose, and succeed in the thing for which I sent it. —Isaiah 55:11

Every morning after an early breakfast, Dick would go with his grandma to help pick peas, beans, and other vegetables for that evening's supper. One morning, as they stood there in the garden, his grandma exclaimed, "Oh, no, it doesn't look as if there are going to be enough peas for dinner tonight." But Dick got down on his hands and knees, and looking under the plants, said, "No, grandma, you're wrong, look at all the pods here underneath." And before long, they ended up picking several pint baskets.

Of all the stories I've been told relating to evangelism over the years, Dick's story about pea pickin' is probably the most valuable because it places the whole process in its proper perspective. It reminds me that there's often much more "fruit" available for pickin' than meets the eye. It's helped me to understand that too often we tend to not only place limits on ourselves, but that we try to "handcuff" God through our unwillingness to share the gospel.

The peas (those who need to hear the word) need to be picked. They need to not only be gathered in, but freed from their pods so that they can be used to feed others the food of the good news. Isaiah reminds us that our efforts will never be in vain. When we go out into garden or the field, there will be something to harvest.

Lord, make me one of your pea pickers. Amen.

Day 312 / Acts 5:1-6

Whole Lot of Faking Going On

You did not lie to us but to God! —Acts 5:4

I have spent a good deal of time in the local and wider church teaching and leading workshops and events. I'll be the first to admit it that it felt good to get this notoriety and be respected by others. But as I look back on some of those times and experiences, I realize that there were times where I was more or less "faking it." My belief in Christ was genuine, but the things I said and did weren't always for the right reasons.

A preacher named A. W. Tozer once said, "Many a solo is sung to show off; many a sermon is preached as an exhibition of talent; and many a church is founded as a slap to some other church."

Annanias and his wife Sapphira wanted to be part of the early Christian community that lived together on the proceeds of property sold by individuals in the group. But rather than bringing all the proceeds of their sale, the couple held some back. When found out, Annanias had a seizure and died. No wonder those who witnessed this were seized by fear.

We all are fakes regarding faith at times. It's tempting to put on a show to look better than we are. We might fool a few people, but we never fool God. God would rather have us be honest about our shortcomings. Faking it with God is futile. Only when we admit our failures and our weaknesses can God forgive and renew our faith.

Lord, make my faith genuine, my love complete, and my service for you alone. Amen.

Day 313 / 1 Kings 19:1-10

Getaway

[Elijah] sat down under a solitary broom tree. He asked that he might die: "It is enough; now O Lord, take away my life. . . ." —1 Kings 19:4

In my opinion, I don't think Elijah was, in any way, serious about wanting God to end his life under that broom tree. But he had been through a lot. After defeating Jezebel's prophets, he had a price on his head. He must have been tired and more than a little scared. He probably thought he couldn't run from his enemies forever. He may even have been frustrated with God, who had gotten him into this situation in the first place. Who can blame Elijah for wanting to just get away from it all?

Who, in this crazy and demanding world, doesn't feel the need to just escape, to get away from it all? Work, health issues, marital problems, and other intense challenges can drive us to the brink. Even those who serve God professionally can overextend themselves and face burn-out.

Elijah had to run away to save himself. Our situations may not be so extreme, but getaways with God are key to our spiritual survival. Even Jesus often left the crowds behind to refresh and refuel through prayer and time alone with God. A line from a contemporary Christian song prompted me to start my journey of prayer and writing reflections:

> A quiet time is all I need, a quiet time of prayer;
> A quiet time alone with Jesus; he will find me there."
> Find time to get away; find time for prayer. God will find you, and you will be refreshed.

Gracious Lord, grant me a quiet heart to hear you, a quiet mind to perceive your word, a quiet resolution to do your will. Amen.

Day 314 / John 1:1-5, 14

Listening to the Divine Word

In the beginning was the Word, and the Word was with God, and the Word was God. —John 1:1

This remarkable introduction from John's Gospel reminds us of the intimate connection between God's word by which we come to faith, and the incarnate Word who is Jesus. The Word is living and creative, present with God from the beginning and present in our lives. How do we connect with that Word on a regular basis? Study, worship, and receiving the sacraments are the most common ways. To these I would add an ancient practice of contemplative prayer called *Lectio Divina* ("listening for the divine Word").

This prayer practice involves four basic stages: *Lectio*—a selection or reading; *Meditatio*—thinking or meditation; *Oratio*—speaking or praying aloud; and *Contemplatio*—contemplation. While it may seem intimidating at first, if you're willing to try it, I can guarantee you will soon sense God speaking to you as you pray. Reserve about 30 minutes of time and choose a text such as a favorite psalm. Then try on this new practice.

As you open yourself up to the Scriptures in this way during quiet time, you'll also come to realize that the Bible is an active, living thing. Praying will not simply be about telling God what you want, but it will be about listening for God's voice. It will take some time to be still and listen, but the rewards will be great.

Great and majestic God, God of all mysteries, lead me into your quiet presence and lay wide open my whole being to the power of your Word. Teach me to be quiet, and teach me to listen for your voice. Amen.

Day 315 / Colossians 1:12-13

Catch Me If You Can

He has rescued us from the power of darkness and transferred us into the kingdom of his beloved Son. —Colossians 1:13

The 2002 movie *Catch Me If You Can* was adapted from the true story of Frank Abagnale Jr., who, in the 1960s, spent four years of his late adolescence impersonating an airline pilot, a doctor, and a lawyer, while writing bad checks around the world to the tune of 2.5 million dollars. The movie depicts these escapades, and shows Abagnale relentlessly pursued by an FBI. agent named Carl Hanratty, who eventually captures Abagnale. After Abagnale spends some time in prison, Hanratty works to get Abagnale released into FBI custody. Upon release, Abagnale is then transformed into a key FBI expert on identifying fraudulent checks.

This movie's plot reminds me of the way God pursues us when we live outside God's purposes for our lives. Through the Holy Spirit, God pursues each of us relentlessly regardless of how far we've strayed. We can try to keep running, try to keep trying to live a particular fiction, but eventually we know that God will track us down. And we are thankful that, like agent Hanratty, God persists until the chase is over.

So why not stop running? Let God catch you, and let God begin to work in you to transform your life. Running with God is so much more fulfilling than trying to run away.

God, I'm tired of being on the run. Find me, transform me, and use me for the work of your kingdom. Amen.

The Jesus Olympics

Therefore, since we are surrounded by so great a cloud of witnesses, let us also lay aside every weight and the sin that clings so closely, and let us run with perseverance the race that is set before us. —Hebrews 12:1

My favorite part of the Olympics closing ceremony is when the athletes congregate in the middle of the stadium in informal celebrating and international exchange. I like it because the country divisions are forgotten, and they no longer see each other as competitors. There aren't medal winners or losers, but people together in celebration of a common purpose. It's probably a good example of what the world is going to be like when Christ makes his triumphal return . . . a world in oneness all ready to "party hearty"!

The writer of Hebrews makes that clear in our passage for today when he says, "let us also lay aside every weight and the sin that clings so closely, and let us run with perseverance the race that is set before us, looking to Jesus the pioneer and perfecter of our faith . . ." There's a race to be run, and we're all entered in it. But our prize is not some gold, silver, or bronze medal, or a laurel wreath placed on our head . . . our prize is the chance to share the heavenly kingdom with our Lord and Savior, Jesus Christ. No flags will be raised or national anthem played; instead all eyes will be focused on the symbol of the risen Christ, the cross, and there will be a heavenly host choir singing, "Glory to God in the highest, and peace to God's people on earth!"

So set your sights on the finish line where Christ awaits you, and run with perseverance, and with all the strength and endurance with which God supplies you . . . and go for the gold(en) streets of the kingdom of Heaven!

Almighty and powerful God, my Nikes are laced up, and I'm ready to run! Fire the gun that will set me running toward the glorious prize that awaits me . . . . . . to live forever with you in Kingdom of God. Amen.

Day 317 / Isaiah 40:25-26

Go Tell It on the Mountain—and Everywhere Else

"Lift up your eyes on high and see: Who created these? He who brings out their host and numbers them, calling them all by name; because he is great in strength, mighty in power, not one is missing." —Isaiah 40:26

For our family, it was a weird but good Christmas. The four of us had attended the late Christmas Eve service. Our son had to work all of Christmas Day, so we didn't start dinner until 9:00 p.m., and we finished opening gifts five hours later. But ours wasn't as unusual as that first Christmas—in a borrowed barn, with visiting shepherds and sheep.

Luke doesn't say how many shepherds visited. Matthew doesn't say how many wise men came, although they presented three gifts. The traditional French tale of *L'Enchante*, mixes fiction with important truths. In it, four shepherds visit the Christ child on Christmas Eve. One brings eggs; the second, bread and cheese; the third, wine. The fourth, L'Enchante, brings nothing. The first three present their gifts, chat with the parents, and offer whatever else they might need. Finally someone asks, "Where is L'Enchante?" After a search, L'Enchante—the Enchanted One—is found kneeling at the crib, where he stays in adoration the entire night, whispering, "Jesu, Jesu, Jesu."

Every day is a day to shout the message of Christmas from the mountains, the rooftops, and from all corners of the world.

Go tell it on the mountain, over the hills and everywhere;
Go tell it on the mountain that Jesus Christ is born!
Jesus Christ is born! Hallelujah! Amen.

Day 318 / 2 Corinthians 4:8-9

In All Times and In All Places

We are afflicted in every way, but not crushed; perplexed, but not driven to despair; persecuted, but not forsaken; struck down, but not destroyed. —2 Corinthians 4:8-9

While Nazi warplanes relentlessly bombed England, Prime Minister Winston Churchill offered these powerful words of encouragement to a country in need of hope. "Never give in . . . never, never, never, in nothing great or small, large or petty, never give in except to convictions of honor and good sense. Never yield to force; never yield to the apparent overwhelming might of the enemy."

In today's Bible passage, the apostle Paul offers encouragement to first century Christians whose lives were in great peril because they were followers of Jesus. Paul's words are especially powerful because Paul, himself, was no stranger to suffering. In proclaiming Christ, Paul had been severely beaten on several occasions, run out of more than one town, shipwrecked, imprisoned, and even bitten by a poisonous snake.

Paul doesn't pull any punches. He is brutally honest about the cost believers will pay for their faith in Jesus. This honest assessment is necessary in order to convey the full power of God's promise that, though we will suffer mightily, we will not suffer alone and we will not be destroyed. God will not forget us. God will not abandon us. God will sustain us.

As contemporary Christians in a Western culture, we aren't likely to experience the kind of persecution that believers in other parts of the world endure. But true faith does not come without a cost. What price do you pay for making Jesus Lord of your life?

Lord Jesus Christ, take my life into your hands. Assure me that, no matter what the circumstances, you are with me. Strengthen me, Lord, in my commitment to live my life in faithful witness to your saving love for all people. Amen.

Day 319 / Psalm 80:1-3

But Not till I'm Ready, God

Stir up your might, and come to save us! —Psalm 80:2

The First Sunday in Advent marks the beginning of one of the church year's two penitential seasons, during which God calls us to a time of introspection and self-reflection, to examine closely our relationship with God and the world around us. God also calls us to use this season to prepare ourselves for Christmas and for who is to come—God's Son Jesus, our Lord.

But as we know, these are also weeks during which we prepare for Christmas in our own secular way. The manger of the Christ child must share space with the Christmas tree. The receiving of that most holy of gifts must take its place alongside the personal gifts we receive. The time for private contemplation must be shared with traffic congestion and crowded stores. No wonder the question, "Are you ready for Christmas?" usually elicits a resounding, "NO!"

Have you ever found yourself thinking, "Go ahead and stir up your power, God, and come—but how about waiting until I'm ready? I really would appreciate it if you could hold off sending Christ until I get those last few cards sent, my packages wrapped and mailed, and the Christmas tree put up. I should be done with all of it by Christmas Day."

If we can't make ourselves ready for Christmas itself, how can we possibly be ready to receive Christ?

Stir up your power, O Lord, and come into our lives this day and all days. Help us evaluate and reorder our priorities. Come into our lives and bring us your peace! Amen.

Day 320 / Ephesians 4:31-32

We Need More "Sams"

. . . forgiving one another, as God in Christ has forgiven you. —Ephesians 4:32

Sara suffered from chronic schizophrenia. Because of her illness, she found it difficult to control her behavior, or to understand why she did the things she did.

Once during a lengthy stay in a mental health unit, Sara started a small fire in her bathroom. The unit had to be evacuated and evening activities were cancelled. The next morning, staff and residents gathered in the lounge to confront Sara about her actions. For nearly an hour, staff and residents alike expressed feelings of frustration and anger. Over and over, they asked Sara to explain why she had done what she had done. But Sara sat mute, refusing even to lift her head and look at those around her.

Finally, a man named Sam got up from his chair, walked across the room, knelt down before her, and said, "It's all right, Sara. Sometimes I don't know why I do the dumb things I do either. But you're part of this group, and we're all here to help you."

With that, Sara began to cry, and then she began to speak saying, "I'm so sorry about what happened . . . " Sam's willingness to try to understand Sara, his willingness to put aside his anger and listen to her and forgive her in spite of what she'd done made it safe for Sara to share herself with that group.

Sam's simple act of compassion provided Sara the forgiveness she so desperately needed. For where there is forgiveness, there is hope. And where there is hope, there is life. God gives all these—forgiveness, hope, and life—to us in Jesus.

Dear Jesus, thank you for the "Sams" in my life. Help me be "Sam" to another who needs to know the life-giving power of forgiveness. Amen.

Day 321 / Genesis 3:7-10

Tape, Tissue, and Fig Leaves

Then the eyes of both were opened, and they knew that they were naked; and they sewed fig leaves together and made loincloths for themselves. —Genesis 3:7

The father noticed a tissue taped to the wall in his young daughter's bedroom. Curious, he paused to investigate. Underneath the tissue was the tell-tale sign of a red crayon marring the finish of the clean wall.

We understand only too well what the little girl was trying to do because we've been there and done that. Instead of tape and tissue, we use a variety of means—lies, distractions, excuses, blame—to hide our sins from each other and from God. Judging from today's text, it's the oldest trick in the book. Just ask Adam and Eve.

Caught with our "hand in the cookie jar," we try to hide in the bushes, thinking God will never know that we are the ones who did the deed. But God does know. And as long as we keep pretending otherwise, our lives are going to be spent on one cover-up after another.

It's time to stop hiding behind fig leaves and taping tissue to the wall. God is waiting to offer us the forgiveness we need to come out of hiding and truly live. Believe it! Come with humble and contrite hearts, trusting fully that God will forgive us for Jesus' sake.

Heavenly Father, I am ashamed of my attempts to hide my sins from you. Please forgive me for the things I have done, and for the things I have neglected to do. All this I ask in Jesus' name. Amen.

Day 322 / Psalm 46

Be Still!

Be still, and know that I am God! —Psalm 46:10

It was long past her bedtime and Rachel was obviously tired, but she just could not settle down. Jumping about the room, she prattled on about nothing until finally her mother caught her up into her arms and said in no uncertain terms, "Rachel, be still!"

I think today's psalm delivers that very same message to you and to me. "Be still!" God shouts as we move frantically through each day, becoming increasingly stressed-out and anxious with each passing moment. "Be still," God tells us as our lives spin out of control. "Be still, and know that I am God!"

But do we dare take the time to be still? Jesus did. The Bible tells us that Jesus often took the time he needed to go away by himself to pray and to renew his relationship with God. On the night before he died, Jesus prayed in the Garden of Gethsemane that God would somehow save him from the agony that was to come, but ultimately that God's will be done, even if it cost Jesus his life.

I'm sure that Jesus understood that it takes discipline to walk away from the things that demand our attention in order to spend quiet time with God. Perhaps we should ask him to help us take time each day to spend in quiet communion with God.

Help me, Jesus! My life is moving a breakneck speed and I'm terrified of falling off. Help me take the time I need to re-center my life in God. Help me in the midst of all the madness to be still. Amen.

Day 323 / Isaiah 40:3-5

Prepare the Way

A voice cries out: "In the wilderness prepare the way of the Lord, *make straight in the desert a highway for our God." —Isaiah 40:3*

Perhaps you have a pre-Advent routine in your house. In ours, it begins with the parade of boxes up and down the stairs beginning at noon on the day of Thanksgiving. Into the evening, the unpacking and careful placement of Christmas decorations continues. The prophet's cry in Isaiah 40 is often used to usher in the Advent season. We prepare for the Lord's coming, both as the Christ-child and as the returning Savior.

Preparing ourselves for the coming of Christ means more than decorating our houses and doing our Christmas shopping, and it requires of us much more than sending out to our friends and relatives our Christmas greetings. If we are to truly prepare our lives to receive him, we need to create once again that preeminent place in our lives, to clear our busy schedules of all the "necessary" time users. To prepare for and to wait with great anticipation once again the glory of his coming, we need to come before God with humility and openness.

Columnist George Will has said, "The future has a way of arriving unannounced." In some ways, he is absolutely right, and his is a reminder to be watchful and ready at all times. On the other hand, the Bible has announced with ringing clarity that the Lord has indeed come. God's future is no secret, even if the details are yet to be written. Each day is a day of preparation, and because the future is ours, we can embrace it in faith.

Lord, in the midst of all the hustle and hurriedness of our lives, help us to take time to prepare the way for your coming—to us and to others. Amen.

Day 324 / Psalm 148

Praise God

Praise the Lord*! Praise the* Lord *from the heavens; Praise him in the heights! —Psalm 148:1*

The Doxology is a familiar hymn of praise that has been set to a variety of different tunes. One of my favorites is by a Christian a capella group called "Glad."

Praise God from whom all blessings flow.
Praise him all creatures here below.
Praise him above ye heavenly host.
Praise Father, Son and Holy Ghost.

The Bible offers us many reasons for praising God. Here are just a few.

Praise God for the beauty of his creation! (Psalm 19)
Praise God for the power of the Holy Spirit! (Acts 1:8)
Praise God for the blood of Christ for our redemption! (Revelation 5:9)
Praise God for healing the broken-hearted! (Psalm 147:3)
Praise God for the cross and his sacrificial love! (Romans 5:8)
Praise God for his mighty acts of power! (Deuteronomy 3:24)
Praise God for his unsurpassed greatness! (Psalm 150:2)
Praise God for his Word! (1 Peter 1:24-25)

We are reminded that the language of praise fills us with joy and gratitude and brings the power of God's Holy Spirit into our lives. So, choose a tune you like and begin right now to sing praise to God from whom all blessings flow.

For all I have been given, I praise the Lord. For all whom I love and who love me, I praise the Lord. For gifts without number, and grace without end, I praise the Lord. Amen.

It's "E" Day

What will they give in return for their life? —Matthew 16:26

Traditionally, the day after Christmas is the sacred, high holy day known as "E Day"—the day when you enter the store and are greeted by long lines standing at a table labeled, "Exchanges and Returns." For many people, exchanging gifts after Christmas has almost become a ritual to which they actually look forward.

But what about other exchanges in your life? Do you have anything that maybe you need to exchange with God (and I don't mean returning the gifts God's given to you)? Is there anything that's going on in your life that's become a burden? If so, then God wants to let you exchange that burden for the comfort of Christ's presence. That is one line where we all should find ourselves.

If you have to head out today to take your place in that long exchange and return line, then take a few minutes to pray before you go; or pray to yourself as you while away the hours in that long line. Hopefully, your prayer will give you a new perspective on the whole process of exchanging things: Take a minute to give up your will to the will of God. Only the Lord can take whatever you want to give to God and exchange even the heaviest of loads with the lightness of God's peace and presence.

God, I exchange my weariness for your strength, my weakness for your power, my darkness for your light, my burdens for your freedom, my turmoil for your calm, my questions for your answers, my doubt for your assurance, my fear for your love, my sinful self for your forgiveness. Amen.

Day 326 / Isaiah 11:6-7

Cat and Griz

The wolf shall live with the lamb, the leopard shall lie down with the kid, the calf and the lion and the fatling together, and a little child shall lead them. —Isaiah 11:6

Cat was an abandoned kitten and Griz was a 650-pound grizzly bear. Both had lived at the wildlife center since shortly after they were born.

One day Cat got into Griz's pen during his mid-day meal. Workers watched in horror as Cat approached the huge bear. Suddenly, Griz raised one of his massive paws, tore a wing from the chicken he was eating and dropped it in front of Cat!

Thus began the very unique relationship of Cat and Griz, a relationship that provided great entertainment for their human caretakers. Often Cat would hide in wait in the bushes for Griz to pass. Then Cat would leap out and swat Griz across the nose, or hitch a ride on the bear's back. At other times, Griz would lie down beside Cat and gently caress her with his massive tongue.

Cat and Griz offer us a picture of the kind of life Isaiah is talking about in today's text, which is aptly named "The Peaceful Kingdom." The rules, expectations, and norms that seek to control our lives have no power over us in God's kingdom. Jesus has freed us from having to live by the rules and norms dictated by the world. Because we are secure in Jesus' love for us, we can risk loving others. Just imagine how wonderful life will be when enemies become friends, competitors become playmates, and adversaries learn to care for one another!

God, help us act with surprising grace toward those we meet this day. Amen.

Day 327 / John 14:1-7

One Way Only

I am the way, and the truth, and the life. No one comes to the Father except through me. —John 14:6

I know all about good intentions. I'm also well acquainted with the fits and starts, wrong turns, and roadblocks that keep me from following through on even the best of my good intentions. So, if the old saying about the road to hell being paved with good intentions were true, I would be toast!

Today's text is about a road that heads in the opposite direction. The name of this road is "Jesus, the Christ" The writers of all four Gospels tell us that John the Baptist arrived on the scene before Jesus. Like the surveyor who figures out the lay of the land before the road crew arrives, John preceded Jesus' coming in order to "make straight the way of the Lord." Make no mistake. John came to prepare the way. Jesus IS the way.

We deceive ourselves if we believe that the road to God can be paved with our good works. Good works, like good intentions, count for nothing in terms of our salvation. By God's grace, we are saved.

Thank goodness we're not given the impossible task of paving the road to heaven. Praise God for Jesus who is "the way, and the truth, and the life."

Lord, you not only guide our steps and accompany us along the way, you are the way to God. Help us to travel faithfully, Jesus. Amen.

Day 328 / Psalm 40:16-17

Special "G"

But may all who seek you rejoice and be glad in you; may those who love your salvation say continually, "Great is the LORD!" —Psalm 40:16

My favorite breakfast cereal is Kellogg's Special K. It's fortified with iron, rich in calcium, low in fat, and it tastes great. This morning while eating a bowl of Special K, I thought about today's Bible verse from Psalm 40. I know it sounds corny, but as a munched on my breakfast and chewed on this text, it occurred to me that my favorite cereal and God have a lot in common.

Like Special K, God fortifies us—not with iron, but with the power of the Holy Spirit. God fills us with spiritual food —his body and his blood. And, while God doesn't help us lose pounds, God does free us from the weight of sin through Jesus' death and resurrection.

It does our bodies good to start each day with a wholesome breakfast. But we must also take care to partake of spiritual sustenance each day with a healthy dose of God's Word. Special K and Special G—the perfect combination to make sure the rest of your day is GRE-E-E-E-E-A-A-A-A-T!

Lord, you provide daily food for our bodies and for our souls. Thank you for these gifts that give us the strength we need to do the work to which you call us. Amen.

Day 329 / 1 Corinthians 12:24-26

No One Can Go It Alone

If one member suffers, all suffer together with it; if one member is honored, all rejoice together with it. —1 Corinthians 12:26

In his "Letter from Birmingham City Jail," the Rev. Dr. Martin Luther King Jr. wrote: "I am in Birmingham because injustice is here. . . . I am cognizant of the interrelatedness of all communities and states. . . . Injustice anywhere is a threat to justice everywhere. . . . Whatever affects one directly affects all indirectly."

King wrote the letter while sharing time in a Birmingham jail with a group of demonstrators arrested because they did not have a permit. In word and deed, he personified Paul's words in today's text: "If one member suffers, all suffer together. . . ."

Jesus did the same. He saw the inequities in the ways certain people and groups were being treated in his day, and he set an example for those who would call themselves his followers. He hung out with the rabble of his day. He extended a hand of compassion to the ragamuffins of his world. He fought for fair treatment for the displaced and disadvantaged. And he calls us to that same task.

May the legacies of such people as Dr. King, Mother Theresa, Ghandi, Jesus, and so many others who have lived their lives for the freedom and dignity of others be the legacies we both pass on to our children and live through our daily words and actions.

Dear God, may your power and healing love draw us together in community with your Son, Jesus Christ our Lord. Amen.

Day 330 / John 20:26-31

The Difference a Week Makes

A week later his disciples were again in the house. —John 20:26

The Church of England calls the Sunday after Easter "Low Sunday," not least for the incredible contrast between the crowds at Easter's high celebration of the resurrection and the quiet, smaller attendance of this day's regular liturgy. Why should this be? Isn't Jesus' resurrection important anymore? Has Jesus suddenly become the "taken-for-granted Christ"? What a difference a week makes!

There was no "low Sunday" for the disciples the week after Jesus' resurrection, for this time all eleven were together in the presence of the risen Christ. Their belief in him, and their need to celebrate together, brought them there. So, what does that say about "Low Sunday"? Is attendance low because we didn't think he'd show up?

Jesus has told us that he's always going to be there for us, so doesn't he deserve our presence for him? Easter isn't a one-time remembrance and time for celebration. Christ is ready to make us his "Easter People," not just on that high and holy celebratory day, but on Low Sunday, on every Sunday, and on every day of our lives.

So why not try starting out each morning from this day on by letting the first words that come out of your mouth be, "Christ is risen; he is risen indeed! Hallelujah! Amen!" Try it, and see what a difference it makes in your day.

God, make us Easter people everyday. May each Sunday be a "high" and glorious celebration of your resurrection. Amen.

Day 331 / Ezekiel 3:22-27

Maybe God's Napping

Thus says the Lord God, "Let those who will hear, hear." —Ezekiel 3:27

Does God really tune us out sometimes, and just take a nap? Sometimes Scripture makes it seem that way; even Jesus questioned from the cross if God had forsaken him. Then again, who is it that's really not listening? Sometimes we simply refuse to listen to God, and sometimes we're just too tired to listen. And maybe that was the same problem that our scriptural forebears encountered: they'd had it with their particular situations. Even though they tried to pass the blame on to a sleeping God, it was they who were tired of their condition, and just weren't in the mood to listen,

In such times, it's good to remember those "shepherds keeping watch over their flocks by night," when, "suddenly, there was with the angel a multitude of the heavenly host, praising God and singing, "Glory to God in the highest heaven, and peace among those whom he favors!" Maybe that's our problem: We won't listen until the angels sing. But can their voices be any sweeter, or any more compelling, than that of God? Must we wait for the angels to cry out, or do we need to un-busy ourselves so that the glorious voice of God can reach our ears and make that blessed pronouncement that Jesus has been born?

It's me who's napping, God, and not listening to your message of salvation and grace. Shake me awake, God. Slow down my frenetic pace and bring me into your presence. And there, fill me with the joy of new life born in a manger and nestled in my heart. Amen.

Day 332 / Mark 6:45-46

The Calm Before the Storm

After saying farewell to them, he went up on the mountain to pray. —Mark 6:46

I looked at my calendar today and discovered, to my amazement, that later this week I have a whole day with no scheduled appointments or activities! Coming as it does just prior to an extremely busy time in my life, I am thrilled to receive this unexpected gift of a calm before the storm.

Life moves at breakneck speed. I rarely drive without the radio, tape player, or a CD blaring. At our house, at least one TV is on from early morning to late evening. Cell phones ring and emails keep coming. It's hard to find even a few seconds of silence for God. Are periods of peace and tranquility heading the way of the dinosaur and the dodo?

Jesus understood how important it was to find times he could be alone, without distractions, so that he could listen to the voice of his Father and be renewed, revitalized, and refreshed. One of the most important things you can do for yourself as a Christ-follower is to find and create ways to nurture the practice of silence. Whatever and wherever it is, find your "mountain," where you can be alone with God. Even a few moments of regular silence can give us the opportunity to train our hearts, ears, and lives to hear a far sweeter sound—the sound of the Master's voice.

Lord of love, stop my feet, still my heart, and quiet my anxious and hurried mind, so that the clear sound of your voice can fill me, renew me, and prepare me to serve you. Amen.

A Virus Warning!

And the shepherds returned, glorifying and praising God for all they had heard and seen, as it had been told them. —Luke 2:20

Do you have any of the following symptoms?

- A tendency to think and act spontaneously despite past experiences
- An unmistakable ability to enjoy the moment
- A loss of interest in judging other people
- A loss of interest in conflict
- A loss of the ability to worry
- Frequent, overwhelming episodes of appreciation and thankfulness
- Contented feelings of connectedness with others and God's nature
- Frequent attacks of smiling
- An increasing tendency to let things happen rather than to make them happen
- An increased susceptibility to the love extended by others as well as the uncontrollable urge to extend it

If you have experienced these symptoms, you have contracted a virus whose cause eludes medical science. But according to today's account from scripture, the virus seems to strike those who have been in the presence of Jesus, and leaves them feeling filled with hope, peace, joy, and love. I strongly urge you to pass this virus warning on to everyone you know. And if you feel that you've been infected by this virus, rejoice, for there appears to be no cure!

Lord of love, let your love infect our hearts, our souls, our whole beings, that we might show your love and share your word with all those around us. Amen.

First God National Bank

Give to everyone who begs from you, and do not refuse anyone who wants to borrow from you. —Matthew 5:42

Shrove Tuesday, according to an old English custom, is the last day to rid one's self of fatty foods before Lent begins on the next day. The revelry and feasting of Fat Tuesday, (*mardi gras*, in French) ends at the stroke of midnight when Ash Wednesday begins.

Lent comes from the Old English word *lencten*, which probably refers to the lengthening of daylight and the coming of spring. It may be coincidental that *lent* also is the past and past perfect tense of *lend*, but it's not inappropriate think about lending and borrowing during this period of penance and reflection on the Christian life. After all, our physical bodies and everything we have in this life, including life itself, are on loan to us from our Creator. We may "give up something for Lent" as a reminder the Jesus gave up his life for us. But frequently what we give up is something we don't need anyway—like a bad habit or a few extra pounds. And more often than not, our "sacrifice" ends abruptly on Easter morning.

As followers of Jesus, we might think less about giving up something for 40 days and more about serving God by *lending* to others every day. Start today by lending an ear, a hand, or a dollar to someone in need of the touch of God's love.

Dear God, help us value the days of our lives, to let go of the things that hurt us, and to use the gifts with which you've blessed us to enrich the lives of those around us this day and always. Amen.

Day 335 / Matthew 2:9-11

Then He Smiled at Me

On entering the house, they saw the child with Mary his mother; and they knelt down and paid him homage. Then, opening their treasure-chests, they offered him gifts of gold, frankincense, and myrrh. —Matthew 2:11

Do you ever pop in a Christmas CD when it's no where near Christmastime? There's no shame in that! I love Christmas carols, especially "The Little Drummer Boy," which tells the story of a boy who visits the newborn Jesus. Seeing that others have brought costly gifts for the baby, he feels terrible that he's come empty-handed. Lacking anything else, the little drummer boy offers Jesus a very special gift. He interrupts the silence of that holy night with the joyful rhythms of his drum.

What a humble gift, especially when compared to the treasure-chests of gold, frankincense, and myrrh that had already been given. Would it have been better if the little drummer boy hadn't given a gift at all? Was Jesus annoyed by the "pa rum pum pum pum" of the little boy's drumming? Obviously not, since in the final verse of the song, the little drummer boy sings joyfully, "Then he smiled at me . . ."

Of course, there's no drummer boy in the Gospel accounts of Jesus' birth Christmas night. The writer is describing a deeper truth: that God is pleased when we're willing to give our best. Please don't wait until next Christmas to do so!

Thank you, most generous and loving God. Thank you for giving to us your best, for it is more than enough. Amen.

Hey, I Know You!

To you, O Lord, I lift up my soul. —Psalm 25:1

We will never, with our limited understanding, be able to comprehend or fully appreciate God. After all, to use several "nickel words," God is omniscient (all knowing), omnipotent (all powerful), and omnipresent (everywhere present). On the other hand, we have limited knowledge and power, and can only dream of having the ability to be in more than one place at a time!

Given these differences, how is it even possible for us to know God? The answer is that God comes to us in relationships . . .

- in our relationship with God's holy word which offers us countless examples of God's faithfulness throughout the ages
- in our relationships with other believers who bear witness to God's presence and activity in their lives
- in our relationship with water, wine and bread—means of God's grace to grant forgiveness and restore broken relationships
- in our relationship with Jesus, God's beloved son

God—all knowing, all powerful, everywhere present—reveals himself in Jesus to be all loving. In Jesus, the "Omni" Creator of all reveals himself to be a father who loves his children with a love beyond our limited power to understand. And that is just fine with me!

Thank you, God, for stooping down to where we can come running into your waiting arms. Inspire in us both awe and faith. Amen.

Day 337 / Genesis 22:1-8

In the Between Times

"The fire and the wood are here, but where is the lamb for the burnt-offering?" Abraham said, "God himself will provide a lamb for a burnt-offering, my son." So the two of them walked on together. —Genesis 22:7-8

We live our lives in the busy hours *between* morning and evening; in the up and down days *between* Sundays; in the ever-changing seasons *between* birth and death; in the inevitable valleys *between* the mountaintop experiences of life. Faith is for these "between times."

Today's text illustrates the importance of faith for the between times of our lives. Abraham clung desperately to faith in those terrible hours between God's command to sacrifice his son, Isaac, and God's last-minute reprieve.

Of course, faith is important for all the times of our lives. In the good times—the mountaintop times—it gives us someone to thank. But in the difficult times—in the valleys between the mountains—faith assures us that we have not been forgotten. God remembers us in the between times and comes to us in Jesus, who is well acquainted with life in the between times. On the brink between life and death, Jesus called out to God, "Eli, Eli, lama sabachthani?" (My God, my God, why have you forsaken me?) Who among us hasn't set up the same plea when the fears, doubts, pain, and sorrow of living in the between times threatened to overwhelm us? Such honesty with God is born of faith that God exists, that God knows us, that God knows our need . . . and that is enough.

Thank you, Lord, for your gift of faith for all the times of our lives. May we remember to praise and thank you in the good times as earnestly as we cry out for your presence in the times in-between, trusting that all time belongs to you. Amen.

Keeping the Promise

"For this is my blood of the covenant, which is poured out for many for the forgiveness of sins." —Matthew 26:28

We talk a lot about contracts, but not much about covenants anymore. But covenants were integral to the relationship between God and the chosen people. The disciples would have understood the significance of Jesus' words, "this is my blood of the covenant . . . " But even they would not grasp what Jesus was really saying until later—after Jesus' death and resurrection.

This covenantal relationship began with God's promise to Abraham of a land, a nation, and a blessing. God later renewed that covenant through Moses and the giving of the law. During the Last Supper, Jesus used the imagery of this "old" covenant to establish a "new" covenant with his disciples. This "new" covenant has no ethnic boundaries, but is offered to all who believe that Jesus "is the lamb of God who takes away the sins of the world." This "new" covenant is of the heart, with bread and wine—body and blood—as its visible reality.

Make no mistake, this covenant isn't an agreement between peers. Rather, it is a promise made by God to sinful people—a promise that even when we are not faithful to God, God will be faithful to us.

I've made lots of promises to God, and I'll bet you have, too. Our relationship with God is most certainly based on promises. But, thankfully, it's not based on our promises to God but God's promise to us: "I will be your God, and you will be my people." God keeps his promise. Jesus is the proof.

Thank you, God, for loving us in your promise of forgiveness and salvation through your crucified and risen Son, Jesus Christ our Lord. Amen.

Day 339 / John 2:1-10

No Watered-Down Gospel

"Everyone serves the good wine first, and then the inferior wine after the guests have become drunk. But you have kept the good wine until now." —John 2:10

One of the oldest tricks in the cookbook involves adding water and a little more seasoning to stretch a pot of soup to accommodate unexpected dinner guests. While this works quite well with soup, I wouldn't recommend diluting wine with water. But that's what the wine steward would have been instructed to do in many situations like the one described in today's text.

How fortunate that Mary and her son Jesus were guests at this particular wedding. Instead of watering down what was left of the wine to make it last a little longer, Jesus turned water into wine—and very good wine at that. The Cana wedding guests weren't served watered down wine. They were served the very best.

As guests at God's banquet table, we, too, are served the very best that God has to offer—unconditional love, forgiveness of sins, and life eternal. And from there, God sends us out into the world to serve others. Do we offer them the life-giving promise of God's grace? Or do we serve a watered-down version that puts limits on God's love and says that God's grace must be earned?

We don't need to be stingy. There will be plenty for everyone. God will make sure of that.

Lord, forgive me when I fail, either knowingly or unknowingly, to offer to others the grace and forgiveness that you have poured out for me. Amen.

Day 340 / Isaiah 60:1-3

Morning Glory

Arise, shine; for your light has come, and the glory of the LORD has risen upon you. —Isaiah 60:1

I have fond memories from camping excursions in my youth of waking up to the smell of breakfast being prepared over an open fire. The aroma of scrambled eggs, bacon, pancakes, and coffee was an effective alarm clock for a hungry boy. But it was also an enticing invitation to begin a new day that held the promise of good things to come—beginning with a delicious breakfast with people I loved.

Today's passage from Isaiah is a wake-up call, delivered first to an ancient people in need of hope and now to us. Like the aroma of long-ago breakfasts, the prophet's words *invite* us to consciousness with the promise that something wonderful awaits us—the glory of a new day in God's presence, doing the work to which God calls us.

Listen. God is calling. "Christian, arise, shine! I want you to share with others the joy of knowing the risen Christ. Let your voice carry the good news that Christ died that all might live. By your loving deeds, invite others to see Jesus at work in their lives."

Now that's the way to wake up a sleeping world!

Wake me, God, and let your light shine through me on this day and every day of the life you give me. Amen.

Day 341 / *John* 13:31-35

A 24/7 Disciple

By this everyone will know that you are my disciples, if you have love for one another. —John 13:35

I read something the other day about how much time the average person spends sleeping, eating, working, exercising, parenting, communicating with others, pursuing personal interests, commuting, and a variety of other things. I didn't check, but I assume that the times added up to 24 hours.

For a variety of reasons, some good . . . some not so good . . . we all compartmentalize our lives to some degree according to the activities we pursue and the roles we play each day. So, what compartment does "being a disciple" fit into? How much time should we allot in each day to loving one another?

Those seem like silly questions, don't they? We know that following Jesus is a full-time calling. And there's no time limit on loving others. As the kids say, that's a 24/7 job—twenty-four hours a day, seven days a week.

Jesus is very clear that love and discipleship go hand-in-hand. In fact, the first is evidence of the second. Followers of Jesus follow his example. That means we don't just love those who are near and dear to us, we love everyone—even those who aren't easy to love. It means that we act with care and compassion all the time, not only when it's convenient for us.

Frankly, I know I can't live up to this 24/7 calling. But with the Spirit's power, I may be able to handle the next few minutes. How about you?

Dear Jesus, help me take one minute at a time in my commitment to follow you and love others 24/7. Forgive me when I fail, and help me begin again. Amen.

Martha Fife

But Martha was distracted by her many tasks. —Luke 10:40

The actor Don Knotts died recently. Many remember Don as the nervous, bumbling deputy sheriff in the 1960s television program, "The Andy Griffith Show." One of my favorite episodes was when Sheriff Taylor and Deputy Fife learned that a notorious crook was going to be staying in their small town jail for two nights. Barney, star-struck by the man's celebrity, immediately began cleaning and decorating the cell for his arrival. In the flurry of activity and preparation, Barney lost sight of the reason for the man's visit.

I get the feeling that Martha and Barney had much in common. Today's text suggests that she, too, was a worrier. And, like Barney, Martha got carried away with her preparations for Jesus' coming. She was so focused on getting everything "just so" for Jesus' visit, that she lost sight of who Jesus was and why he was coming.

I see some similarity between myself and Barney and Martha. How about you? Do you ever get so caught up in the details of life that you lose sight of the big picture? Are you so busy running from one task to the next that what's truly important fails to get done? Are you so concerned about getting ready for Jesus that you miss the opportunity to get to know him?

"Martha, Martha," Jesus said, "there is need of only one thing." Replace Martha's name with your name. Then take to heart what Jesus is saying. Truly only one thing is needed, and that is Jesus.

God, stop our feet, close our mouths, and open our ears and our hearts to your message of love and forgiveness that comes to us in Jesus. Amen.

Day 343 / John 8:12

Light of Hope

Again Jesus spoke to them, saying, "I am the light of the world. Whoever follows me will never walk in darkness but will have the light of life." —John 8:12

There are many accounts of "near death" experiences. With only slight variation, all involve walking toward a brilliant light at the end of a long tunnel or passageway. People who have experienced this describe a sense of being enveloped in the most incredible feeling of love.

What are we to make of these experiences? Are they actual occurrences, or figments of an overly active imagination? Is there any validity to the descriptions of a light at the end of a tunnel? Is this really what happens when we die?

I don't know what to think about near death experiences, but scripture assures us that we don't have to wait until death to experience the light. Jesus is the light of the world. Those who know Jesus walk in his light everyday. Those who know Jesus know the power of love to bring light to the darkest corners of our lives.

I find it interesting that those who experience "near death," no longer fear death. "Fear not!" was the message proclaimed on that first starry Christmas night and again on the morning when Friday's darkness gave way to the light of Easter. In Jesus—the light of the world—the power of death has been destroyed. God's perfect love casts out all fear.

Loving God, draw us from the darkness of what surrounds us into the glorious light of your presence. Amen.

The Sounds of Silence

Be silent, all people, before the Lord; *for he has roused himself from his holy dwelling. —Zechariah 2:13*

What would you do if you could spend one full hour in complete quiet—no noise, no distractions—just you and the quiet? You and I both know that is almost impossible to experience in our "hurry up" world. Yet, there is something to be both said and appreciated about such an experience. The "sounds" of silence can speak more loudly to us than words. A quiet place apart is needed sometimes, if we want to hear God's voice.

Mother Theresa of Calcutta has said about silence: "See how nature . . . grows in silence; see the stars, the moon and sun, how they move in silence . . . we need silence to be able to touch souls."

At some point today, find a place away. Take a cup of water or something else to satisfy your thirst, a Bible, a journal or paper, and a pen. Choose a passage and read it slowly, pausing to let the message sink in. Read it again, and then stop and listen. Listen for what God's Spirit is saying to you in the silence of your heart. If you want to remember it later, write it down. How does it apply to your life?

Being silent before God is not about being quietly passive; it's about active listening. God wants to be heard.

God, lead me to the quiet, to the silent places in this crazy world. And there, fill me, renew me, and refresh me for the work of your kingdom. Amen.

Let It Shine

In the same way, let your light shine before others, so that they may see your good works and give glory to your Father in heaven.
—Matthew 5:16

A while back, an observer went to a Christian rock and culture festival. What he found dismayed him. It seemed that the performers spent much of their time hawking their cds and merchandise. There's certainly nothing wrong with artists and speakers at a large event promoting their Christian products. But it made the observer ponder what the world really sees when it looks at Christians.

Does the world see the light of Christ? And what would that light look like? Hopefully, it would look like people engaged in real worship and praise, people with sleeves rolled up serving their neighbors, or people seeking peace and justice. It would look like people feeding the hungry and taking care of the lonely and downhearted.

So much of the world lives in the dark. The nightly news is a constant reminder of that. But we who have been washed in the baptismal waters have been invited to "let [our] light shine," so that we might glorify God in all we do.

So, today, let us imagine what the world sees when it looks at us. What do our words and deeds communicate about Jesus to the world around us? How do we carry the light?

God, let your light shine through me. Help me to shine with the light, hope, peace, and love. Amen.

Go and Be

Go therefore and make disciples of all nations. —Matthew 28:19

Imagine what it must have been like to be one of Jesus' first disciples. I imagine it might have been exciting and perhaps even simple in one sense. Why simple? Following Jesus was for the disciples their entire life vocation. They left work and family behind and spent their days walking beside, learning from, and ministering with Jesus. If only when Jesus calls us to "go and make disciples" we could just drop everything else and do what the disciples did.

Can you even begin to imagine doing that today? How do you think family members or employers or coworkers would react? No doubt many would question what we were doing.

True discipleship is costly. In his classic work on discipleship, Dietrich Bonhoeffer has said, "A Christianity that no longer took discipleship seriously remade the gospel into only the solace of cheap grace." So often we want to follow on our terms. In this world of plenty and complexity, it seems like such a stretch to simply drop it all and follow Jesus.

It seems like such a tall order, but we need to keep our eyes on the possibilities. Making and being disciples opens us to the abundant life. We are not promised that it will be easy, but we are assured that we will experience life to the fullest.

Lord, as you called the twelve, call us to walk with you. And give us strength to go and make disciples, baptizing and teaching in your name. Amen.

Day 347 / Isaiah 55:6-9

In Who's Image?

For my thoughts are not your thoughts, nor are your ways my ways, says the LORD. For as the heavens are higher than the earth, so are my ways higher than your ways and my thoughts than your thoughts. —Isaiah 55:8-9

From the late poet Edward Arlington Robinson comes this line: "The world is not a prison house. Rather, it is a kind of spiritual kindergarten where millions of bewildered infants are trying to spell *God* with the wrong blocks." If you lay that quote alongside Isaiah's words from today's passage, we realize just how difficult it is for us human beings to describe God and understand God's ways.

Many years ago, the author J. B. Phillips wrote a book entitled *Your God is Too Small*. In it, Phillips examines this very issue, that we humans can only feel comfortable as long as we feel we have control over God, that we can compartmentalize God, that we can turn God off and on at our convenience, and that we can only feel safe if we're able to put God in a box.

We were created in the image of God (Genesis 1:27), not the other way around. Still, we keep trying to recreate God to suit our needs, and when life doesn't go exactly as we wish, we question God's motives. We will never solve the mystery that is God. We live with the mystery because that is our place as the "created" ones. We do not try to work our way up to God's level. Those who built the Tower of Babel tried that and failed. No, we rejoice in the knowledge that God has come down to our level. If we need an image of God, we need look no further than Jesus.

God of all power and might, forgive our selfish and controlling ways. Continue to mold us into your image, so that those who would seek to envision you might see you through us. Amen.

Day 348 / Psalm 37:1-7

S.T.O.P.

Be still before the Lord, *and wait patiently for him. —Psalm 37:7*

One Sunday afternoon, I had my usual list of things to get at the store before closing time. Naturally, I managed to end up having to stop at all seven traffic lights on the way there, and just managed to make it to the store before closing time.

Needless to say, I wasn't real thrilled about having to stop at every light along the way. I caught myself offering up a totally selfish prayer: "Come on, God, cut me a break, please make the rest of them green!" What a ridiculous act! In my selfish praying, did I even once think that some other driver on the road might well be praying to God *for* a red light so that he or she could deal with a squirming child or check out some directions on a map? And what if one of those other drivers really could have used that time at a red light to offer up to God some very serious prayer?

It's a shame that we get so caught up in life that we can't use those moments of "lifeus interruptus" at a red light to look around at God's world, seek out the needs of his people, and then use that time to offer it all up to God in prayer.

In today's passage, the psalmist invites us to "Be still before the Lord, and wait patiently for him." Not bad advice . . . to S.T.O.P., to take a **S**econd or **T**wo **O**ut for **P**rayer.

God, help me to stop my fretting and my fussing. Help me to practice a lot more patience as I go about my days. Help me to use the S.T.O.P. signs in life to take that second or two out for some meaningful prayer time. Amen.

Day 349 / Luke 5:12-13

Leave It Up to God

Once, when he was in one of the cities, there was a man covered with leprosy. When he saw Jesus, he bowed with his face to the ground and begged him, "Lord, if you choose, you can make me clean." Then Jesus stretched out his hand, touched him, and said, "I do choose. Be made clean." Immediately the leprosy left him. —Luke 5:12-13

When I drove past one of the Methodist churches in town, the slogan on their signboard caught my attention. It read: "Who Is Your Leper?"

Normally when I pass one of these signboards, I can usually figure out the sense of the statement. I rattled it around in my mind the entire time I was driving around town, but I just couldn't figure what the person was implying. The very next morning while reading *God's Joyful Surprise* by Sue Monk Kidd, I came across a section about using one's imagination when reading Scripture. One of the texts used as an example was the healing of the leper from Luke's Gospel. Talk about one of God's joyful surprises. I read Monk's own imaginings abut the leper and thought again about the signboard.

Who is your leper? The leper is any person or persons in your life and mine whom we shove aside—the AIDS victim, the disabled child, an older person, someone with the "wrong" skin color, or the smelly street person. Why do we shove them aside? Why do we pull back from touching them and providing care and love for them in Jesus' name?

I thank God for that church sign question, and for the joyful discovery I made the next day. Both remind me that many in the world are seeking a loving touch and that when faced with big challenges, God will provide answers.

God, I never cease to be amazed about the way you work. Continue to surprise me and shake me out of my Christian complacency, so I may reach out to all who need a healing touch. Amen.

Day 350 / Daniel 1:1-7

What's in a Name?

The palace master gave them other names: Daniel he called Belteshazzar, Hananiah he called Shadrach, Mishael he called Meshach, and Azariah he called Abednego. —Daniel 1:7

Think for a moment of the following names, what images or emotions these names conjure up in you: Donald Trump . . . Osama Bin-Laden . . . Brittany Spears . . . George W. Bush . . . Jesus Christ. Isn't it interesting how the mere mention of someone's name evokes emotions and feelings? We connect meaning with names.

In today's lesson, this was certainly the case. When King Nebuchadnezzar defeated the northern kingdom of Israel, he captured and brought to Babylon some of Israel's best and brightest. He proceeded to change some of their names, hoping to change their loyalties. *Daniel* ("God is my judge") was changed to *Belteshazzar*, which meant "Bel (who was the chief Babylonian god, also known as Marduke) protect his life." *Hananiah* ("The Lord shows grace") was changed to *Shadrach*, which in Babylonian meant "under the command of Aku, the Babylonian moon god." *Mishael* ("who is like God") became *Meshach*, or "who is like Aku." *Azariah* ("The Lord helps") was changed to *Abednego*, which in Babylonian meant, "servant of Nego/Nebo, or Nabu, the Babylonian god of learning and writing." Of course, the book goes on to tell how the plan backfired. The young men remained faithful to God.

How you live your life, the things you accomplish, the way you treat people—all these will be forever connected with your name. But, thanks be to God, in baptism we have received the most important name of all—"child of God." This is the name we need to be willing and proud use, even if there isn't a space for it on a form!

God, thank you for naming your child in baptism. Help me to proclaim your name and the name of your Son Jesus Christ proudly and boldly at all times and in all places! Amen.

Day 351 / Isaiah 30:18

Between Jesus and You

Yet the LORD longs to be gracious to you; he rises to show you compassion. For the LORD is a God of justice. Blessed are all who wait for him! —Isaiah 30:18 (NIV)

During a discussion that took place between two monks in a Franciscan monastery, one of the monks challenged the other: "Do you ever reflect upon the fact that Jesus feels proud of you? Proud that you accepted the faith he offered to you? Proud that you chose him for a friend and Lord? Is he proud of you that you haven't given up? Do you ever think that that Jesus appreciates you for wanting him, for wanting him to say no to so many things that would separate you from him? He said, 'I do not call you servants, but friends.' Therefore, there is the possibility of every feeling and emotion that can exist between friends to exist here now between Jesus and you."

For just a minute, put yourself in the place of that monk who was being questioned. What would your response be to those probing questions? Do you think Jesus is proud of what you say and do in his name? If not, can you talk it over with him? That's what true friends do—talk and support one another in tough times. And when we disappoint each other, we ask for forgiveness.

It is amazing to think that, even when I turn away from God, the Lord longs to be gracious to me and rises to show compassion. I couldn't ask for a better friend.

Gracious Lord, may I live in a way that makes you proud, and when I disappoint, please rise to show compassion. Amen.

Day 352 / Luke 12:22-31

Good Morning, Lord!

He said to his disciples, "Therefore I tell you, do not worry about your life, what you will eat, or about your body, what you will wear." —Luke 12:22

For the most part, I am a "morning person." But I don't find myself popping right out of bed as briskly anymore. Some days I'm somewhat reluctant for the day to begin. Maybe that's an aging body, or maybe it's fueled by the fact that most nights I only get about four and a half hours sleep. Then there are the mornings (most, if the truth be told) when that "Good Lord, Morning!" attitude is fueled by the thousand and one things that are on my mind the minute my eyes open.

As I lay there in bed trying to put some semblance of order to what I know is going to be a crazy and hectic day (and this is even before the potential myriad of interruptions and surprises), that feeling of being overwhelmed leaves me reluctant to face the day.

If you're like me, and this is the way your day often starts, then consider beginning everyday with a prayer of praise. Give thanks for something in your life. Seems like a much better way to start one's day than worrying "about your life, what you will eat, or about your body, what you will wear" or whether someone's going to do their chores or violate a house rule, don't you think?

It is so easy to let the worries of the day cloud our perspective. But we know that none of us can add a single hour to our life by worrying.

Father, help me to wake each morning as your grateful servant. Amen.

Day 353 / Psalm 30:1-5

More Than a Good Breakfast

Weeping may linger for the night, but joy comes with the morning.
—Psalm 30:5

I take great joy in eating breakfast, but I don't think that's the kind of joy the psalmist is talking about. I've been reading *The Christian Handbook*, and in a small section called "Five Ways to Put God First Daily," there are some powerful suggestions for assuring ourselves joy in the morning . . . and all day long.

Begin the day by opening the Bible. But don't just open it—allow some quiet time to read and reflect on God's word. Perhaps you could "chew" on it while you eat breakfast.

Pray about your day. I've found that taking a moment before I even get out of bed to talk with God about the day ahead helps me focus better and worry less.

Take stock of sins that might be keeping you from putting God first and repent. The "baggage" we tote around weighs us down and makes it hard to be joyful. As you throw back the covers on your bed each morning, throw off the weight of sin by confessing to God the things you've done, and left undone, and asking God's forgiveness.

Remind yourself that God has a purpose for you. How long is your "to do" list for today? Remember that within and beneath your daily activities lies the deeper purpose of serving God by loving neighbor.

Be mindful of the "onionskin factor." Life is like an onion that every day, when "peeled away," reveals a new day filled with the promise of God's presence where joy abounds in the morning, at noon, and at night.

Lord, thank you for your care in the night and for the promise this new day offers. Grant me joy in your presence and in my calling to serve you. Amen.

The Christian Handbook, © 2005, Augsburg Books, p. 107

Day 354 / Hebrews 9:11-14

We Are Repairable

How much more will the blood of Christ, who through the eternal Spirit offered himself without blemish to God, purify our conscience from dead works to worship the living God!
—Hebrews 9:14

During a fantastic after-Christmas sale, I purchased a couple of medium-weight jackets thinking I would wear one in the spring and save the other for fall. I used my new spring jacket a lot. But in the fall, I discovered that the sleeve of the other jacket was torn along the seam. Since I no longer had the sales receipt, I couldn't return the jacket. I thought I would just have to throw it out, but my wife assured me that she could repair it so it would be as good as new. She did, and now I'm enjoying my "new" fall jacket as much as my spring one.

My jacket experience got me thinking about my relationship with Jesus. What if Jesus had decided that it wasn't worth his effort—or pain—to die on the cross in order to repair my broken life? Would Jesus have thrown me out?

As today's passage tells us, in the Old Testament people sacrificed animals in atonement for their sins and to be made right with God once again. By his death on the cross Jesus did away with the need for such sacrifice. No more animals need to die because Jesus—the Lamb of God—died once and for all. Through Jesus' death, our sinful lives are repaired and we are made good as new. Through his sacrifice, the torn fabric of our relationship with God has been sewn together again.

I got a really good bargain at last year's post-Christmas sale—and a theology lesson as well!

Lord, I confess to you that I'm broken and in bondage to sin. There isn't anything I can possibly do on my own to change that, but you can . . . and you have. Thank you for making me whole through your sacrifice on my behalf. Help me truly live in newness of life. Amen.

Day 355 / 1 Samuel 3:19-4:1

Scraped Knees

As Samuel grew up, the LORD was with him and let none of his words fall to the ground. —1 Samuel 3:19

Like our journey through life, our walk in faith is full of risks. It's inevitable that we're going to suffer plenty of bumps and bruises, cuts and scrapes as we seek to traverse its treacherous ways. Is there no consolation for our pain? Is there no assurance that the risks are worth taking?

In today's passage, we read about God's providential care of Samuel. God called Samuel at a very young age to be a prophet to his people. What a daunting responsibility that must have been for the young boy! But from the beginning, Samuel put his trust in God, and God supported him as he grew and as he prophesied. Did Samuel ever fall down and scrape his knees? Many times. But from the fact that "God let none of [Samuel's] words fall to the ground," we know that God was there to cushion Samuel's fall.

We will trip and fall. We will earn plenty of bumps and bruises as we seek to be faithful to God and to the work to which God has called us. God will make sure that our precious witness is never wasted. And God will be with us to bandage our skinned knees and heal our pain with his kiss of love.

When we stumble and fall, Lord, pick us up, dust us off, and send us on your way once again. Amen.

Day 356 / Romans 12:1-2

Good Work

Do not be conformed to this world, but be transformed by the renewing of your minds, so that you may discern what is the will of God. —Romans 12:2

How many people do you know who enjoy their job? Do you? Do you look forward to going to work in the morning? If we're honest, we will admit that we don't always appreciate our work . . . or feel appreciated at work.

I consider myself very fortunate to have known a great deal of satisfaction in the work I've done for over twenty years. It has given me the chance to use my skills and to develop new ones. But most importantly, I enjoyed my work because of the opportunity it gave me to serve God.

One of my favorite scripture passages is Paul's appeal to Christians in Rome in which he says, "Do not be conformed to this world, but be transformed by the renewing of your minds, so that you may discern what is the will of God—what is good and acceptable and perfect." I believe that Paul's words are helpful to all of us who, at one time or another, lack enthusiasm for our work—or question the value of what we do.

According to Martin Luther, God calls us where we are—meaning that all work is valuable for the opportunity it offers to serve God and love our neighbor. So, instead of "conforming" to worldly measures for job satisfaction—salary, benefits, perks, and advancement opportunities—we should "be transformed" to God's understanding of "good work." This new perspective brings purpose to every job—even on the days when we really don't enjoy what we're doing.

Lord, your gifts to me include food and clothing, home and family, and daily work. Help me to be more appreciative of my daily work, and to see it as an opportunity to share your love with those I meet today. Amen.

Day 357 / Luke 24:36-39

Knock on Wood

Why are you frightened, and why do doubts arise in your hearts?
—Luke 24:38

The phrase, "knock on wood," derives from an ancient belief that gods lived inside trees, and waited eagerly to frustrate happy lives with a little unholy mischief. It became customary to rap on trees to drive away the gods. Even though we no longer believe in mischievous tree gods, we continue to perpetuate the superstition. When was the last time you had the impulse to "knock on wood"?

Superstition is alive and well in these modern times, and it's based in fear. We fear that God may not be working for our good, and so it is up to us to make sure that good things happen in our lives. So we "knock on wood," just in case there is something to the evil spirits thing. And when good moments come, we can't fully enjoy them because we live in fear that they won't last. Eventually, "the other shoe will drop."

Does this picture of a stingy and mean-spirited God bear any resemblance to the God revealed to us in Jesus? Of course not! So why do we continue to hold onto it so tightly? Jesus came to cast away our fears by assuring us—with his own body and blood—of God's immeasurable love for us. Jesus frees us from sin, death, and the power of the devil . . . and from the need to be "knock on wood" people.

God, keep me from succumbing to fear and superstition. Let me live, instead, in the promise of your love for me, and your presence with me. Amen.

Be It Resolved . . .

But Daniel resolved that he would not defile himself with the royal rations of food and wine; so he asked the palace master to allow him not to defile himself. —Daniel 1:8

Once each year our Lutheran synods meet in assembly to deal with the business of the church. Part of that process often involves the introduction of "memorials" (motions needing action) to the assembly. These memorials involve two parts. The first section explains both the rationale and the purpose behind the petition for action; the second half, beginning with "Therefore, be it resolved" expresses the action(s) the petitioner desires to have taken.

When Daniel lived in court of the Babylonian king, Daniel would not defile himself (and reject his faith in God) by eating and drinking the royal food and wine. In order to do this, we read in today's passage that he "*resolved* that he would not defile himself with the royal rations of food and wine."

To be "resolved" means to be committed to a course of action. It means backing up our words with actions. When we resolve to accept God's vision, we are also resolving to live out our lives according to God's word. To make such a resolve requires more than lip service. Its requirements can be summed up in the words of our own Affirmation of Baptism, in which we commit ourselves to live among God's people, hear God's word and share in the Lord's Supper, proclaim the good news in word and deed, serve all people following Jesus' example, and strive for justice and peace in all the earth (*Lutheran Book of Worship*, 201). Now that's a resolve!

Through the power of your Holy Spirit, Lord, draw me each day to your word. Let your word be my guide and my direction, leading me away from life's temptations and into strength and comfort of your loving arms. Amen.

Day 359 / Matthew 11:28-30

Anybody's Welcome

Come to me, all you that are weary and are carrying heavy burdens, and I will give you rest. Take my yoke upon you, and learn from me; for I am gentle and humble in heart, and you will find rest for your souls. For my yoke is easy, and my burden is light. —Matthew 11:28-30

During his three years of ministry, Jesus spent a lot of time hanging around the "wrong kinds of people," at least in the eyes of the religious leaders. He ate with tax collectors, socialized with prostitutes and lepers, and he was accused of being a liar, a drunkard, and a glutton. In short, Jesus got himself in trouble for hanging out with and accepting the "wrong people."

I recently read an article about Heather Veitch, the cofounder of "J.C.'s Girls, Girls, Girls." While the article didn't offer any specific information about her conversion to Christianity, this former stripper now shares her faith with others still involved in the business. She goes to strip clubs and conventions related to the industry, taking with her both Bibles and her own testimony about God's message of salvation. I'm sure she has as many detractors and she does supporters.

The closing sentences in the written article I found online about Veitch's ministry says: "Veitch said strippers and porn stars don't have to quit their jobs before entering a church. 'Do we ask gluttons to stop eating too much before they come to church?'"

It would seem to me that we would need to be that type of church. Just as Christ welcomed all who sought to hear his message and to receive his gift of salvation and forgiveness, our doors need to be open wide to welcome the "unwelcomed" of our world.

Gracious God, we confess that we are quick to pass judgment about whether a person is "worthy" to be among us in the church. Help us to extended your invitation to all you who are weary and carrying heavy burdens. May we be true expressions of your hospitality and grace. Amen.

Day 360 / Psalm 116: 5-7

Rested

Return, O my soul, to your rest, for the Lord *has dealt bountifully with you. —Psalm 116:7*

I recall a day when I felt fully rested. It's easy to recall since I seldom seem to get enough rest. Proper rest is both important and necessary. Our bodies need physical rest so that we're able to meet the demands of each day. Yet, our frenetic lifestyles and our constant list of things to do have us running. And when we have become too busy to rest, we have become far too busy. We need rest for our bodies and, even more importantly, we need rest for our souls. We only have one of each.

The psalmist reminds us of the need for rest: "Return, O my soul, to your rest, for the Lord has dealt bountifully with you." Our souls need rest from the constant barrage of thoughts and demands that this life creates. We need to seek out those times of quiet, those prayer times with God, to speak and to listen. Bodily rest prepares us for our work; soul rest prepares us to do the work of God.

A quote by that famous Anonymous says, "If your day is hemmed in prayer, it is less likely to come unstitched." The crazier our schedules, the more we need time to be with God. As you consider what to pour into your life, consider the space left for rest, especially rest in God's refreshing presence.

O God of rest and peace, draw me to you and fill me with your presence. Remind me to stop and rest, so I can be renewed and energized to serve you. Amen.

Day 361 / Colossians 1:15-20

Out of Sight, But Not Out of Presence

He is the image of the invisible God, the firstborn of all creation; for in him all things in heaven and on earth were created, things visible and invisible . . . —Colossians 1:15-16

In 1867 Walter Chalmers Smith, a pastor of the Free Church of Scotland, wrote the words of this familiar hymn:

> Immortal, invisible, God only wise,
> in light inaccessible hid from our eyes,
> Most blessed, most glorious, the Ancient of Days,
> Almighty, victorious , thy great name we raise.

God the invisible. How do we maintain faith in a God that seems unable to be reached by any of our human senses—hearing, seeing, touching, smelling, or tasting? How are we expected to connect with this immortal, invisible, and wise God?

In his book, *Reaching for the Invisible God: What Can We Expect to Find,* author Philip Yancey suggests that these questions may not be the right ones to ask. Yancey suggests that, as Christians, we need to seek more from this "invisible God" than simple pat answers. He concludes that our relationship with this "invisible God" is less about our questions and more about God, who is the answer, who invites us reach out for him and find him in the very real and very visible living Jesus Christ.

Because we are connected to the risen Christ, we are the image of that invisible God to those around us. We embody the risen Christ who calls us to feed the hungry, clothe the naked, visit the sick, give shelter to the homeless, reach out to those who are the "least." When we serve others in Jesus' name we make God visible to one another.

God of all wisdom and power, let us touch you, taste you, smell you, hear you, and see you in the faces of those whom we serve in the name of your Son Jesus Christ. Amen.

Day 362 / Ecclesiastes 3:10-15

A One-Winged Butterfly

[God] has made everything beautiful in its time. He has also set eternity in the hearts of men; yet they cannot fathom what God has done from beginning to end. —Ecclesiastes 3:11 (NIV)

As I reflected on today's text, I was reminded of words from the chorus of pop singer Ray Steven's song: "Everything is beautiful in its own way."

The words were especially fitting as I sat down to write this morning. A beautiful light coating of snow covered everything, and to top that, our beloved Steelers won last night's Super Bowl! As I puttered around the kitchen, my eyes caught sight of an old cookie jar. On the top of the jar's lid sits a very colorful butterfly with its wings spread wide open. Actually, that butterfly now sits on top of that lid with *one* of its wings spread wide open. The wing broke off years ago, and we've never been able to glue it back on so it will withstand the constant opening and closing of the jar. Because of its damaged condition, it would probably be something that someone would overlook if they saw it at a yard sale. But to us, it is beautiful for two reasons.

First of all, it's beautiful because we deeply value the friendship of the person who gave it to us nearly 33 years ago as a wedding present. Secondly, even with its damaged lid, the one remaining wing of that butterfly still allows us to gain access to the many sweet treats contained in that jar throughout the year.

It's true, under heaven, beauty lies in the eyes of the beholder. God has made everything beautiful. We simply need to look beyond our skewed perceptions and preconceived notions.

Loving God, open the eyes of our hearts that we might see beyond the superficial to find your beauty in the hearts of all your people. Amen.

Day 363 / 2 Samuel 24:10-14

In God's Hands

Then David said to [the prophet] Gad, "I am in great distress; let us fall into the hand of the LORD, for his mercy is great; but let me not fall into human hands." —2 Samuel 24:14

I was reminded of these words of David during the coverage of the funeral for Coretta Scott King. One of speakers made reference to the gospel hymn, "He's Got the Whole World in His Hands." Seated in the congregation were four presidents, a host of senators and congresspersons, foreign dignitaries, blacks, whites, rich and poor, famous and obscure, Republican and Democrat, liberal and conservative. They became a testament to the fact that, no matter what our particular political or economic position in life, God's got all of us in his hands.

I also recalled a weekend retreat years ago that included a softball game. My friend Dwight chased after a foul ball and ended up landing face first against some rocks in a shallow stream. He sustained severe facial injuries that necessitated a trip to a nearby emergency room and an overnight stay.

Later that evening, we gathered around a campfire to sing and relax. One of the songs that we sang was "He's God the Whole World in His Hands." After having gone through the standard verses, others began to offer up specific individuals and concerns as alternate verses. I remember offering up Dwight. What started out as a song of affirmation of God's abiding strength became a sung prayer for the hurting and the needy of our world, including Dwight.

Especially when we are in distress, we need to remember to let go and fall, fall into the hands of the Lord, whose hands will catch and comfort.

Lord, while insurance ads claim that we are in "good hands," we have assurance that in you we are held in the "best hands"! Thank you, Lord, for your love and your protection. Amen.

Day 364 / Matthew 14:28-33

Walking on the Water

Peter answered him, "Lord, if it is you, command me to come to you on the water." He said, "Come." So Peter got out of the boat, started walking on the water, and came toward Jesus. —Matthew 14:28-29

Sometimes, writing these devotions feels a bit like walking on water. I search for something helpful, if not profound, to say. I want to reach the hearts and needs of those who are on a journey with Christ. But some days, the gap between starting the devotion and completing it feels like the distance between the panicking Peter and Jesus. My friend Kerry also writes daily devotions, and he has remarked, "The reality is that I can no more produce a 'devotion a day' than Peter can walk on water. . . . It is impossible for me. I don't have that much to say! But it isn't impossible for God. Nothing is impossible for God."

So, just like Peter, each day I climb out of my safe little boat, and I respond to Jesus' bidding me to come across the water to him, prepared to receive from him the words that he would have me share. Like Peter, I find myself becoming distracted by the winds, I lose my focus, and I end up drowning in that tumultuous sea of doubt and uncertainty. Like Peter, I end up screaming, "Lord, save me!" And the Lord does just that. He reaches out his hand and pulls me close to him.

Do you need to walk on water? Are you called to do something that seems impossible? Step out of the boat. The Lord of possibility stands ready to help.

God, my protector, give me the courage to be willing to step out in faith, knowing that your hand is always there to save me if I begin to drown. Grant me the courage to try and do great things in your name. Amen.

Day 365 / Isaiah 55:6-12

Tell the Story

[My word] shall not return to me empty, but it shall accomplish that which I purpose, and succeed in the thing for which I sent it.
— Isaiah 55:11

A young coworker of mine brings his Bible to work with him and reads from it occasionally throughout the day. So, on one of the mornings we were working together, I asked him about his practice of daily Bible reading and learned that this is something new for him. As we talked, I was reminded anew of the power of God's word to transform lives and nurture faith. And that made me think about how it is both a privilege and responsibility for us to share the word—to tell the story of Jesus and his love.

Today's passage from the Old Testament book of Isaiah leaves no doubt about the power of God's word, but I think there are some things that we "storytellers" can do to help others hear God's promise of forgiveness and life. Here's my short list.

Avail ourselves of opportunities to hear the story through personal devotions and corporate worship. Use both our words and our actions to share the good news of God's love for all people. Speak plainly—in language that the hearers will understand—of both the joys and the struggles of following Jesus. Witness openly and honestly of God's activity in our lives, without judging others.

And most importantly of all, remember that it isn't our words but the word of god revealed in Christ Jesus that saves storytellers and story-hearers alike.

Lord, write your story upon my heart so, with the whole of my life and being, I might proclaim your blessed word to others. Amen.

Another Year or a New Year? (New Year's Day)

He said to me, "Mortal, can these bones live?" I answered, "O Lord God, you know." —Ezekiel 37:3

How might people react if, instead of saying, "Happy New Year!" we said, "Another year?" We'd likely get some strange looks. But many people start the new year with that attitude. They have few plans or aspirations. At best they have vague resolutions, without plans or steps, about losing weight, quitting smoking, or becoming a better person. Most of those resolutions end up as a pile of "dry bones" in the valley. No real effort is made to breathe life into them—or to ask God if the bones can live.

Those folks aren't as bad off as the ones who don't even bother to make a list of potential life changes. They're content with, or resigned to, the prospect that the new year will be a continuation of the old one.

In the verses following today's text, Ezekiel prophesies as instructed, then God breathes life into the dead bones. God does so because he knows there's the potential of vibrant life in that pile of bones.

There's *power* in the words of scripture, and words of hope, prosperity, comfort, and guidance. But if we're not willing to seek out God's breath of life for our lives, we're going to end up a lifeless pile of bones.

May you live this year in a renewed relationship with your Lord and Savior!

God of hope and promise, come into our mundane and stagnant lives and make them new again. Fill us with the promise of your presence and the power of your spirit. Renew us each day and breathe life into us through your word, whether it be spoken or read or through the quiet insights of your Holy Spirit. In the name of your Son Jesus we pray. Amen.

Aha!
(Epiphany)

Opening their treasure-chests, they offered him gifts of gold, frankincense, and myrrh. —Matthew 2:11

Once when I commented to a friend about that day being Epiphany, she replied, "It's what?" Only when I explained that this day—and season—is when we celebrate the Wise Men's arrival at Jesus' manger could she relate the word "Epiphany" with something she understood.

Many people don't understand Epiphany. It's not a commonly used word outside of the church, and when it does appear, it is usually described as a startling insight that changes one's life. Yet a true epiphany is much more. For the Wise Men, being in the presence of the Christ child, God's Son, was a life-changing experience. What began as a journey of curiosity ended in an overwhelming sense of the divine.

Our lives are filled with moments of grace in which God reaches out and touches us. These may not be life-changing experiences, but they are nonetheless epiphanies, when we realize the power and the majesty of the one who loves even us. In such precious and enlightening moments we find ourselves in awe and wonder at God's presence and power.

Perhaps, instead of just celebrating the day or season of Epiphany, we should celebrate its wonder every day. Being surprised anew by God's presence in the most unlikely of places, we may experience an epiphany and say, "Aha! Now I understand; thanks, God!"

Gracious and loving Lord, as I live in your transforming light, let each day of this new year be filled with "Aha" moments, epiphanies through which you reveal yourself and your love for me in wonderful, startling ways. Amen.

The Source of All Love (Valentine's Day)

The greatest of these is love. —1 Corinthians 13:13

Today the world is caught up and bubbling over with love. Candy and flower sales are probably at their peak, and restaurants are jammed with thousands of couples taking this day to express their love for each other.

Paul's words are both a powerful expression and description of what the shared love of a relationship should be. He lays out a pretty complete list of love's characteristics: "Love is patient; love is kind; love is not envious or boastful or arrogant or rude. It does not insist on its own way; it is not irritable or resentful; it does not rejoice in wrongdoing, but rejoices in the truth. It bears all things, believes all things, hopes all things, endures all things. Love never ends" (1 Cor. 13:4-8).

Those words can be the benchmark by which we gauge our love, not just for others, but also for God. But remember also the words of 1 John, which remind us of the source of love: "Beloved, let us love one another, because love is from God; everyone who loves is born of God and knows God. . . . God is love. . . . We love because he first loved us" (4:7-8, 19).

So let God be the source of your love, and then share that love with everyone around you.

Lord, fill us with your love, and let that love flow out to others. Amen.

How About Some Green Eggs and Ham? (St. Patrick's Day)

He answered, "The man called Jesus made mud, spread it on my eyes, and said to me, 'Go to Siloam and wash.' Then I went and washed and received my sight." —John 9:11

My car radio was tuned to the talk/advice/soft-rock station. It was St. Patrick's Day, and the deejay talked about using food coloring to create green potatoes, milk, and scrambled eggs. That got me thinking about Dr. Seuss's *Green Eggs and Ham.* Remember?

> Do you like green eggs and ham?
> I do not like them Sam-I-am.
> I do not like green eggs and ham.

The classic children's story is, like the healing of the man born blind, a story of *conversion and transformation.*

Every moment of every day, God is inviting us, as he did that blind man, into his love. And we, like those religion authorities, resist and object. We need to learn from the blind man—to trust in Christ and be ready to move from blindness to sight.

In the end, Seuss's character caves in to Sam's badgering, hoping Sam will then leave him alone. And he discovers he likes them: "I will eat them here and there, say, I WILL EAT THEM ANYWHERE! I do so like green eggs and ham. Thank you! Thank you, Sam-I-Am!"

And we will say: "I will follow you here and there, say, I WILL FOLLOW YOU ANYWHERE! I will follow you, even to the cross, great God-I-Am!"

I bind unto myself today the power of God to hold and lead, his eye to watch, his insight to stay, his ear to hearken to my need. Amen. (Attributed to St. Patrick)

Are We Willing? (Good Friday)

As they led him away, they seized a man, Simon of Cyrene, who was coming from the country, and they laid the cross on him, and made him carry it behind Jesus. —Luke 23:26

My Good Friday often involves watching "The Way of the Cross," a reenactment on the streets of Greensburg of Jesus' arrest, trial, and walk to Golgotha. Using volunteer actors, it was started more than a decade ago by some downtown churches. In one scene, Roman soldiers snatch Simon of Cyrene from the crowd and force him to carry Christ's cross. Every time I watch, I hear Jesus' words: "If any want to become my followers, let them deny themselves and take up their cross and follow me" (Mark 8:34). Only if we take up our own cross and walk with Jesus can we be his followers.

Last year, when our family attended the Good Friday Tenebrae service at our church, the pastor, in the opening prayer, asked God to "look with mercy on your family for whom our Lord Jesus Christ was willing to be betrayed. . . ." The word *willing* jumped out at me. Simon of Cyrene was *forced* to carry the cross. Jesus went *willingly* to Calvary, *willingly* endured the pain and humiliation of hanging on the cross, and *willingly* gave up his life for us.

Our Lord was willing to be betrayed and to be given over to the hands of sinners and to suffer death on the cross. As I ponder all these things in my heart and mind, questions arise: Am I willing? Are you?

God, I doubt that I able to accept Jesus' challenge to deny myself, take up my cross, and follow him, completely and without reservation or fear. God, I'm just not sure. Help me. Amen.

March Madness (Easter)

"And so, because it was the Jewish day of Preparation, and the tomb was nearby, they laid Jesus there." —John 19:42

Last year, Easter was early—March 27. It was the day before Easter, and I wasn't a happy camper. I'm a basketball junkie, and it was the "March madness" of the National Collegiate Athletic Association playoffs. I'd printed out my trusty bracket and was making my picks. In most years I had predicted about seventy-five percent of the winners in each round. Now, going into the final round, my record was sixty-six, sixty-three, and—gulp!—thirteen.

Whether Easter ends up in March or April—in A.D. 325 the Council of Nicea decreed that it falls on the first Sunday after the first full moon on or after the vernal equinox—the period from Lent through Easter is often a rush, especially if you're involved in or work in the church. A lot happens in this forty-plus-day period. Factor into the mix the emotions that are part of holy week, and, for the Christian, it's an intense time—sometimes the church's own version of March Madness.

As a basketball junkie, I always look forward to the madness and intensity of the playoffs because I know they'll culminate in a championship game full of energy, excitement, and—for many—joy. The same holds true for us Christians as we anticipate celebrating Christ's victory over death and the grave—except that we'll *all* be joyous as we together shout, "Alleluia!"

We're filled with expectation, Lord. We're waiting with bated breath, and we're waiting to celebrate. Let the Son arise! Amen.

All Is Calm, All Is Bright? (Christmas Eve)

And she gave birth to her firstborn son and wrapped him in bands of cloth, and laid him in a manger, because there was no place for them in the inn. —Luke 2:7

I was listening the end of "Silent Night," sung by the Three Tenors. I couldn't help but think about some of the words and the tranquil scene they depict: "all is calm . . . round yon virgin . . . sleep in heavenly peace." That's how the manger scene is usually depicted. Hushed silence. The animals stand motionless, in awe of what's occurring. Mary and Joseph kneeling in silent wonder.

The reality must have been much different. "Yon virgin" was a scared early adolescent, Joseph a frightened spouse. Their audience that night included no kings, only smelly, perhaps noisy farm animals and some shepherds who wandered in with their sheep. We've prettified and sentimentalized the manger scene, robbing it of its shock value. Christmas *needs* to be shocking. It *was* scandalous—because God chose to come to us as a helpless infant born in a lowly place.

But one line in "Silent Night" rings with truth about the reality of the manger: "shepherds quaked at the sight." I'll bet they quaked from the thunderous angelic pronouncement until they left the stable in awe. We, too, should be quaking with joy as we leave Christmas worship. We need to let Luke's words speak anew to our minds and our hearts, letting God bring the true heavenly peace into the chaos of Christmas.

Draw us to that stable, Lord, to be disturbed by the raucous noises, to be offended by the awful smells, to feel uncomfortable around "those people," and then to be blessed by the power and the glory of the child who was born to set us free. Amen.

Traditions
(Christmas Day)

. . . stand firm and hold fast to the traditions that you were taught . . . —2 Thessalonians 2:15

Every child—and sometimes many adults!—regard some product or another as the greatest Christmas gift of all time, but they would be wrong. Long ago in Bethlehem, God gave us the most incredible gift we will ever receive: Jesus Christ.

This holiday season likely has been a very busy time for you. In the midst of that busyness, it's easy to lose sight of just why we celebrate Christmas. If you would ask people why they celebrate Christmas, one of their most common responses would be, "Because it's tradition." And indeed, the traditions that are part of our lives are very important. They help us to remember the people and events that have shaped our being and provide a connection both with our ancestors and our heirs. But while we each have traditions that are a part of our Christmas celebrations, Christmas itself is much more than just tradition. Christmas is the celebration of a new life we can all have in Jesus Christ.

I pray that, on this Christmas Day, you've been able to take at least a little bit of time to look beyond the mounds of wrapping paper and boxes and put it into perspective, that lying beyond that huge pile of gifts lies the greatest gift of all time: God's Son, the risen Savior, Christ the Lord.

Thank you, Lord, for the chance to celebrate together your Son's birth, a time we will cherish long after the season has officially ended. You've reminded us that sharing is what this time is truly about—sharing lives and sharing your Son. Amen.

The Beginning and the End (New Year's Eve)

I am the Alpha and the Omega, the beginning and the end.
—Revelation 21:6

Tonight, many people will be out reveling at a New Year's Eve party; others will be content to stay at home and usher in the new year more quietly. Either way, what you are welcoming is the beginning of another year of your life, filled with new experiences and challenges, a year of uncertainties, doubts, triumphs, and tragedies. We who confess Christ can be certain that it will be a year blessed by God's presence and power sustaining us through challenging times and rejoicing with us in the year's many joys. For God has assured us that he who has been in existence from the beginning of time will be there during each day of our life, and in the end as well.

This is also that time of year when many of us will sit down and think about new year's resolutions—those promises to do things to better our lives. Whatever you personally choose to do for your life, above all, choose to draw closer to the God who created you, to the God who is the beginning, the now, and the end of all life. Take time out of each day to read God's word, to reflect upon it, and to act upon it, for the good of your own life and for the lives of those around you.

God, grant me a blessed and joyous New Year; and may I find your hope and promise for my life in these quiet times with you. Happy New Year, God! Amen.

9 780806 652306